Small Business Success Through TQM

Also available from ASQC Quality Press

Principles and Practices of TQM
Thomas J. Cartin

The Change Agents' Handbook: A Survival Guide for Quality Improvement Champions
David W. Hutton

Managing the Process, the People, and Yourself
Joseph G. Werner

Mapping Work Processes
Dianne Galloway

The ASQC Total Quality Management Series

> *TQM: Leadership for the Quality Transformation*
> Richard S. Johnson
>
> *TQM: Management Processes for Quality Operations*
> Richard S. Johnson
>
> *TQM: The Mechanics of Quality Processes*
> Richard S. Johnson and Lawrence E. Kazense
>
> *TQM: Quality Training Practices*
> Richard S. Johnson

To request a complimentary catalog of publications, call 800-248-1946.

Small Business Success Through TQM

Practical Methods to Improve Your Organization's Performance

Terry Ehresman

ASQC Quality Press
Milwaukee, Wisconsin

Small Business Success Through TQM
Terry Ehresman

Library of Congress Cataloging-in-Publication Data

Ehresman, Terry, 1960–
    Small business success through TQM: practical methods to improve
your organization's performance / Terry Ehresman.
        p.   cm.
    Includes bibliographical references and index.
    ISBN 0-87389-309-3 (alk. paper)
    1. Small business—Management. 2. Total quality management.
I. Title
HD62.7.E38   1994
658.5'62—dc20   94-21676
                                                                      CIP

10 9 8 7 6 5 4 3 2 1

ISBN 0-87389-309-3

Acquisitions Editor: Susan Westergard
Project Editor: Jeanne W. Bohn
Production Editor: Annette Wall
Marketing Administrator: Mark Olson
Set in Stone Serif and Avant Garde by Montgomery Media, Inc.
Cover design by Paul Tobias
Printed and bound by IPC Publishing Services

ASQC Mission: To facilitate continuous improvement and increase customer
satisfaction by identifying, communicating, and promoting the use of
quality principles, concepts, and technologies; and thereby be recognized
throughout the world as the leading authority on, and champion for,
quality.

For a free copy of the ASQC Quality Press Publications Catalog, including
ASQC membership information, call 800-248-1946.

Printed in the United States of America

   Printed on acid-free recycled paper

  ASQC
Quality Press
611 East Wisconsin Avenue
Milwaukee, Wisconsin 53202

To Joan, Matt, and Ryan.
Thanks for the fun, the lessons
you teach me, and mostly for
the love you show me

CONTENTS

List of Figures...xv
List of Worksheets...xix
List of Activities xxi
Preface...xxiii
Acknowledgments xxvii

Chapter 1: Introduction to Total Quality Management 1
    Total Quality Management in Small Business....................................1
    What Is Total Quality Management?..1
        Ensuring Customer Satisfaction 2
        Managing Processes...3
        Continuously Improving..5
        Working Together 6
        Encouraging Personal Initiative..7
        TQM Checklist..8
    Can It Work in My Small Business?..8
    Why Is Quality Important? 9
        Customers 9
        Competition 10
        Costs 11
    Summary..13

Chapter 2: The Continuous Process Improvement Cycle..........15
    The Need for a Methodology 15
        Avoid False Starts..16
        Build a Stable Foundation..16
    The Methodology..17
        Plan for Customer Satisfaction 18

Understand Processes 18
Measure Performance 19
Take Action to Improve 20
The Cycle Is Continuous 20
The First Cycle 20
Subsequent Cycles 21
Getting Started 22

Chapter 3: Understand Customer Requirements 23
Quality Is Defined by the Customer 23
Customers Can Be Fickle 24
Customers for Life 24
Internal and External Customers 25
Customer Satisfaction or Delight? 27
Basic Customer Expectations 27
Customer Desires 28
Customer Exciters 29
The Steps in Understanding Customer Requirements 32
List Team Outputs 32
Types of Outputs 33
Develop the List 34
Keep the Output List Current 34
List Customers 36
The Boss Is Not the Customer 36
No Customers? 36
Everyone Is a Customer? 38
Identify Output Requirements 38
List the Requirements for Each Output 38
Think from the Customer's Point of View 39
The Output Requirements Worksheet 39
Meet with the Customers 41
Verify Output Requirements 43
Determine Requirement Importance 44
Determine the Current Level of Requirement Satisfaction 45
Methods for Receiving Customer Feedback 46
Calculate Output Priority 49
Conduct Regularly Scheduled Customer Meetings 50
Summary 50
Review Questions 51

Chapter 4: Develop Team Plans 53
Purpose of Team Plans 53
Receive and Understand Team Mission 54
Developing a Team Mission 54
Understanding the Team's Role in the Organization 57

Elements of Team Plans..58
    Goals..58
    Obstacles 60
    Strategies 60
    Objectives...62
Relationship Between Plan Elements....................................63
Cascading Plan Elements..64
Using Team Plans 65
    Communicate Purpose and Direction 65
    Document Responsibilities 65
Updating Team Plans...65
Summary..66
Review Questions 66

Chapter 5: Define Processes 67
All Work Is a Process 67
Process Definitions 67
    List Team Outputs 69
    Group Similar Outputs...69
    Name the Process...70
    Define Process Boundaries 71
    List Process Activities...71
    Identify Inputs 73
A Completed Example 73
Define All of Your Team's Processes.....................................75
Prepare a Process Map for the Entire Organization...........75
Look for Gaps and Overlaps 76
    Identify Areas of Duplication...76
    Verify Output/Input Matches..76
Prioritize Processes for Improvement...................................76
    Calculate Process Priority Scores....................................77
    Identify Priority Groupings..77
Summary..79
Review Questions 79

Chapter 6: Provide Supplier Feedback 81
You Are Dependent on Your Suppliers..................................82
Meeting with Your Suppliers..82
Input Requirements 83
    List the Requirements 83
    Be Willing to Negotiate 85
Level of Importance 85
Level of Satisfaction...85
Using the Supplier Feedback Worksheet 86
    The Priority Column 86

Conducting the Meeting 86
Provide Regular Supplier Feedback...86
Summary...88
Review Questions 88

Chapter 7: Document Processes...89
Select Processes to Document...89
Use Process Flow Diagrams...89
    Identify Proper Level of Detail...89
    Ensure Process Definition Compatibility..............................90
Process Flow Diagram Symbols 90
Types of Process Flow Diagrams...90
    Operations Process Flow Diagrams.......................................90
    Functional Process Flow Diagrams 91
    Layout Process Flow Diagrams 92
Uses of Process Flow Diagrams 92
    Document a Process 93
    Highlight Variances Between Actual and Planned Methods......94
    Enhance Understanding of Other Team Members' Jobs............94
    Understand Interrelationships and Dependencies....................94
    Increase Personal Accountability..94
    Train New Employees...94
    Analyze the Impact of Proposed Changes 95
Updating Process Flow Diagrams 95
    Management Must Encourage Updates.................................95
    Schedule Periodic Reviews 96
Summary...96
Review Questions 96

Chapter 8: Improve Processes...97
Waste Reduction 97
    Assess the Value-Added for Each Activity 97
    Minimize Checks and Inspections 100
    Minimize Administrative Tasks..101
    Minimize Storage and Transportation Activities....................102
    Optimize Internally Required Activities 103
Process Simplification 103
    Combine Similar Activities 104
    Analyze Decision Points..104
Cycle Time Reduction..105
    Analyze Queues 105
    Conduct Activities in Parallel 106
    Modify the Sequence of Activities.......................................106
    Consider Time Deadlines..106

Standardization 107
    Review/Create Work Procedures 107
    Develop Standard Report Formats...........................107
    Use Forms, Worksheets, and Checklists 107
Summary..108
Review Questions 108

Chapter 9: Develop Process Measures 109
Measure Processes, Not People 109
Why Measure? 110
    Understand What Is Happening 110
    Provide Objective Performance Feedback...........110
    Evaluate the Need for Improvement.......................111
    Evaluate the Impact of Changes.............................111
    Set Meaningful Schedules and Performance Targets 111
Understand Process Variation 112
    What Is Process Variation? 112
    Process Variation Is Undesirable.............................114
    Variation Causes Loss...114
    Causes of Variation 117
Develop Measures 118
    Types of Process Performance Measurements 118
    Identify Critical Process Performance Characteristics...............119
Document Measurement Decisions....................................121
Summary..122
Review Questions 122

Chapter 10: Collect and Analyze Data...........................125
Types of Data...125
    Attributes Data...125
    Variables Data 126
    Comparing Attributes and Variables Data................126
Data Collection and Analysis Tools 126
Check Sheets..126
    Decide What Data Will Be Collected 126
    Select the Time Period..128
    Create a Data Collection Form 128
    Record the Data 128
    Uses...129
    Activity 130
Pareto Charts 130
    Collect the Data to Be Analyzed.............................130
    Select the Time Period to Analyze 132
    Sort the Data 132

List the Categories on the Horizontal Axis 132
Draw the Bars 132
Uses 132
Histograms 133
Collect the Data to Be Analyzed 134
Divide the Data into Classes 134
Create a Frequency Table 134
Draw and Label the Axes 134
Draw the Bars 134
Uses 134
Activity 137
Scatter Diagrams 137
Collect Data on Variables That May Be Related 139
Draw and Label the Axes 139
Plot Points on the Graph 139
Analyze the Data for Possible Correlations 139
Uses 139
Run Charts 141
Determine the Process Characteristic to Measure 141
Select an Appropriate Data Collection Frequency 141
Plot Points in Time-Order Sequence 141
Calculate and Draw the Process Average 142
Identify Process Patterns 142
Uses 142
Summary 142
Review Questions 143

Chapter 11: Use Statistical Methods 145
Introduction to Control Charts 145
Uses 145
Control Limits 147
Types of Control Charts 147
Attributes control charts 147
p Charts 147
c Charts 154
Variables Control Charts 159
Average and Range Charts 159
Individuals Charts 166
Selecting the Most Appropriate Chart 172
Identifying Out-of-Control Conditions 172
Nonrandom Patterns 175
Out-of-Control Rules 176
Activity 179
Working with Out-of-Control Processes 186
Determining Process Capability 186

Using Process Measurements...188
  Process Measurements Must Be Timely 188
  Display Process Measurements 188
  Use Measurement Data to Make Process Decisions 188
Summary...189
Review Questions 189

Chapter 12: Solve Problems 191
Overview of the Problem-Solving Approach....................................191
Define the Problem 191
  What Is the Problem?..193
  Where Is the Problem Occurring? 193
  When Is the Problem Occurring?..195
  The Problem Definition Worksheet 196
Identify the Root Cause 196
  The Importance of Determining the Root Cause......................196
  List Possible Causes 196
  Test Possible Causes..203
Select the Best Solution..204
  Identify Selection Criteria 204
  Generate Solution Ideas 208
  Compare Solution Ideas..210
  Analyze Risks Associated with Implementation.......................211
  Select the Best Overall Solution..214
Develop an Action Plan 217
  Document Planned Activities..217
  Identify Obstacles 217
  Revise the Plan...218
  Follow the Plan...219
Verify the Solution Results 219
Summary...219
Review Questions 219

Chapter 13: Use Creative-Thinking Techniques........................221
The Role of Creative Thinking 221
  Escape from Patterns 221
  Provide a Means for Restructuring 222
  Challenge Assumptions 222
Techniques...224
  Application 224
  Brainstorming...224
  Reversals..225
  Characteristic Changing 229
Summary...234

Chapter 14: Make Quality Everyone's Job............................235
    ISO 9000...236
        Uses..236
        TQM and ISO 9000 238
    Malcolm Baldrige National Quality Award 238
        Learn from the Best 238
        Assess Your Performance..240
    Now It's Up to You..241

Epilogue 243

Bibliography 245

Index 247

FIGURES

P.1   Overview of book contents...xxv

1.1   The key elements of TQM...2

1.2   Customer satisfaction checklist 4

1.3   Continuous improvement checklist 6

1.4   Total quality management checklist.............................9

1.5   The three Cs..10

1.6   The quality/profit chain reaction 12

2.1   The continuous process improvement cycle...............17

2.2   The first cycle...20

3.1   Internal customer/supplier relationships....................25

3.2   Every team serves as both a customer and a supplier.....26

3.3   "How do you treat your internal customers?" test......27

3.4   The customer satisfaction/delight model 28

3.5   Basic expectations vs. exciters 30

3.6   Achieving customer delight..31

3.7   Understanding customer requirements steps............32

3.8   Identify output requirements 38

3.9   Customer feedback methods 46

3.10   Review questions 52

4.1   "How are plans used?" survey 54

4.2   Mission statement elements 55

4.3   Mission flowdown through the organization 57

4.4   Plan elements...58

4.5   The relationship between plan elements.....................63

4.6   Cascading plan elements to ensure compatibility 64

4.7   Review questions 66

5.1   Process definition steps 68

5.2   The elements of a process definition 68

5.3   Possible output groupings..70

5.4   Alternate output groupings..70

5.5	An organizational process map	75
5.6	Inputs to calculating process priority totals	77
5.7	Review questions	79
6.1	The steps leading to providing supplier feedback	81
6.2	The steps in providing supplier feedback	83
6.3	Identify input requirements	83
6.4	Review questions	88
7.1	Process flow diagram symbols	91
7.2	Operations process flow diagram	91
7.3	Functional process flow diagram	92
7.4	Layout process flow diagram	92
7.5	Process flow diagram uses	93
7.6	Review questions	96
8.1	Process improvement methods	98
8.2	Value-added assessment checklist	99
8.3	Inspection challenge questions	100
8.4	Administrative task assessment checklist	102
8.5	Process simplification steps/checklist	103
8.6	Cycle time reduction methods	105
8.7	Serial vs. parallel process activities	106
8.8	Review questions	108
9.1	Process measurement purposes	110
9.2	Mail receipt distribution	112
9.3	The traditional view of loss	115
9.4	The realistic view of loss	116
9.5	Critical process performance characteristics identification methods	120
9.6	Review questions	122
10.1	Data collection and analysis tools	127
10.2	Check sheet	128
10.3	Location check sheet	129
10.4	Pareto chart	130
10.5	Stratified Pareto chart	133
10.6	Histogram	133
10.7	Using histograms to view variation	135
10.8	Using histograms to view process skewness	136
10.9	Stratified histogram	136
10.10	Histogram caution	137
10.11	Scatter diagram	139
10.12	Types of correlations visible on scatter diagrams	140
10.13	Run chart	141
10.14	Run chart patterns	143
10.15	Review questions	143
11.1	Measurement of process variation	146
11.2	Control chart selection flowchart	172

11.3   Nonrandom patterns 175
11.4   Control chart zones...176
11.5   Out-of-control rule 1 177
11.6   Out-of-control rule 2 177
11.7   Out-of-control rule 3 178
11.8   Out-of-control rule 4 178
11.9   Process capability...186
11.10   Process capability examples 187
11.11   Review questions 189
12.1   The five-step problem-solving approach 192
12.2   Problem definition questions 192
12.3   The "asking why" technique...200
12.4   A cause/effect diagram 200
12.5   Using multiple cause/effect diagrams 202
12.6   A relationship diagram..203
12.7   Select the best solution steps 205
12.8   Potential obstacle identification suggestions 218
12.9   Review questions 219
14.1   ISO 9000 documents...236
14.2   ISO 9001 clauses 237
14.3   MBNQA winners 239

WORKSHEETS

Output List Worksheet 35

Customer List Worksheet 37

Output Requirements Worksheet 42

Output Requirements Worksheet (completed example)...........51

Process Definition Worksheet 72

Process Definition Worksheet (completed example) 74

Process Priority Scoring Worksheet 78

Process Priority List Worksheet...80

Supplier Feedback Worksheet 87

Measurement Decision Documentation Worksheet...............123

Problem Definition Worksheet...197

Problem Definition Worksheet (completed example) 198

Selection Criteria Development Worksheet.............................207

Selection Criteria Development Worksheet
       (completed example)...209

Solution Comparison Worksheet 212

Solution Comparison Worksheet (completed example).........213

Risk Analysis Worksheet...215

Risk Analysis Worksheet (completed example) 216

Reversal to Identify Causes Worksheet 227

Reversal to Identify Solutions Worksheet 228

Reversal to Identify Causes Worksheet (completed example)..............230

Characteristic Changing Worksheet...232

Characteristic Changing Worksheet (completed example).................233

ACTIVITIES

Output Requirement Listing Activity 40

Check Sheet Activity 131

Histogram Activity 138

p Chart Activity 150

p Chart Activity Control Chart 151

p Chart Activity Control Chart (Solution) 153

c Chart Activity 155

c Chart Activity Control Chart 156

c Chart Activity Control Chart (Solution) 158

$\bar{X}$–R Chart Activity 162

$\bar{X}$–R Chart Activity Control Chart 163

$\bar{X}$–R Chart Activity Control Chart (Solution) 165

X–R Chart Activity 168

X–R Chart Activity Control Chart 169

X–R Chart Activity Control Chart (Solution) 171

Control Chart Selection Activity 173

Control Chart Selection Activity (Solution) 174

Control Chart Activity 180

Control Chart Activity (Solution) 183

PREFACE

The concepts and techniques of total quality management (TQM) traditionally have been limited to large manufacturing companies. This is no longer the case. Now, more and more people are realizing the concepts and techniques of TQM are the same for any business, regardless of its size or type. Total quality management can help companies small and large, manufacturing and service.

Although the concepts and techniques are the same, it can be difficult to understand and apply the techniques until they are presented directly to a specific audience. Up to this point, such a source has not existed for small businesses. For those in small businesses, this book is for you. The aim of this book is to provide you with a complete reference for implementing TQM in your company. With this said, I will be the first to admit that this book does not cover everything associated with TQM (such a book would be thousands of pages long). I have attempted to boil down what I think you need to know to get started and successfully apply the concepts and techniques for positive results in your business. My hope is that this book, and the success resulting from following the steps prescribed, will stir your interest in the subject of TQM and encourage you to continue your journey toward continuous quality improvement. The bibliography at the end of the book contains a list of recommended books. Look there to find a book to continue your study on the subject(s) of special interest to you.

One of my greatest disappointments is to hear TQM discussed as just a set of theories or the latest management craze. It is neither! TQM, when implemented completely and systematically, offers practical methods to improve your organization's performance. For this reason, the discussion of theory has been included in this book only when necessary to introduce a tool or technique. This is a practical, how-to book.

Throughout the book you will be encouraged to act upon the information presented to you. The information provided and the steps prescribed are based on my experience implementing TQM and helping others do the same. The steps have been used with success by others before you. For those who read, and do not apply the techniques suggested, TQM will be just a theory or craze. Those who take the time and effort to apply the techniques will be rewarded with improved performance.

HOW TO USE THIS BOOK

This book has been designed to provide a step-by-step guide for anyone in a small business wanting to implement TQM. Figure P.1 presents a tree diagram of the layout of this book, showing the sequence of topics covered. The how-to portion of this book starts in chapter 3, after the first two chapters provide the introductory information you need to get started. The last chapter introduces ISO 9000 and the Malcolm Baldrige National Quality Award as two final subjects to which you should be introduced.

This book is written with the assumption that your company has not implemented the concepts and techniques of TQM. Many readers may be part of organizations that have started implementation, but had their efforts stall. Based on my experience, these stalls often are due to a lack of a structured approach to implementation. This book presents a proven, successful approach to implementation. In most cases, companies already started on the journey toward TQM will not have to start over. Much of what has been accomplished can be built upon. I recommend that companies in this situation follow the steps prescribed in the order they are presented. When you come to an area where you already have made some progress, build upon the work already performed.

Worksheets

Worksheets are included throughout this book. The book has been formatted to make use of the worksheets as easy as possible. The worksheets are visible representations of the steps called for or information provided in the text. They are provided as an aid to the reader since some people can understand a concept better once they can see it.

Completing the worksheets should be done as a team. This teamwork not only results in a better product, but helps everyone to feel like a part of the group. Encourage everyone on the team to participate, everyone's ideas are important.

Use the worksheets only if they are helpful. Completing the worksheets should not be your aim. Worksheets are a means to the end, not the end itself. Your aim is process improvement. If the worksheets help you to improve your process, use them. Your job is not complete just because you have completed a worksheet; your job is done when you have performed the steps prescribed.

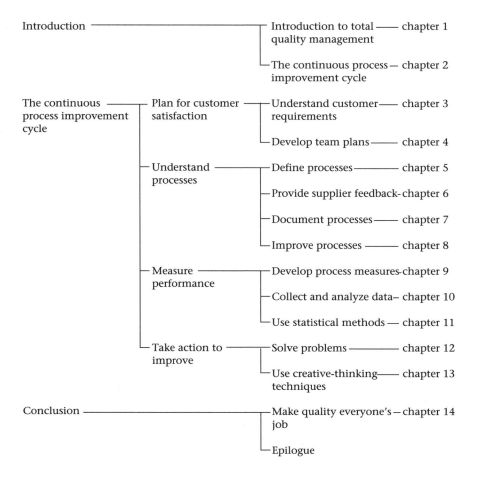

Figure P.1. Overview of book contents.

In some cases, you may find the worksheets more helpful once you have made some changes to customize them for your organization. Great! Do whatever helps you. The only caution is that I strongly recommend you do not get off the path prescribed by the steps presented in the text. The steps have been developed over time, and tested by many companies, to accomplish specific ends. The results of the steps are used later to accomplish the overall aim of process improvement. Modifying the steps recommended or the sequence in which they are presented may have an adverse effect later in your process improvement efforts.

(*Author's note:* I would like to see the worksheets you have customized for your organization. At your request, I will provide you my thoughts on your modifications. Fax copies to 316-945-9696 or call me at 800-962-9799.)

Make a Team Notebook. I recommend that you create a team notebook to store your worksheets and other documentation generated from your improvement initiatives. You will need a way to easily access the documentation for reference and to make necessary updates. Make the following four tabs.

- Plan for customer satisfaction.
- Understand processes.
- Measure performance.
- Take action to improve.

You will see the significance of these four titles in chapter 2. Get the notebook and make the tabs now; you will need it in chapter 3.

Activities

Activities also are presented throughout the book. They are designed to allow you to practice the concepts or techniques after they are introduced. I suggest you perform each of the activities as they are presented before continuing your reading. The activities are based on my experience training teams in the same concepts and techniques presented here. Each of the activities have been performed by many before you, so the bugs have been worked out. Use the activities to test your understanding before you continue reading. The point of the activities is the best time to identify any misunderstandings. Proceeding with misunderstandings likely will result in confusion. It is better to clarify any misunderstandings on the examples presented in the activities rather than experience problems when you apply the concepts and techniques to your job.

Review Questions

Questions are listed at the end of chapters 3 through 12. They are provided to help you check what you have done with the information provided in the chapter. Remember, this book is a guide to action. Because the chapters rely on information and action from the previous chapters, the questions can help you decide if you are ready to continue on to the next chapter. The questions also can be used by members of management to encourage use of the tools and techniques. Asking these questions can demonstrate management's commitment to the use of the concepts and techniques taught.

ACKNOWLEDGMENTS

I have been privileged to meet and work with many people in my lifetime who have helped me considerably. There are many people to thank at the completion of a project such as this. At the risk of leaving someone out, I would like to offer my appreciation to those listed below.

First, I am thankful to everyone at the Vought Aircraft Company, Dallas, Texas. It is with you that I first had a chance to develop and put into practice some of my ideas. Special thanks to Drew, Leigh, and David. I am proud to have been associated with you.

Thanks to Gonzalo Mendieta, Ph.D., and Jeffrey Stewart for your review and comments on chapter 11. Your comments reassured me that I was on the right track and ensured that I had all of the technical details straight.

Thanks to Evelyn Thompson. Miss Thompson, I hope your student has made you proud.

Without the support from Chuck, Jackie, Gwen, and Byron at Spectrum, Inc., Wichita, Kansas, I never could have completed this book. Thanks for your support and encouragement as my thoughts and ideas were transferred to these pages.

Finally, thanks to my wonderful family. Thanks for being especially patient the last few months as I have worked on this book. To Joan, Matt, and Ryan: Daddy's book is done.

INTRODUCTION TO TOTAL QUALITY MANAGEMENT

Total quality management. What is it? Can it really be applied and work in my small business? If so, how? This book has been written to answer these three questions. The first two questions are addressed in this chapter. The remainder of the book is devoted to answering the "how" question.

TOTAL QUALITY MANAGEMENT IN SMALL BUSINESS

The concepts and techniques of total quality management (TQM) are the same for any business, large or small. To date, the benefits of TQM primarily have been enjoyed by large manufacturing companies. Many small businesses are now beginning to realize they too can benefit from implementation. In some cases, companies are requiring implementation by their suppliers (many of whom are small businesses). Whatever the motivation, small businesses are becoming increasingly interested in TQM. This book presents a systematic approach for understanding and successfully implementing the concepts and techniques of TQM for any small business. Let's start with a discussion of what TQM is.

WHAT IS TOTAL QUALITY MANAGEMENT?

Many people think TQM is just the latest management craze, and that it will fade like the fads preceding it. In fact, I am often asked what I think will come after TQM. My answer is that it is here to stay. We may call it something else, and we will advance beyond what is now referred to as TQM, but the basic concepts will remain. With this said, let's work on defining TQM.

1

The first issue to address is what to call it. I have been using the phrase total quality management (TQM). Others prefer total quality leadership (TQL), continuous quality improvement (CQI), or any number of other three letter acronyms (TLAs). It seems to me that those who argue over the best name for the concepts and techniques being discussed are missing the main point. What difference does it really make what you call it, as long as you know what it is?

The problem with trying to define any subject, especially one with as many different understandings as TQM, is the tendency to argue or struggle over single word choices rather than focus on the important, overall meaning. For this reason, I define TQM by describing its five key elements shown in Figure 1.1 rather than introduce a one-sentence or paragraph definition. Each of the elements will be described.

Ensuring Customer Satisfaction

In recent advertising campaigns, Southwestern Bell Yellow Pages has poked fun at fictitious companies that chose not to advertise in its book because they don't want to overwork mom in the diner or sell their only rug. The rest of us want customers. Customers are the reason you are in business. Does this sound incredibly obvious? If so, why have so many businesses lost sight of the importance of customer satisfaction? One does not have to look far for stories of malfunctioning products or incompetent service. The subject of many horror stories mentioned at my seminars are auto dealerships, specifically their service departments.

The dealership where I *used* to take my car for service has, unfortunately, provided me with many examples. On one occasion, on the way home from picking my car up after the service was completed, I noticed that the speedometer and odometer were not working (I'm embarrassed to say how far I had driven before I noticed the problem). I knew the

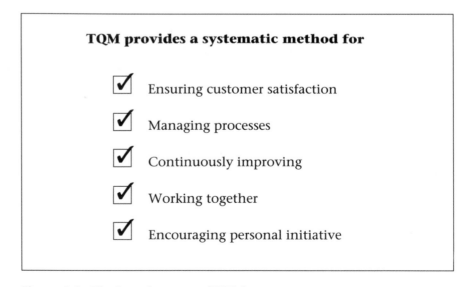

Figure 1.1. The key elements of TQM.

office of the service department was full of people picking their cars up after work and the office personnel were ready to quit for the day, so I continued home and called to report the problem the next day. After receiving several excuses about how the problem could have occurred, the service manager offered to fix the problem whenever I could return. The next time I had service performed on my car at the same dealership, I got home only to realize my car's radio antenna was missing. My call to the service manager resulted in more excuses.

A closer look at this example may reveal some reasons why we tend to think so many businesses have lost interest in customer satisfaction. I have no doubt that the service manager I was dealing with was attempting to satisfy his customer (me) by offering reasons (I interpreted as excuses) for the problems and offering to remedy the situations at no cost to me. The point he missed was that I was a dissatisfied customer because the problems occurred in the first place. It did not matter to me what his reasons were or that he so generously offered to fix the problems. I still had to make the trips across town for them to fix something that should not have needed fixing!

Needless to say, I have not returned to that dealership for service or to purchase a new car. Satisfied customers, on the other hand, not only return to do business again, they are likely to tell others of the outstanding service they received.

Look at the checklist in Figure 1.2. How does your organization rate? Do you have a customer focus? Is customer satisfaction your aim? Are you doing what is necessary to accomplish this aim?

Managing Processes

As part of the introduction to the seminars I present on TQM, I ask my audiences what comes to mind when they think of quality. Much to my surprise, the word *inspection* has not been mentioned once in the last year! Didn't we used to think quality and inspection were synonymous?

The Clara Johnson Test. This reliance on inspection was evident even in television commercials. Do you remember a lawn mower commercial that featured Clara Johnson? She was the inspector at the end of the line for this lawn mower manufacturer. Her job was to pull the cord of each lawn mower as it came off the line. As the mower started on the commercial, she proudly said, "Ship it!" We were all supposed to feel better about buying this brand of lawn mower, because they would not ship their product unless it passed the Clara Johnson test.

What is wrong with this way of thinking? What if the mower did not start (other than filming the actress pulling the cord on another mower)? How could the manufacturer know what is wrong with it? How many other mowers had been produced with the same problem?

How does your organization rate? ✔

☐ "We know what is best for our customers."   —*or*— ☐ "We can never know enough about our customers."

☐ Satisfaction is defined as the absence of dissatisfied customers   —*or*— ☐ Satisfaction means understanding and exceeding customer expectations

☐ The customer service department is responsible for satisfaction   —*or*— ☐ Customer satisfaction is everyone's responsibility

☐ Training emphasizes "smile school" and problem solving   —*or*— ☐ Training emphasizes customer and expectation identification

☐ Customer satisfaction is viewed as a program   —*or*— ☐ Customer satisfaction is an attitude, a way of life

☐ Procedures are designed for the convenience of the organization   —*or*— ☐ Customer convenience is the driver for all procedures and practices

☐ Decisions are based on cost, payback, and budgets   —*or*— ☐ Decisions are based on satisfying customers

---

Figure 1.2. Customer satisfaction checklist.

Process Focus. By the time the Clara Johnsons of the world find a problem, it is too late! A more proactive approach is to *manage the processes* that produce the products and services that reach your customers.

Processes exist in every part of an organization. Many people mistakenly think of only production or manufacturing operations when process improvement is discussed. Production processes often come to mind because it is easy to visualize the systematic progression of activities from receiving parts to assembling the parts to produce the product. But every part of an organization performs work that also can be systematically described. There will be more discussion about work processes beginning in chapter 5.

Managing processes is the second element of the TQM definition. Organizations must change from relying on detecting errors (inspection) to preventing errors. This shift is an easy concept to understand and agree with, but often can be difficult to implement. The key for implementation is acknowledging that employees need to be prepared to manage the processes they perform. This preparation involves training in the concepts and techniques of TQM.

PROCESS

A series of tasks that produce a result. Requires the transformation of inputs into outputs.

Continuously Improving

You may have heard the phrase: "If you do what you've always done, you'll get what you've always gotten."

Well, I have news for you: whoever said this was an optimist. This is the best you can hope for! The phrase should be rewritten for today's business climate. Something like the following probably would be more appropriate: "If you do what you've always done, you'll get run out of business."

There Is Always Room for Improvement.   In sporting events, fractions of a second or fractions of an inch can mean the difference between a gold medal and no medal at all. For some reason, we seem to think we need to look for the big improvement ideas in business. Study the checklist in Figure 1.3. Which side of the checklist best describes your organization?

The checklist contrasts business's traditional approach of thinking big with the concept of continuous improvement that focuses on small, incremental improvements. The biggest difference probably is the realization that searching for improvements does not have to be driven by programs, events, or problems. Quite the contrary, everyone should continuously be searching for improvements to the work they perform.

To use another sports analogy, the traditional approach is similar to hitting home runs in baseball. Home runs are exciting, and they are one way to score runs. Those striving only for home runs exhibit an all or nothing attitude. In fact, hitters who rely on home runs often suffer a high number of strikeouts. Another strategy is to rely on contact instead of power. The focus on making contact can lead to many singles. Singles may not be as exciting as home runs, but a string of singles can score runs. The search for continuous improvement is like hitting singles. Implementing many small, incremental improvements can have a compounding effect.

The purpose of this discussion is not to say that big improvements are bad or that you should avoid them, just that there is significant benefit from those small, incremental improvements as well. Consider this a challenge to your current thought process. Do you look for ways to improve the little things?

Systematic Process Reviews.   You may be thinking: "This sounds great, but how do I go about finding these small, incremental improvements?" The answer is in conducting systematic process reviews. These reviews will reveal opportunities for improvement. The specific how-tos for conducting these reviews are covered in detail throughout this book.

How does your organization rate? ☑

☐ Focus on big improvements   —*or*—   ☐ Focus on small, incremental improvements

☐ Search for improvements drivenby programs, events, problems   —*or*—   ☐ Continuous search for improvements

☐ Improvements made intermittently, in spurts   —*or*—   ☐ Gradual and constant improvements

☐ Individual ideas and efforts   —*or*—   ☐ Everyone involved, team approach

☐ Look for improvements to others' jobs   —*or*—   ☐ Focus on job-related improvements

☐ Driven by cost/benefit, profit   —*or*—   ☐ Driven by desire to make the job easier, quicker, safer

---

Figure 1.3. Continuous improvement checklist.

Base Improvement Decisions on Cost/Benefit Analyses. Improvements should not be implemented just for improvement sake. The cost associated with implementation should be compared to the expected benefits. These calculations do not need to be performed with a great deal of accuracy. Don't make this activity too scientific, just make sure you are not spending $100 for a $.05 benefit that goes unnoticed by your customers.

Working Together

The fourth element of the TQM definition is teamwork. The whole really can be greater than the sum of the parts. Teams can achieve more if the individuals work together than if they all act independently.

TEAM

A group of individuals who work together on one or more common processes.

What Is a Team? A team is a group of individuals who work together on one or more common processes. These individuals may all be from the same department, represent several departments, or involve an external supplier or customer. The team members already work together to produce their work outputs. The department at a bank that processes and mails customer statements, the department responsible for drilling holes and installing rivets, and the group that makes an organization's travel arrangements are all examples of teams.

Differing Views Must Be Valued.   Effective teamwork requires that everyone understand that different ideas and points of view are good—the team actually is strengthened by its diverse backgrounds and experiences. By valuing diversity, team members realize they are important and that they can contribute to the team.

Consensus Decision Making.   Effective teams make decisions based on consensus. Consensus is a general agreement by everyone involved. Consensus is achieved when all members of a team understand a decision, and, even if they don't completely agree with the decision, accept and support it. Consensus means everyone has a chance to voice their opinions and concerns, and everyone else listens and considers different ideas.

Decisions made by consensus do not involve voting. A 6 to 5 vote should not automatically mean the decision passes. The key is to understand why the five do not support the decision, their concerns should be probed and addressed. Attempts should be made to reconcile all issues and concerns expressed. The aim of consensus decision making is to make a decision everyone can support. There is no room on a team for "I told you so."

For a complete discussion of teams including many examples and case studies, how teams work best, and how to enhance their effectiveness, I recommend *The Wisdom of Teams*.[1]

CONSENSUS

A general agreement by everyone involved. Achieved when all members of a team understand a decision, and, even if they don't completely agree with the decision, accept and support it. Everyone has a chance to voice their opinions and concerns, and everyone else listens and considers different ideas.

Encouraging Personal Initiative

One of the most common words in the business community today is empowerment. After talking on this subject with a small group, one manager from the audience asked: "Isn't empowerment like letting the inmates run the asylum?" We all got a laugh from the question, but I think he was serious. I know many members of management share this way of thinking. This point of view, I think, comes from a lack of understanding of the concept of empowerment and a poor perception of the employees (why else would they be referred to as inmates?). Part of the misunderstanding comes from the "power" portion of the word empowerment. Some members of management feel like they have worked too hard to give up some of their power.

According to Stephen R. Covey, author of the best-seller *The 7 Habits of Highly Effective People,*

> An "empowered" organization is one in which individuals have the knowledge, skill, desire, and opportunity to personally succeed in a way that leads to collective organizational success.[2]

Isn't this what everyone in the company wants? Why don't we see more empowered organizations?

Appropriate Personal Initiative.   I prefer the phrase "appropriate personal initiative" to empowerment. This phrase offers a better description of the concept being endorsed, and does not contain the word power. Let's take a closer look at this concept.

No Need to Micro-Manage.   Based on my discussions with managers from many small businesses, I believe few managers want to micro-manage the activities of their employees. They do so out of a perceived necessity. They feel that if they are not involved in all the details, something will go wrong. If this is indeed the case, the way to encourage appropriate personal initiative is to address this concern for management.

The way to address this concern is to look at the key word in the phrase "appropriate personal initiative" for management: *appropriate.* If managers were convinced the action taken by employees would be appropriate to the situation, they would encourage action to be taken. This reasoning leads to the conclusion that the key to empowerment is preparing employees to take appropriate personal initiative.

Preparing Employees.   The key to preparing employees to take appropriate personal initiative is to train them in the concepts and techniques of TQM. Through this training, employees are prepared to manage the processes they are responsible for performing. This book presents a structured approach to training the employees in your organization in the concepts and techniques of TQM.

TQM Checklist

I have suggested that TQM can be defined by the five elements just introduced. How does your organization rate? The TQM checklist shown in Figure 1.4 is provided as a means for you to quickly assess your organization's starting point for implementing TQM.

CAN IT WORK IN MY SMALL BUSINESS?

Since you bought this book, you must be interested in implementing TQM in a small business. Your first question may be: "Can TQM be applied and work in my small business?" YES! The concepts presented so far in this chapter are the same for *any* company: small or large, service or manufacturing. (Who would dare contend that customer satisfaction is not relevant to their business?) The techniques presented throughout this book are also the same for any company. What makes this book unique is the method and sequence in which the concepts and techniques are presented and the examples used to help those of you in small businesses understand and know how to apply the techniques in your business for results.

How does your organization rate? ☑

☐ Has a product-oriented definition of quality	—or—	☐ Has a customer-oriented definition of quality
☐ Emphasizes maintaining the status quo	—or—	☐ Emphasizes daily improvements
☐ Focuses on the short term	—or—	☐ Attempts to balance the short and long term
☐ Measures people	—or—	☐ Measures processes
☐ Emphasizes error detection	—or—	☐ Emphasizes error prevention
☐ Asks: "Who made the error?"	—or—	☐ Asks: "What allowed the error to occur?"
☐ Relies on managers to solve problems	—or—	☐ Encourages teamwork and group problem solving involving everyone
☐ Assigns the responsibility for quality to the quality control department	—or—	☐ Realizes that everyone is responsible for quality
☐ Views managers as dictators and controllers	—or—	☐ Views managers as coaches, facilitators, and problem solvers
☐ Blames workers for poor performance	—or—	☐ Realizes management is responsible for the system

Figure 1.4. Total quality management checklist.

Let's continue with a look at why producing quality products and providing quality service is important. See if you don't agree that the reasons presented are certainly applicable to your business.

WHY IS QUALITY IMPORTANT?

The reasons for improving quality can be summarized by considering the three Cs shown in Figure 1.5.

Customers

Customers are the reason any business exists. The primary reason for producing quality products and delivering quality service is customer satisfaction. This may sound obvious, but few would say it sounds easy. The frustrating part about the customer-quality connection is that the customer may have difficulty defining quality. How can you provide quality products and services if your customers cannot even

Why Is Quality Important?
The three Cs

 Customers
   –Your customers may not be able to define quality or even
      explain what they consider to be "high quality," but they
      know it when they see it.
   –Customers vote with their feet.

 Competition
   –Advances in transportation and communications
      technology are making the world smaller.

 Costs
   –It costs less to provide quality products and services.

Figure 1.5. The three Cs.

tell you what "high quality" is to them? Herein lies the challenge. Chapter 3 offers some techniques for addressing this dilemma.

Competition

The geographic boundaries that used to define competitive zones are disappearing. A couple of years ago, when I wanted to purchase some office supplies, I had two options depending on which direction my other business required me to go. As a consumer, my options were clear. As suppliers, the two companies were familiar with each other as their competition. It is not so clear-cut now.

The Effects of Technology.   The world of toll-free telephone numbers, fax machines, and overnight delivery have changed the competitive boundaries. Technology has, in effect, made the world smaller. (From what I understand about interactive television and other new technologies, the changes we have already seen are just the beginning.) Consumers are no longer limited to suppliers in their geographic area to fulfill their needs. It is just as easy, if not easier, to shop in a catalog or through an on-line computer shopping network, place an order by calling an 800 number, and receive the product the next day courtesy of an overnight package delivery company. If you have not checked lately, you can purchase almost anything this way now.

Service Companies Are Affected, Too.   This discussion so far has focused on products. Has technology had the same effect for services? Sure. For example, I have never personally met my investment advisor. We have conducted all of our business over the telephone (long distance through an 800 number) and the mail. By choosing to conduct my business in this manner, I am not limited to the investment advisors in my city, I can choose from any in the country.

Even more hands-on services are affected. Computer software support is a good example. I used to be a computer programmer. As part of my job, I provided support to customers by helping them with any software problems or questions. I was able to provide some of my services over the telephone, but most of the time the situation required me to travel to where the computer was to be able to diagnose and fix the problem. This travel requirement made it necessary for me to be geographically close to the customers to provide the prompt service they expected. In other words, my area of coverage was limited. Today, this same type of service can be provided without traveling to where the computer is. The computer experts can log on to the problem computer from wherever they are, experience the problem for themselves, perform their diagnosis, and fix the problem.

Costs

There are many benefits to implementing TQM. Some of the benefits are intangible. Improved employee morale and company reputation are two good examples. These types of intangible benefits often are cited as the benefits of TQM. Although it is true these benefits exist and are important, I want to emphasize the financial benefits of improved quality.

You can't afford *not* to implement TQM! Improved quality has a direct impact on improved profits. Figure 1.6 shows how improved quality results in improved profits.

Reduces Waste.   Probably the most obvious result of improved quality is the reduction of the waste associated with producing a product or providing a service. Waste includes the costs of scrap materials and the time required to redo work. These costs usually are associated with a manufacturing company, but there are occasions in any organization where time is spent doing things over again. The direct result of reduced waste is reduced costs. It is then easy to see the next link, the one between reduced costs and increased profit.

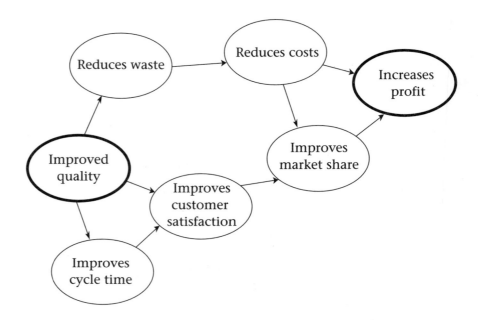

Figure 1.6. The quality/profit chain reaction.

Improves Customer Satisfaction.   Another result of improved quality is improved customer satisfaction. As already illustrated, views of quality may vary between consumers. This means that quality is in the eye of the beholder. But, consumers know quality when they see it. Do you think improved customer satisfaction would have a positive effect on your profits? Sure. Satisfied customers not only return to do business with you again, they tell their friends, family members, and coworkers about their positive experiences. Improved customer satisfaction results in improved market share which, in turn, results in increased profits.

CYCLE TIME
The time required to produce a product or provide a service from the point of order.

Improves Cycle Time.   Cycle time is the time required to produce a product or provide a service from the point of order. Anytime you can reduce the cycle time of your products or services, your customers will notice. This idea means improved cycle time leads to improved customer satisfaction, and the merits of improved customer satisfaction have already been discussed.

The bottom line is that improved quality leads to increased profits. It actually costs less to provide quality products and services.

SUMMARY

This chapter has presented a description of TQM by describing its five key elements: ensuring customer satisfaction, managing processes, continuously improving, working together, and encouraging personal initiative. This definition provides a working model of TQM for any small business.

The next chapter provides an introduction to the continuous process improvement cycle, the structure around which this book is built.

NOTES

1. Jon R. Katzenbach and Douglas K. Smith, *The Wisdom of Teams: Creating the High-Performance Organization* (Boston, Mass.: Harvard Business School Press, 1993).

2. Stephen R. Covey, *Principle-Centered Leadership* (New York: Summit Books, 1990), 212.

THE CONTINUOUS PROCESS IMPROVEMENT CYCLE

Before getting into the how-tos of implementation, we need to get organized. Many business get started with initiatives like TQM, but few follow through to realize the benefits. Initial desires fizzle, excitement wanes, and momentum disappears. Why does this happen, even to the most well-intentioned people?

The source, at least in part, is a lack of structure to the initiative. Without structure, progress requires constant attention to detail and daily decisions. Focus on this level can be exhausting and very time consuming. Structure provides the path to follow so course chartering decisions do not have to be constantly made. The course is set (but not inflexibly mandated) by the structure.

The importance of having and following a structure exists for a company of any size. Do not think that just because your company is small you do not need to follow a structure for successful implementation of TQM. In fact, a methodology may be even more important to small companies since they can rarely afford the luxury of a full-time quality expert to guide them through the steps of implementation.

THE NEED FOR A METHODOLOGY

A methodology is a system or collection of methods. A methodology, containing a collection of the proper methods in a logical sequence, can provide the structure helpful to implement TQM. Such a methodology is presented in this book.

METHODOLOGY
A system or collection of methods. A methodology can provide the structure helpful to implement TQM.

Avoid False Starts

Build a Stable Foundation

As soon as a commitment to implementing TQM has been made, the first question is rather obvious: What do we do first? Getting a good start is important to allow you to avoid false starts and build a stable foundation upon which your improvement activities can be built.

After employees know a little about TQM, they are likely to be excited about the prospects of implementation. Employees want to do a good job. They want to be able to improve the quality of their products and services, they just need to know how.

Depending on your company's history, the employees may also be a little apprehensive. If the employees perceive this new effort as the latest in a string of programs they have seen come and go, they will likely be skeptical. They may also try to test management to see if they are serious this time.

This apprehension is common in new initiatives. Years ago I was the administrator of a large company's suggestion program. I was responsible for redesigning the existing program to encourage more participation. A key element in the new program was to significantly reduce the time required for idea suggestors to receive feedback on their ideas.

The employees were skeptical about the new program; they were not at all sure things were going to be any different than what they had experienced under the old program. Guess what happened at the start of the new program. We received hundreds of ideas in a very short period of time. In retrospect, I can see that the employees were testing the new program to see if it could live up to its advance billing. We knew it was critical to handle these initial ideas as promised to demonstrate the company's commitment to the new program. We had to convince everyone that things really were different. Just think how hard it would have been to get the employees to believe in any new programs down the line if we did not deliver this time.

This same level of criticality exists for you as you begin your TQM implementation. You cannot afford any false starts. Getting started on the right foot is critical. Skeptical employees will watch your actions to see if they match your words. They may even test the system. Don't blame the employees for this skepticism, it is based on what they have experienced in the past. Your responsibility is to prove through actions that this initiative is for real, not just the latest program of the month.

The first steps of implementation also need to lay a stable foundation for your future activities. Implementation should be designed so each step builds upon the previous. Actions should not be independent or separate from previous actions.

Building this foundation requires an understanding of future activities so the initial actions can prepare the way. Visibility of future activities is impossible without personal experience or advice from someone with the necessary experience. That is where this book comes in. The book outlines a tested, structured approach to implementation you can follow to get a good start.

THE METHODOLOGY

Training in the tools and concepts of TQM requires a structure—a sequenced set of activities to follow. This chapter introduces the continuous process improvement cycle as a structure around which TQM training can be structured for small businesses. The cycle is shown in Figure 2.1.

Those familiar with the plan-do-check-act (PDCA) cycle may notice some similarity between the continuous process improvement cycle and the PDCA cycle. The PDCA cycle is sometimes called the plan-do-study-act (PDSA) cycle or the Deming cycle[1] after quality pioneer Dr. W. Edwards Deming (although Dr. Deming called it the Shewhart cycle after Walter Shewhart). The continuous process improvement cycle is a modified version of the PDCA cycle.

Each step of the cycle is summarized in the following text. Descriptions of each chapter are provided to introduce you to the sequence of topics covered in the rest of the book.

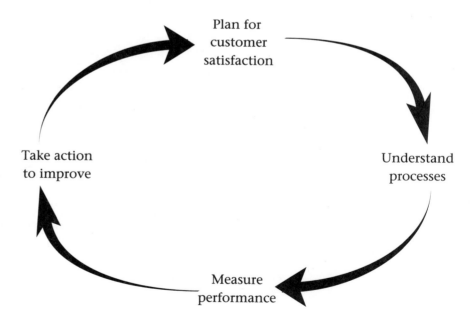

Figure 2.1. The continuous process improvement cycle.

Plan for Customer Satisfaction

The first step of the continuous process improvement cycle is plan for customer satisfaction. As we stated in the first chapter, customers are the reason your business exists, so it makes sense that your TQM implementation begins by focusing on customer satisfaction. By beginning with this emphasis on customer satisfaction, all of the activities performed throughout the rest of the cycle can be focused toward this aim.

Understand Customer Requirements.   The starting point for achieving customer satisfaction is to know who your customers are and understand their requirements and expectations. Chapter 3 introduces the concept of internal customers and compares customer satisfaction with delight. A structured approach to achieving customer satisfaction also is presented.

Develop Team Plans.   After the voice of the customer has been heard, plans can be developed to document a team's planned activities. Plans can be used to help coordinate and focus a team's activities. Chapter 4 provides a list of recommended elements for team plans and provides examples for each.

Understand Processes

After you understand who your customers are and what they expect, you are ready to look at the processes you perform to produce the products and services provided to your customers.

Define Processes.   The first step in understanding your processes is to define each of the processes you perform. Chapter 5 presents a structured method for defining the work processes of any team or organization.

Provide Supplier Feedback.   Since you are dependent on your suppliers to provide what you need to satisfy your customers, it is important to communicate with them. Make sure they know what you need, what is important to you, and how you think they are doing. Chapter 6 describes the information you should communicate to your suppliers.

Document Processes.   A key step in understanding a process is to be able to document it by listing the steps involved. Chapter 7 introduces process flow diagrams as a means of graphically describing a process. These diagrams serve as excellent process analysis tools and will be used in several subsequent chapters. Three types of process flow diagrams are introduced to provide different types of information. The symbols to use and steps to follow to prepare the diagrams are discussed.

Improve Processes.   A quick review of process flow diagrams often reveals simple, immediate improvements that can be made to the process. This type of improvement is the focus of chapter 8. Methods for reducing waste, simplifying processes, reducing cycle time, and standardizing processes are detailed.

Measure Performance

Process performance must be measured to understand what is happening, provide objective performance feedback, evaluate the need for improvement, evaluate the impact of changes, and set meaningful schedules and performance targets.

Develop Process Measures.   Objective, accurate information about process performance is required to make proper decisions. Chapter 9 discusses the focus of measurements, why process measurements are important, and the effects of process variation. Methods to follow in selecting critical process characteristics to measure are introduced.

Collect and Analyze Data.   After you know what process characteristics you are going to measure to monitor process performance, the next step is to collect and analyze process performance data. Chapter 10 introduces and explains several tools that can be used to collect and begin analyzing the data. Specific steps to follow to use each of the tools are offered.

Use Statistical Methods.   Proper interpretation of time-sequenced data requires statistical data analysis. Chapter 11 introduces control charts as the means for analyzing the variation present in any process. The uses, elements, and types of control charts, as well as step-by-step instructions for four common control charts, are provided. Methods for determining whether a process is in-control or out-of-control also are listed.

Take Action to Improve

The result of the previous activities will likely be the identification of actions to take to improve the process. Chapter 12 provides a structured approach to problem solving and decision making. Creative thinking techniques are introduced in chapter 13 to help identify possible root causes and generate new solution ideas.

THE CYCLE IS CONTINUOUS

The cycle has four steps, but remember from Figure 2.1 that the cycle is continuous. There is no way that anyone could make all of the possible process improvements after completing the four steps once. In fact, the activities described in the cycle are designed to help you prioritize your improvement efforts and focus your resources on the areas requiring immediate attention. Continuous improvement is the name of the game.

The cycle is the structure around which your improvement efforts are based. The first time through the cycle is important. There is a delicate balance between spending too much time the first time through (by spending a significant amount of time on many processes rather than making progress on a single process) and rushing through (by not covering all of the topics and spending enough time on a process to have impact). The following paragraphs contain recommendations for the level of detail you should consider as you apply the concepts directly to your job.

The First Cycle

The aim of the first cycle is to prepare you to know the contents of the cycle and how to apply the concepts and techniques to your job. This aim is accomplished by introducing you to the concepts and techniques and applying the techniques directly to your job.

Because there are many opportunities for improvement in any organization, improvement efforts must be focused. Figure 2.2 shows

Cycle Step	First-Time Focus
1. Plan for customer satisfaction	List *all* customers and outputs, talk to *all* customers, develop a complete plan
2. Understand processes	Define *all* processes, document *one* process
3. Measure performance	Collect and analyze data on *one* process
4. Take action to improve	Implement a solution to *one* problem with the process being measured

Figure 2.2. The first cycle.

how I recommend you approach your first time through the cycle. Some of the items listed under First-Time Focus may not make sense now, but they will as you reach the part of the book covering that portion of the cycle. Refer back to the figure as you work through the book. Use it as a guide for the recommended level of detail to focus on as you implement the concepts and techniques to your job.

The focus of the *plan for customer satisfaction* step is very broad. You should list all of your customers and outputs, and even talk to all of your customers. This level of detail is required the first time through the cycle because this information is used later in the cycle to define your processes and help prioritize processes for improvement.

During the *understand processes* step your focus begins to narrow. I recommend that you begin this portion of the cycle by defining all of your processes. These definitions provide the structure you need to look at the work you perform. The next step is to document just one of the processes you have defined. This process will be the focus of the rest of your efforts through the first cycle.

The *measure performance* step of the cycle continues with the process documented in the previous step. The next step is to select critical performance characteristics for the process. After the characteristics are selected, process performance data are collected and analyzed.

The focus of the *take action to improve* step is the most narrow. The aim of this step is to implement a solution to one problem identified from the process measurements.

Subsequent Cycles

The focus of subsequent cycles is threefold: continue to monitor process performance, broaden emphasis on the initial process, and analyze additional processes.

Continue to Monitor Process Performance. Do not forget about the process(es) addressed the first time through the cycle. Even though you have implemented a solution to a problem, your work is not complete. You need to make sure you have truly eliminated the problem. Did your solution have the desired effect? Are any undesirable side-effects present?

In the spirit of continuous improvement, continue to monitor the performance of the process. Is the process performing at the level required to satisfy your customers? Even if the answer to this question is yes today, your customers' requirements or expectations may change tomorrow.

Broaden Emphasis on the Initial Process. Since the *take action to improve* step of the first cycle focused on a single problem with the initial process, some work may remain on the process. Other problems may remain, or new problems become visible from continued monitoring of all of the process's critical characteristics.

Analyze Additional Processes. The obvious need for additional cycles is due primarily to the limited focus of the first cycle. Since significant analysis is only performed on one process, many other processes remain for analysis. Over time, your team may also become responsible for new processes. As these processes are added, you should follow the steps of the cycle, at least to the point where the new process is included in your prioritization list.

GETTING STARTED

These first two chapters have laid the foundation for your improvement efforts, so now you are ready to get started. The next chapter is the first of the how-to chapters.

NOTE

1. W. Edwards Deming, *Out of the Crisis* (Cambridge, Mass.: MIT Center for Advanced Engineering Studies, 1986), 88–89.

UNDERSTAND CUSTOMER REQUIREMENTS

The continuous process improvement cycle begins with planning for customer satisfaction. Who are your customers? In your business, customers may be called clients, patients, students, guests, passengers, or some other name. Whatever you call them, customer satisfaction is critical for the long-term success of any business. This is especially true for small businesses where the impact of losing even a single customer can be serious. The first step in planning for customer satisfaction is to understand what your customers need and expect from the work you provide them. Before getting into the specific techniques, some important, foundation-building concepts should be introduced.

QUALITY IS DEFINED BY THE CUSTOMER

Who would you say defines the quality of your products and services? Who determines whether a customer does business with your organization or one of your competitors? Since the customers make purchasing decisions, they define quality.

A good example of customers defining quality is the Susan B. Anthony dollar coin. The U.S. government, for several seemingly sound reasons, thought a one-dollar coin would be a good idea. The reality is that a dollar coin is only a good idea if people use it. Many Americans did not like the new coin because they thought it was too much like a quarter. What was the government's response? "This dollar coin is nothing like a quarter! It is not the same size, weight, shape, or design! How could you say the Susan B. Anthony dollar coin is similar to a quarter?"

In the end, who was right? When was the last time you saw a Susan B. Anthony dollar? It does not matter how "right" you are (logically, technically, or on any other basis) if your customers do not agree. Remember, quality is defined by the customer.

In some cases, you can help your customers define quality by helping set their expectations. Customers are likely to be disappointed if you fail to meet their expectations and pleased if you meet (or exceed) their expectations.

Everyone has probably been in a doctor's office waiting room and had a nurse say, "The doctor will see you in a few minutes." How do you feel when you are still in the waiting room 30 minutes later? The same situation takes place in lines waiting to be seated at a popular restaurant. The hostess may tell you that she will have a table for you in 20 minutes. If you are still waiting 45 minutes later, you probably are not very pleased.

The point to be made is: Avoid giving customers expectations that you cannot meet. Some people will gladly wait in line 45 minutes for a special meal at a great restaurant if they are expecting to wait 45 minutes or more.

Customers Can Be Fickle

The frustrating part about acknowledging that quality is defined by the customer is that customers can be fickle. They may not even be able to describe what quality is to them. Customers may be able to state what *poor* quality is, but still be unable to articulate what they mean by *good* quality. Even if they can define what they mean by quality, their definitions may change over time (maybe even from day to day). These facts are not presented to make the case that attempting to satisfy your customers is futile, just to stress the importance of staying in touch with your customers to understand how they define quality today.

Customers for Life

Some may ask: "Is it worth it? If the customers get to define quality, and they can change their minds if they want, I might as well not even try!" Let me challenge you with another question. How much is an existing customer worth to you and your business? Carl Sewell is a highly successful luxury automobile dealer in Dallas. He says, in his book *Customers for Life*[1], that he figures each of his customers represents the potential for $332,000 in business (from new car sales and parts and service over their lifetime). No wonder he emphasizes customer service in his dealership.

Any businessperson knows it is easier to sell new or additional products and services to existing customers than to develop new customers. Now, with all this in mind, how much are your existing customers worth to you? Are you treating them like the valuable asset they are? What are you willing to do to keep them? Think of the benefits of making them customers for life (reduced marketing expenses, a ready market for new products and services, a reliable source of feedback, and so on). Are you willing to change the way you do business and treat your customers? This book documents steps you can take to change the way you do business and develop lifetime customers.

INTERNAL AND EXTERNAL CUSTOMERS

INTERNAL CUSTOMER
The individual or department within an organization to whom another department provides its products and services.

When most people think of customers, they think of the ultimate purchaser or end user of their product or service. This is probably because we have all experienced being customers in retail stores and restaurants. We are the customers, and the store or restaurant employees are the suppliers. In these cases we are the organization's external customers. The organization exists to serve these customers. But, another group of customers exists—internal customers.

Internal customers are those individuals or departments within an organization to whom another department provides their products and services. In most large organizations, only a few departments actually have direct contact with external customers. The situation can be quite different in small businesses. Some of these companies have management perform the customer contact duties. Their approach is based on management's need to understand customer desires so it can properly direct the employees. In other small businesses, most (if not all) of the employees have contact with external customers. This method offers a direct, personal approach in dealing with customers. Those directly contacting the customers are the most visible, but they are certainly not alone in producing the organization's product or service. Figure 3.1 shows the sequence of teams involved in the process of converting an organization's inputs into the outputs provided to their customers.

The aim of every organization is to satisfy its external customers (so they will not only return to do business, but also will tell others about

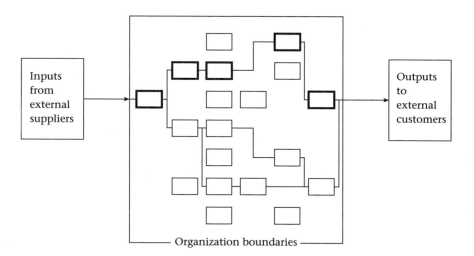

Figure 3.1. Internal customer/supplier relationships.

this great company with whom they are doing business). External customer satisfaction results from a chain of satisfied internal customers. In some large companies, this chain may include over 50 teams. Small businesses will likely have between three and 15 teams in their chain.

This chain consists of many internal customer/supplier relationships. In fact, every team serves as both a customer and a supplier as part of the chain. Figure 3.2 shows how teams begin as customers, receiving inputs from their suppliers, then become suppliers by providing their outputs to their customers.

This view of an organization's work flow is significantly different from the traditional approach. The traditional view of work flow is full of interdepartmental barriers and results in each department optimizing its work for its own, limited benefit. No consideration is given to surrounding departments (as customers and suppliers). This approach, of course, leads to overall suboptimization.

This customer/supplier chain view of work requires teams (or departments) to continually talk to each other, as customers and suppliers, so they can provide each other with better products and services. This approach extends the concept of teamwork from just local departments to across the entire organization. The organization is one team, all working together, to produce the products and services that will satisfy the customers utilizing the minimum amount of the organization's resources (no suboptimization).

Later this chapter will look at ways to analyze your relationships with all of your customers. For now, take a minute to take the "How do you treat your internal customers?" test in Figure 3.3.

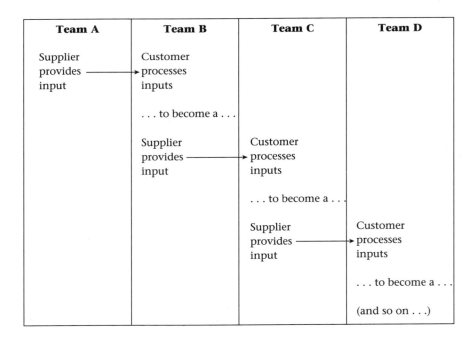

Figure 3.2. Every team serves as both a customer and a supplier.

| Emphasis on providing the product or service | | | Emphasis on satisfying the customer | |
| 1 | 2 | 3 | 4 | 5 |

| Attitude of "I'm the only game in town." | | | Attitude of "We're all in this together. How can I help?" | |
| 1 | 2 | 3 | 4 | 5 |

| They get what I give them. | | | I provide what they need and want. | |
| 1 | 2 | 3 | 4 | 5 |

| My products/services are good enough. | | | I'm always looking for ways to improve. | |
| 1 | 2 | 3 | 4 | 5 |

| Customer meetings are viewed as interruptions. | | | Customer meetings are viewed as opportunities for improvement. | |
| 1 | 2 | 3 | 4 | 5 |

| Feedback is discouraged, ignored if offered. | | | Feedback is encouraged, prompt action is taken. | |
| 1 | 2 | 3 | 4 | 5 |

Figure 3.3. "How do you treat your internal customers?" test.

CUSTOMER SATISFACTION OR DELIGHT?

What emotion would you like to generate on the part of your customers? Would you like for them to be satisfied or delighted? The customer satisfaction/delight model, shown in Figure 3.4, shows the progression of elements that lead to customer delight.

Basic Customer Expectations

BASIC CUSTOMER EXPECTATIONS

The "must haves." Basic features or attributes that the customer expects the product or service to have. Customer may assume you will handle them.

Basic customer expectations are at the base of the pyramid; they are the "must haves." The customer expects the product or service to have these basic features or attributes. The expectations may be so basic, in fact, the customers may not even mention them. This omission does not mean they are not important. Quite the contrary, it means the customers are just assuming you will handle them.

Customers at a restaurant, for example, rarely ask for a glass of water in a clean glass. The absence of this request, of course, does not mean receiving their drink in a dirty glass is acceptable.

Receiving a clean glass is just one of many unspoken, basic expectations restaurant customers have for their dining experience. In fact, someone requesting water in a clean glass has probably been served a drink in a dirty glass somewhere (or they would not verbalize the request).

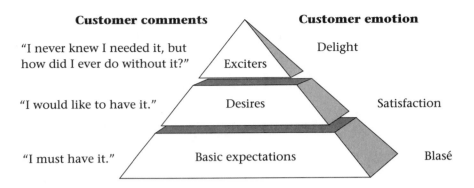

Figure 3.4. The customer satisfaction/delight model.

Addressing basic customer expectations is not always glamorous. In fact, you probably will get little feedback from your customers regarding their basic expectations. They just assume you will handle them. Herein lies the danger—everyone just expects the basic expectations will be addressed. It can be easy to overlook the simple, ordinary, run-of-the-mill features for the more flashy, high-tech features. Avoid the temptation. Any organization that does not satisfy the basic expectations of its customers will very likely lose customers to the competition whose products or services do satisfy the basic expectations.

Customer Desires

CUSTOMER DESIRES
Product or service attributes that are nice to have, but not necessarily required. Addressed only after basic customer expectations are satisfied.

Understanding and satisfying these basic expectations is crucial, but may not be enough. Organizations that satisfy only basic expectations are especially susceptible to having their satisfied customers switch to competitors for many reasons. Customers may be willing to switch to a competitor if they are convinced the competitor can not only satisfy their basic expectations, but also offer more color selections, more frequent delivery times, and so on.

The next element of the customer satisfaction/delight model reveals that customer satisfaction can be enhanced by considering customer desires—those product or service attributes that are nice to have, but not necessarily required. These attributes often are the difference that cause customers to return. Customers are likely to have a positive recollection of their experience with an organization that understands and satisfies their desires in addition to their basic expectations.

A simple example may help. I get my hair cut at a local shop associated with a national hair cut chain. In my neighborhood there are several places I could choose to get my hair cut. They are all about equally close and convenient to get to, have minimal wait times, charge about the same price, and do a good job of cutting my hair the way I like it cut (these are my basic expectations). There is one simple difference that separates the company I use and the others: the manager of the store recognizes me and calls me by name when I come in. (I almost feel like

Norm on the television show *Cheers*.) After only two or three visits she knew my name and how I like my hair cut so she didn't have to ask every time. Does this sound like a big deal? Probably not, but I appreciate being recognized and called by name. Being recognized is not one of my basic expectations, but when it is time to get my hair cut, where do you think I go?

How can this simple example relate to your business? Everyone likes to be treated with courtesy and respect. Treating your customers this way does not have to be based on your unselfish concern for them; there is something in it for you, too. If they like and appreciate the way they are treated, they will return to do business with you.

Customer Exciters

CUSTOMER EXCITERS
Pleasant surprises or unexpected features that the customer has never experienced or thought to ask for.

Pleasant surprises or unexpected features can often convert a satisfied customer to one who is delighted. When you delight a customer, you not only get the impact of satisfaction, you also gain the benefit of that customer becoming your best salesperson. In most cases, these exciters are features the customer has never experienced or thought to ask for. Once the exciter is introduced, customers may wonder how they ever got along without it.

Exciters sound somewhat exotic, but they do not have to be difficult to provide or expensive. Little touches often make the difference. Every time I use the drive-through window at my bank and my sons are along, the friendly teller sends the boys something (for example, balloons, candy, small magnets). These surprises are certainly nothing I expected or even wanted, but these small items make the day for the boys. They always want to go to the bank with me! Small items like this can make it a delight to go to the bank (I like to see my boys happy).

One time, after using this example at a seminar, a lady from the audience came up after the presentation to tell me of a similar story with a unique twist. She had taken her dog with her to the drive-through window at her bank. The teller returned a dog biscuit with her deposit receipt. She immediately gave the biscuit to her dog. According to her story, the dog jumped into her car every time she was ready to leave for several days after the bank trip.

The first time we received a balloon from the teller, we were pleasantly surprised, but what do you think would happen if we went to the bank this week and did not receive anything for the boys? Disaster! (I'm sure anyone with preschool children can relate.) Over time, exciters become desires and eventually even become basic expectations.

Remember, these exciters are built upon the basic expectations and desires. As much as I like receiving a surprise at the bank, a balloon just cannot make up for a $100 mistake on my bank transaction (one of my basic expectations is transaction accuracy)!

Several travel agencies have been collecting information about their customers' travel preferences for some time. They record each customer's preferences for seat selection (window or aisle, front or back), rental car type and size, and hotel features. (Some men's clothing stores have now started a similar customer preference log documenting their customers' sizes and style and color preferences.) This preparation saves a little time each time travel arrangements are made. The most significant result of this type of log is most likely not the small amount of time saved, but the attention to customer satisfaction demonstrated by the travel agent's efforts.

Achieving Customer Delight.   Figure 3.5 depicts the relationship between customer satisfaction and the level of achievement of basic expectations and exciters. Point *A* shows that basic expectations, even when completely accomplished, can at best result in satisfied (not delighted) customers. On the other hand, basic expectations that are not accomplished result in very dissatisfied customers (point *B*).

Exciters are treated on an entirely different curve. Point *C* shows that exciters not attempted at all still result in customer satisfaction (because they, by definition, were never expected). But, exciters that are completely accomplished can result in delighted customers (point *D*).

The Elements Build Upon One Another.   Each of the elements of the customer satisfaction/delight model build upon one another. In other words, you should concentrate on identifying, addressing, and satisfying your customers' basic expectations first. Then, after these expectations have been satisfied, begin to address the *like to haves*—the customers' desires. This sequence is important. From time to time, you may be tempted to focus on the desires first. This approach seldom leads to lasting customer satisfaction.

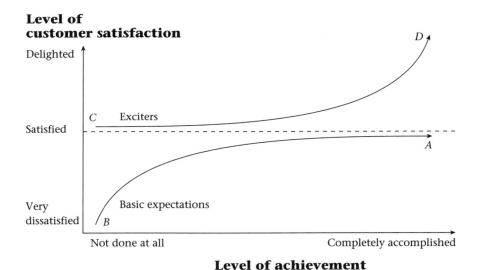

Figure 3.5. Basic expectations vs. exciters.

Have you ever seen or heard an advertisement for a pair of scissors that can even cut a penny? Not many of us would list cutting pennies as one of the requirements we have for a pair of scissors (in other words, not a basic expectation). But, the claim may sound intriguing (a *like to have*). How satisfied with your new scissors would you be if it did a great job of cutting pennies, but did a poor job of cutting more normal items like paper, cardboard, and wire? Focus on satisfying basic customer expectations first.

Another example may help explain the three levels of the customer satisfaction/delight model. One day I picked up some of my dress shirts from the dry cleaners. When I got home, I noticed one shirt was missing two buttons and another had pulled apart at a cuff seam. I took the shirts back to the cleaners and showed the manager the two shirts with the problems I had discovered. He was extremely apologetic and promised to repair the shirts (at no cost to me) by the next afternoon. When I returned the next day, the manager apologized again, presented me with my repaired shirts, and gave me a $15 credit on future cleaning for the inconvenience he had caused me. In this case, my basic expectation was that the shirts would be repaired at no cost. I was hoping (my desire) they would not give me any hassles over my request that they repair the shirts. I never even expected to receive a $15 credit. The cleaner satisfied my basic expectations, addressed my desires (I was treated very well), and exceeded my expectations by surprising me with the $15 credit.

Before going any further, let me challenge you to look at the questions in Figure 3.6. The questions are designed to help you identify ways

---

What could you do to

Basics

1. Ensure factors the customers assume will be handled are indeed handled?
2. Address the issues your customers have said are mandatory?
3. Make it convenient for customers to get your products or use your services?

Desires

4. Provide the additional products/services your customers would like to have?
5. Differentiate your organization from the competition?
6. Enhance your customers' impression of your organization?

Exciters

7. Pleasantly surprise your customers?
8. Make your customers' experiences memorable?
9. Convey an "above and beyond the call of duty" attitude?
10. Generate customers for life?

Figure 3.6. Achieving customer delight.

you can ensure your customers' basic expectations are addressed and actions taken to change their emotion from blasé to delight.

THE STEPS IN UNDERSTANDING CUSTOMER REQUIREMENTS

The introduction of internal customers and customer delight provide the background necessary to understand customer requirements. The remainder of the chapter focuses on the steps listed in Figure 3.7 for understanding customer requirements.

LIST TEAM OUTPUTS

A key step in satisfying your customers is to list all of the products and services you provide to your customers—your team outputs. The outputs for your team are the results of the work performed that are provided to the team's customers. What is the result of everything you have done?

Examples of team outputs include

- Reports
- Parts
- Computer programs
- Assemblies
- Advice
- Information
- A prepared meal
- A clean room

OUTPUTS

The results of the work performed that are provided to the team's customers.

---

1. **List team outputs**
   to document the results of the work performed.

2. **List customers**
   to identify everyone who receives the outputs.

3. **Identify output requirements**
   to pinpoint the output characteristics the customers want, require, or expect.

4. **Meet with the customers**
   to verify output requirements, determine requirement importance, and understand current level of satisfaction.

Figure 3.7. Understanding customer requirements steps.

Types of Outputs

Most of us think of tangible products (such as parts, tools, widgets, and reports) when we think of outputs, but there are many outputs that are not products. Make sure you list all of your outputs.

Information Is an Output.   Some have called this era the "information age." It is easy to understand why as we often are bombarded by information from many sources. As a part of some of your processes, you may research and/or analyze data you then provide to your customers (written or verbal). Information, even though it is intangible, certainly is an output of many processes.

Services Are Outputs, Too.   Services are work outputs, too. Many of the products produced and provided to a team's customers are services like investment advice, training, and delivery. Do not overlook the services you provide to your customers as you list your outputs.

Listing the services you provide may be more important than listing your products. When providing a service, you (the provider) are the only tangible product. The way you deliver the service can have as much impact on the customer as the service itself. How many times have you heard a stale, unemotional "Thanks for shopping at _____. Have a nice day" from a clerk at a checkout register? Did it make you feel like a valued customer? If you received a genuine "thanks," would your impression of your experience be different? Another good example is the way business telephones are answered. Is the voice cold and robotic? Does it sound like the receptionist is in a race to see how fast the company name can be pronounced? Does the pace and the tone of the voice indicate "I have answered this phone thousands of times; you are just the latest in a long list" or "You and your calls are important to us"? (Certified public accountants and law firms are the worst! It is often hard to know how to pronounce the names, and you seldom get any help from the receptionist answering the phone.)

In some cases, the service you provide (or product you sell) may be similar to what is offered by other companies. Think about how you can differentiate yourself from the competition.

Carl Sewell explains how he knows customer satisfaction is important to him in his book *Customers for Life.*[2] He hired J. D. Power and Associates, the independent research firm well known for evaluating automobile quality, to evaluate his dealership. As part of the evaluation, Power asked Sewell customers, and those at other Cadillac dealerships nationwide, if they were "very satisfied" with the car they bought. Even though the cars sold at Sewell Village Cadillac are no different from the ones that are delivered to any other Cadillac dealership, Sewell's "very satisfied" score was 25 percent higher than the national average. Carl Sewell's conclusion: "Our customers thought more of the car because of the way we treated them before and after the sale." Don't forget that some of your outputs are services.

Develop the List

Use the output list worksheet on page 35 to record your outputs. Take some time with your team to list all of your outputs. Be as complete as possible.

Level of Detail.   List the outputs as specifically as possible. Avoid grouping sets of outputs together, for now. You should not, for example, identify "reports" as one of your outputs. List all of the individual reports your team produces.

List Everything.   Remember, include anything you provide to any of your customers. If you provide a packing slip with your widget, the packing slip is one of your outputs. List everything!

Your team probably does not create all of your outputs from scratch. In some cases, you will add value to something you receive from one of your suppliers and provide the updated product to your customers. These also are your outputs. You may receive some type of checklist or work order with the product you receive. As part of your normal operations, you may update the paperwork and provide it to your customers at the same time you provide them with your product. You have added value to the paperwork—it is one of the outputs you provide to your customers.

Place the Worksheet in Your Notebook.   Remember the notebook you set up earlier? This is your first chance to add something to your notebook. Place the completed output list worksheet in your notebook behind the Plan for Customer Satisfaction tab.

Keep the Output List Current

Make every attempt to make a complete list of all of your work outputs now. This output list is the basis for many of the steps that follow as part of the continuous process improvement cycle, so do whatever you can to make the list complete. You may think of an output missing from your list later, be sure to add it then. From time to time, your team may begin providing new outputs to your customers. Add these new outputs to your output list.

Output List Worksheet

Date: _____

List all of your team's outputs in the space below.

_____   _____

_____   _____

_____   _____

_____   _____

_____   _____

_____   _____

_____   _____

_____   _____

_____   _____

_____   _____

_____   _____

_____   _____

_____   _____

Note:

Be sure to list your outputs as specifically as possible. Identify each of your outputs separately; do not group them together.

LIST CUSTOMERS

CUSTOMERS
The individuals, teams, departments, and companies that receive any of your team's outputs.

The next step is to list *all* of your team's customers. Who are the individuals, teams, departments, and companies that receive any of your team's outputs? Just as with the output list, it is important for you to list all of your customers. This can be a very helpful step; many teams have never really thought about who their customers are. How can you aim for customer satisfaction without first knowing who the customers are? Your customers may be fresh on your mind now that you have listed your outputs. Many times, customers are identified at the same time outputs are listed. Whatever the case, make sure you list all of your customers. Use a worksheet like the customer list worksheet to record your customers (see page 37).

Be specific. List your customers by name, if possible. This list will form the foundation of some analysis later. A specific list will save you a lot of time later. In some cases, everyone on a certain team or within an entire department will be your customer. If so, state the name of the team or department. In other cases, entire groups of employees will be your customers (for example, all managers, everyone in a certain building). A good description of the group, in cases like this, is sufficient.

Update your team notebook. Add the completed customer list worksheet to your notebook.

Some misconceptions exist in identifying customers. The following paragraphs are provided to assist in clarifying these misconceptions.

The Boss Is Not the Customer

Some teams identify their supervisor or department manager as their customer. (This misconception exists mostly in larger organizations since many small business employees have contact with their external customers.) It is true that supervision reviews and evaluates work outputs to make sure the outputs will satisfy the team's customers. In this capacity, supervision is acting as a surrogate for the real customer—supervision is not the customer.

Supervision must be sensitive to the needs of their customers and make sure their team members are sensitive as well. The role of the boss is not to be a customer, but to be the leader of a team serving its customers. This explanation means the boss provides the team with the help it needs to meet its customers' expectations.

No Customers?

At this point, some teams come to the conclusion that they don't have any customers. This is scary! Why does the team exist? Remember, teams (departments, companies, and so forth) exist to serve their customers. Teams with no customers have no reason to exist.

In most cases, the team really does have customers, they just need to be identified. This activity alone can significantly help a team improve the quality of the products and services they provide. Identifying specific teams that rely on them often instills a new sense of purpose. This pur-

Customer List Worksheet

Date: _____

List all of your team's customers in the space below.

_____   _____

_____   _____

_____   _____

_____   _____

_____   _____

_____   _____

_____   _____

_____   _____

_____   _____

_____   _____

_____   _____

_____   _____

_____   _____

_____   _____

Note:
Be sure to list your customers as specifically as possible. List your customers by name if possible, by department at a minimum.

pose often is the driver for improvement efforts. Losing track of why you exist (and therefore who you exist to serve) always adversely affects your performance. Customer satisfaction provides the necessary focus.

Everyone Is a Customer?

On the other extreme, some teams are tempted to claim that everyone within their company is one of their customers. Although it is more common in very small companies (especially those with less than 10 employees), this is rarely the case. You should be as specific as possible in listing your customers. Rarely does everyone within the company receive one of your outputs (unless, for example, you are in the department responsible for mailing announcements to all company employees). Develop a comprehensive, accurate list of all of your customers.

IDENTIFY OUTPUT REQUIREMENTS

Output requirements are the individual characteristics of the outputs the customers want, require, or expect. Specific output requirements answer questions like those listed in Figure 3.8.

List the Requirements for Each Output

The output requirements should be listed for all of the team outputs identified earlier. Yes, *all* of them. The best way to develop the output requirement list is to work together as a team to identify all of the output requirements. Based on different jobs and levels of experience, team

---

What
- What will it be used for?
- What size should it be?
- What color should it be?
- What level of accuracy is needed?

Where
- Where will it be used?
- Where should it be delivered?

When
- When should it be delivered?
- When will it be used?

How
- How often is it needed?
- How should it be packaged?
- How should it be presented?
- How long should it be?
- How much should it cost?
- How much should it weigh?
- How should it be delivered?

Figure 3.8. Identify output requirements.

REQUIREMENTS
Individual characteristics of the outputs the customers want, require, or expect.

members may have different ideas of the requirements customers have for the team's outputs. It is good to hear and discuss all of these ideas. Use the questions from the figure to help you develop your list.

Obviously, this is a big task, but a necessary one at this point. This information will be used later for several purposes. Identifying individual output requirements is a key step in process improvement, so make the lists as complete as possible. It does not matter which output you start with, just get started.

Think from the Customer's Point of View

At this point, you are trying to identify all of the attributes your customers expect from your outputs. Try to put yourselves in your customers' shoes. If you were them, what would you expect, require, or demand from your team? Try to anticipate all of their requirements. You will have a chance shortly to show your list to your customers to make sure you have captured all of their requirements.

An example may help at this point. Everyone receives mail, so we are all customers of the U.S. Postal Service. Examine the activity on page 40 and list the requirements you have of the postal service.

What mail delivery process requirements did you list? Some requirements commonly listed include

- Receiving only the mail addressed to you
- Receiving the mail unopened
- Delivered between 10:30 A.M. and 11:30 A.M.
- Mail received undamaged (for example, torn, folded)
- Placed in the secretary's in-box

The Output Requirements Worksheet

The output requirements worksheet is an important tool in identifying and documenting the requirements that exist for each output. The requirements are listed for one output per worksheet.

Involve everyone on your team in completing the output requirements worksheet on page 42. It is important that the worksheet be accurate and complete. Listen to everyone's ideas and discuss them as a group.

Begin completing the worksheet by writing in the current date. This is the first of many times this worksheet will be completed for this output. Over time, it is a good idea to continue to check to make sure you understand the requirements your customers have for your outputs. Next, list the output and the customers who receive the output. Try to list all of the customers. Abbreviate as necessary, just make sure you know now, and the next time you look at the form, who the customers are. Identify your team on the "completed by" line. Your customers will see the worksheet, and they will need to know which team they are working with (eventually, teams from all over the organization will be working with their customers to complete the form).

Output Requirement Listing Activity

Introduction:
We are all customers of the U.S. Postal Service. As customers, we have certain desires, expectations, and requirements for the postal service.

Instructions:
The U.S. Postal Service provides several outputs to us as customers. For the purpose of this activity, we will analyze the daily mail delivery output (not stamp delivery, overnight or priority mail, and so on). List the requirements customers have for this output.

Output: _Daily mail delivery_

Requirements:

1. _____

2. _____

3. _____

4. _____

5. _____

6. _____

7. _____

8. _____

9. _____

10. _____

11. _____

12. _____

At this point, list all of the requirements you have identified for your output. Leave the Importance, Satisfaction, and Priority columns blank for now.

Remember, list specific output requirements. For example, do not list timeliness as a requirement. What is timely for this output? Within 5 minutes? Anytime this week? Before Wednesday at 4:00 P.M.? List the specific day or time (or day or time ranges) you think the customer needs the output.

The worksheet has room for nine requirements, but there is nothing magic about this number. List all of your requirements (use a second worksheet if you identify more than nine requirements).

MEET WITH THE CUSTOMERS

Now it is time to talk to your customers to make sure your output and output requirement lists are complete. You should not rely entirely on your judgment for these lists—the customer's point of view is critical. The aim of this activity is to make sure you are doing whatever is necessary to satisfy your customers. It is not good enough to think you know what the customers expect—you must know what they expect. The only way to make sure their requirements are being satisfied is to talk to them.

Complete and accurate customer satisfaction assessments are accomplished through direct meetings with your customers to discuss the outputs your team provides to them. This personal touch will make a positive impression on your customers. The meetings will demonstrate your commitment to satisfying them. The result of spending time meeting with and getting to know and understand your customers is the ability to identify and take the actions necessary to increase customer satisfaction and ultimately increase market share and sales.

Customer Reception.   The most common questions asked by teams before they meet with their first customer almost always are

- How will I be received by my customers?
- How will my customers react when I request to meet with them?

Based on hundreds of such meetings, I can tell you to expect your customers to be surprised. Just imagine how you would feel if, after several years, the person who has provided you a weekly report called to ask you what requirements you have for the report. Wouldn't you be surprised? After you had a few minutes to think about the meeting, you would probably be very appreciative of the effort demonstrated. This is how your customers will feel when you approach them. Relax, the first meeting is always the hardest.

Output Requirements Worksheet

Date: _____

Output: _____

Customer(s): _____

Completed by: _____

Requirements	**Importance**	**Satisfaction**	**Priority**
A. _____ _____	[5] Extremely important/critical [4] Very important [3] Important [2] Somewhat important [1] Not important	[1] Extremely satisfied/delighted [2] Very satisfied/pleased [4] Satisfied [6] Dissatisfied [10] Very dissatisfied	_____
B. _____ _____	[5] Extremely important/critical [4] Very important [3] Important [2] Somewhat important [1] Not important	[1] Extremely satisfied/delighted [2] Very satisfied/pleased [4] Satisfied [6] Dissatisfied [10] Very dissatisfied	_____
C. _____ _____	[5] Extremely important/critical [4] Very important [3] Important [2] Somewhat important [1] Not important	[1] Extremely satisfied/delighted [2] Very satisfied/pleased [4] Satisfied [6] Dissatisfied [10] Very dissatisfied	_____
D. _____ _____	[5] Extremely important/critical [4] Very important [3] Important [2] Somewhat important [1] Not important	[1] Extremely satisfied/delighted [2] Very satisfied/pleased [4] Satisfied [6] Dissatisfied [10] Very dissatisfied	_____
E. _____ _____	[5] Extremely important/critical [4] Very important [3] Important [2] Somewhat important [1] Not important	[1] Extremely satisfied/delighted [2] Very satisfied/pleased [4] Satisfied [6] Dissatisfied [10] Very dissatisfied	_____
F. _____ _____	[5] Extremely important/critical [4] Very important [3] Important [2] Somewhat important [1] Not important	[1] Extremely satisfied/delighted [2] Very satisfied/pleased [4] Satisfied [6] Dissatisfied [10] Very dissatisfied	_____
G. _____ _____	[5] Extremely important/critical [4] Very important [3] Important [2] Somewhat important [1] Not important	[1] Extremely satisfied/delighted [2] Very satisfied/pleased [4] Satisfied [6] Dissatisfied [10] Very dissatisfied	_____
H. _____ _____	[5] Extremely important/critical [4] Very important [3] Important [2] Somewhat important [1] Not important	[1] Extremely satisfied/delighted [2] Very satisfied/pleased [4] Satisfied [6] Dissatisfied [10] Very dissatisfied	_____
I. _____ _____	[5] Extremely important/critical [4] Very important [3] Important [2] Somewhat important [1] Not important	[1] Extremely satisfied/delighted [2] Very satisfied/pleased [4] Satisfied [6] Dissatisfied [10] Very dissatisfied	_____

Output Priority Total: [_____]

Avoid Creating False Expectations. Meeting with your customers requires planning. The simple act of meeting with your customers to discuss their requirements automatically creates raised expectations. They immediately become convinced that you are going to do something different to improve the level of service they have been receiving. They will be disappointed if they do not see a change soon. This disappointment will be translated into a lesser opinion of your current level of performance. If you are not ready to take action, you are not ready to meet with your customers.

Conducting the Meeting. The entire team does not need to attend the meeting with the customer. This approach is not only unnecessary, but probably a little intimidating for the customer. Your team should select a member to be the spokesperson for the team. The spokesperson should then call to schedule a meeting with the customer.

It is a good idea to rotate the spokesperson position so everyone on the team has a chance to meet with at least one customer one time. Meeting with the customers can be a very valuable experience, so everyone should get a chance. Additionally, individual team members have different skills and points of view that may solicit different responses from the customer. Any method (including rotating the spokesperson) that can enhance the information gained from the customer should be utilized. The purpose of this step is to understand true customer requirements. The customers themselves may not even know what they really need, so every effort should be made to get at the true requirements.

The meeting itself should be very informal. Once introductions have been made (if necessary), describe the purpose of the meeting, then present the output requirements worksheet to the customer.

Verify Output Requirements

The first step in meeting with the customer is to verify the output requirements you have listed on the worksheet. There are two requirement factors to verify: accuracy and completeness of the list.

Verify the Accuracy of the Requirements List. First, request that the customer review and verify the accuracy of the requirements you already have listed. Make sure all of the requirements, as you understand them, really do exist for the customer. If, for example, you have stated that the output is required by 5:00 P.M. every Friday evening, verify that the customer really does need it *every* week, on *Friday,* and *by 5:00.* You may find out that only one section of the report is used once a month. This is the type of information you hope to gain from the interview.

You also may find that the customer spends a significant amount of time totaling several columns of data you provide as part of the report. Based on this new information, you may be able to suggest a better format or volunteer to add a total field in your spreadsheet. These simple actions cause very little additional work for you, but could save the overall organization a significant amount of time. This is the type of customer/supplier interaction that should be developed throughout the organization.

Verify the Completeness of the Requirements List.   It also is important to verify the completeness of the requirements you have listed. Have you listed all of the requirements the customer has for the output? Ask your customers: "Are these all of the requirements you have for the output I provide to you?" Encourage the customer to be thorough in the analysis of the list. You may even want to reference the questions listed in Figure 3.8 as they may help your customers list all of their requirements. New requirements always can be added, but it is best to add them to the list now. As customers identify additional output requirements, add them to the output requirement worksheet.

Encourage your customers to be as specific as possible in describing their additional output requirements. Ask enough questions to help the customer formalize in his or her own mind what really is required to do the job.

Is the Customer Always Right?   What happens if the customer wants to add a requirement with which you just don't agree? Is the customer automatically right? Not necessarily. (I know this may sound like heresy, but read on.) In some cases, you, as the supplier, may have expertise the customer does not have. In these cases, you have a responsibility to speak up when you think the customer is making a mistake. If, for example, a customer requests that the studs in a new home be placed four feet apart (to save money), the builder should explain why that is not a good idea. With this said, always remember that customers should be afforded respect because, after all, they are the customers.

Determine Requirement Importance

Not all output requirements are equally important, are they? Some are critical to the customer, others are just "like to haves." So a method is needed for denoting the importance of each of the requirements. Use the following five-point scale.

1. Extremely important or critical
2. Very important
3. Important

4. Somewhat important
5. Not important

Ask the customer to identify the importance of each of the requirements using this scale. Check the corresponding block on the output requirements worksheet. Disregard the numbers in the boxes for now; they are explained later.

The Scale Is Absolute.   It is important to note that this rating scale is absolute (as opposed to relative). Each requirement should be assigned an importance rating based on its merits, not based on a comparison to another requirement. An absolute scale is necessary because the same scale will be used for all requirements of all outputs and consistency across all outputs is important. So, instruct your customers to select the rating statement that best describes the importance of the requirement to them.

Encourage Your Customers to Be Honest.   This information is very important—it will be used later to monitor your progress over time. Encourage your customers to be completely honest in assigning their importance scores. Some customers may be tempted to inflate their importance ratings in an attempt to get priority or special treatment from your team. Inflating the importance of a requirement does not help anyone.

Determine the Current Level of Requirement Satisfaction

Also ask your customers to rate their current level of satisfaction with how well your team has been able to address each of the requirements. If they are not satisfied with your work, you certainly want to know it. Use the following five-point scale.

- Extremely satisfied or delighted
- Very satisfied or pleased
- Satisfied
- Dissatisfied
- Very dissatisfied

Request that your customers check the corresponding block on the output requirements worksheet for each requirement.

The Importance and Satisfaction Weights.   The boxes used to check the level of importance and satisfaction have numbers inside. The numbers are weights assigned to each level to help prioritize future improvement efforts. Notice that the importance weights increase as the importance of the requirement increases while the satisfaction weights increase the more dissatisfied the customer is. The weights have been assigned this way to put emphasis (through higher priority scores) on requirements that are very important and with which the customer is very dissatisfied.

Ask for Examples.   When determining your customers' current level of satisfaction, ask them to provide examples of specific situations to help explain their scoring. Often, specific examples can help you relate to what your customers are telling you so you can take appropriate action.

These steps may seem like nothing but extra work. Actually, you probably will find out that these efforts now will significantly reduce the work you perform to satisfy your customers. A customer may decide that a certain output is not important and agree to drop the requirement, or an output provided by more than one supplier may be identified, reducing the amount of work you perform.

Methods for Receiving Customer Feedback

The most effective method for gathering the information described earlier is to have a representative from your team talk personally with every customer. Time constraints and geographic distance sometimes make personal visits impossible or impractical. Methods for receiving customer feedback are summarized in Figure 3.9.

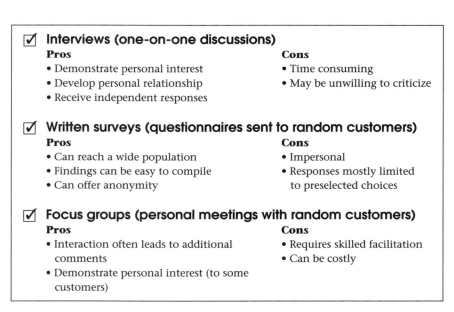

Figure 3.9. Customer feedback methods.

INTERVIEWS

One-on-one discussions between you and your customers. Conducted to receive information for and document findings on an output requirements worksheet.

WRITTEN SURVEY

A written substitute when an interview is impractical or impossible. Especially efficient for receiving feedback from a large group of customers.

Interviews.   Interviews are one-on-one discussions between you and your customers. The interviews may be conducted in person or over the telephone. This personal approach is what has been described so far regarding talking to your customers.

The obvious disadvantage to interviewing your customers is the time involved. Individual interviews can be time-consuming, then multiply this time by the number of customers to be interviewed. Another potential disadvantage is that some of your customers may be unwilling to provide you with criticism. Encourage everyone to be completely honest in providing the feedback.

Written Surveys.   For one reason or another, you may not be able to talk directly to all of your customers. Written surveys provide a means of reaching a wide population. If your customer base is large or geographically disperse, a written survey can allow you to get meaningful inputs without talking to everyone. The aim of using written surveys is to receive accurate feedback on the thoughts and feelings of all customers by talking to only some of them. Normally, surveys are distributed to several customers—randomly selected to represent the opinions of all customers. Care must be taken in the selection of those to receive the survey. They must be selected randomly to ensure that the feedback received is indeed representative of the entire customer base.

The aim of a written survey should be to get the same information discussed earlier for interviews: the accuracy and completeness of the requirements list, the requirement importance, and the current level of satisfaction with the performance on each requirement. Use the output requirements worksheet as your survey document. You could have the general information at the top of the worksheet already filled in and the requirements that you have identified listed. Then, provide the following instructions to your customers.

1. Review the requirements listed and make any corrections necessary. This list is not meant to put words in your mouth, but to serve as a list of your requirements as we understand them. Please make sure that we have accurately listed all of the requirements you have.

2. Add requirements you have that are not already listed. Please state the requirements as specifically as possible (in other words, write "by 9:00 a.m. every Friday morning" rather than "timely delivery" or "prompt service").

3. Check the box that best describes the importance of each of the requirements.

4. Check the box that best describes how satisfied you have been with our performance for each of the requirements.

Since new requirements may be added to the list, it is a good idea to initially distribute a small number of surveys (probably about five or 10). After you have received the responses from this group, you can add any requirements they have added, then distribute the survey to the selected population.

There are two approaches to analyzing the numerical responses for the requirement importance and customer satisfaction ratings. The most common approach is to average the ratings to get single, overall importance and satisfaction ratings. The disadvantage to this approach is that the extremes get washed out. You may be interested in the extremes, especially those on the unfavorable end of the scale. The other approach is to look at the *worst case* by using the highest of the importance responses and the lowest of the satisfaction responses. By focusing on the worst case, your efforts will be targeted toward improving the lowest ratings.

A common approach to surveying customers is to use comment cards like those placed in hotel rooms or on restaurant tables. Although these cards do provide a means of receiving customer feedback, be careful. This type of card has become so common that most of the cards will be completed only by those either very pleased or very displeased with the product or service. This bias does not mean you should not use the cards, just be aware that the responses are probably not representative. You can still learn a lot about where improvement is necessary from negative comment cards.

One benefit to using questionnaires is that they can offer anonymity to the person responding. Often, people will be more complete and honest with their responses when they know the comments cannot be traced back to them. This option creates a dilemma. You certainly want the responses to be complete and honest, but you also want to know who harbored negative thoughts so you can do whatever you can to rectify the situation. The best solution probably is to request that respondents identify themselves on the survey, but also provide a means for anonymous comments to receive the tough comments that otherwise may not be submitted.

Written surveys are not presented as an option to replace the need to meet personally with your customers. Personal interaction always is preferred over any other method, especially for the first few meetings. There is a lot of value gained from demonstrating the personal interest and getting to know one another. You also receive much more information from a personal interview—information that cannot show up on a questionnaire. The words your customers use and the attitude demonstrated provide valuable information. In some cases, circumstances may eliminate personal interviews as an option; this is when written surveys should be considered.

FOCUS GROUP

A meeting in which randomly selected customers are invited to discuss in a group setting the requirements they have for the work you provide them.

Focus Groups. Focus groups provide an opportunity to meet personally with a cross section of your customers. Focus groups are meetings in which randomly selected customers are invited to discuss in a group setting the requirements they have for the work you provide them. The interaction between the customers can be interesting and often leads to additional ideas and comments.

Companies in the snack food industry have used focus groups as a means of getting consumer feedback on proposed new products. The companies offer samples of their new products and ask the participants to offer opinions on size, taste, and other important snack characteristics. This form of feedback allows the snack producer to get an accurate gauge of consumer acceptance of a new product without spending money to produce, package, and distribute the product on a large scale.

Your focus groups should begin with the facilitator explaining to everyone why they have been invited to the meeting and encourage them to be completely honest. The facilitator could then present the initial requirement list to the group and ask for corrections and additions. (Note: the success of focus groups is largely dependent on the skills of the facilitator.) The aim of the meeting is to reach consensus among the customers present as to what the requirements are for the output being discussed. Importance and satisfaction ratings should be developed in the same manner.

Most companies offer some type of incentive to their customers who agree to participate in a focus group. The incentive may be cash, free samples, coupons, free or reduced cost services, or any combination of these. You will need to determine what kind of incentive you need to offer to entice your customers to participate.

Calculate Output Priority

The next step is to calculate the priority for each output. Priority should be placed on areas important to the customer with low satisfaction ratings. The priority score will be used later to help prioritize improvement efforts. First, individual requirement priority scores are calculated by multiplying the number in the box checked in the importance column by the number in the box checked in the satisfaction column. Record the result in the priority column for each requirement. Total the requirement priority scores to obtain the output priority score.

The importance and satisfaction ratings boxes contain weighted factors that are used to calculate the requirement priority scores. The weights are designed such that the highest scores result when a requirement is rated as extremely important and very dissatisfied. This scenario requires immediate attention!

Update Team Notebook.   Add all of your output requirements worksheets to your team notebook. These worksheets will be referenced in later activities, so you will need a way of easily finding them.

All worksheets and documentation you complete should be added to your notebook. From this point on, I will not include recommendations for updating your notebook for each worksheet, just remember that the recommendation stands.

A Completed Example.   A completed output requirement worksheet is provided on page 51 as an example of how the worksheet should be filled out. The example is for airline tickets provided by a travel agency. Notice that this output is only one of many provided by the travel agency (the travel agency also provides travel recommendations and advice, price comparisons, and so on). Additional output requirement worksheets should be completed for these outputs.

Conduct Regularly Scheduled Customer Meetings

The meeting that has been described is the first, but certainly not the last, customer meeting. Just as it is important to meet with your customers for the first time, it is important to continue to meet with them on a regular basis. These subsequent meetings will allow discussion of new or changing requirements and opportunities for performance feedback.

As a supplier, you should look forward to these meetings. The feedback they offer can provide you with the information you need to assess your improvement efforts and prioritize future efforts. You want to focus your attention on activities that are important to your customers. Because their requirements and priorities will change over time, the only way to really stay in touch with their requirements is to continue to meet with them on a regular basis.

SUMMARY

Customer satisfaction is a key for any organization implementing TQM. The first step toward achieving customer satisfaction is understanding customer requirements. A systematic, complete analysis of customer requirements lays the foundation for the steps documented in subsequent chapters.

Output Requirements Worksheet

COMPLETED

Date: _June 1, 1993_

Output: _Airline tickets_

Customer(s): _Terry Ehresman_

Completed by: _Mary Smith (travel agent at ABC Travel Services)_

Requirements	Importance	Satisfaction	Priority
A. _Prepared for the proper date, time, and destination_	☑ Extremely important/critical ☐4 Very important ☐3 Important ☐2 Somewhat important ☐1 Not important	☐1 Extremely satisfied/delighted ☑ Very satisfied/pleased ☐4 Satisfied ☐6 Dissatisfied ☐10 Very dissatisfied	10
B. _Delivered to my office_	☐5 Extremely important/critical ☐4 Very important ☑3 Important ☑ Somewhat important ☐1 Not important	☑ Extremely satisfied/delighted ☐2 Very satisfied/pleased ☐4 Satisfied ☐6 Dissatisfied ☐10 Very dissatisfied	2
C. _Billed to my American Express card_	☑ Extremely important/critical ☐4 Very important ☐3 Important ☐2 Somewhat important ☐1 Not important	☐1 Extremely satisfied/delighted ☐2 Very satisfied/pleased ☑4 Satisfied ☑ Dissatisfied ☐10 Very dissatisfied	30
D. _Received 1 business day before the departure date_	☐5 Extremely important/critical ☑4 Very important ☑ Important ☐2 Somewhat important ☐1 Not important	☐1 Extremely satisfied/delighted ☑ Very satisfied/pleased ☐4 Satisfied ☐6 Dissatisfied ☐10 Very dissatisfied	6
E. _Itinerary of flight, hotel, and rental car information_	☑5 Extremely important/critical ☑ Very important ☐3 Important ☐2 Somewhat important ☐1 Not important	☑ Extremely satisfied/delighted ☐2 Very satisfied/pleased ☐4 Satisfied ☐6 Dissatisfied ☐10 Very dissatisfied	4
F. _Duplicate itineraries for office and family_	☐5 Extremely important/critical ☐4 Very important ☐3 Important ☑2 Somewhat important ☑ Not important	☐1 Extremely satisfied/delighted ☑2 Very satisfied/pleased ☑ Satisfied ☐6 Dissatisfied ☐10 Very dissatisfied	4
G.	☐5 Extremely important/critical ☐4 Very important ☐3 Important ☐2 Somewhat important ☐1 Not important	☐1 Extremely satisfied/delighted ☐2 Very satisfied/pleased ☐4 Satisfied ☐6 Dissatisfied ☐10 Very dissatisfied	
H.	☐5 Extremely important/critical ☐4 Very important ☐3 Important ☐2 Somewhat important ☐1 Not important	☐1 Extremely satisfied/delighted ☐2 Very satisfied/pleased ☐4 Satisfied ☐6 Dissatisfied ☐10 Very dissatisfied	
I.	☐5 Extremely important/critical ☐4 Very important ☐3 Important ☐2 Somewhat important ☐1 Not important	☐1 Extremely satisfied/delighted ☐2 Very satisfied/pleased ☐4 Satisfied ☐6 Dissatisfied ☐10 Very dissatisfied	

Output Priority Total: 56

The next step is to take the information learned from your customers and develop a plan of action for your team. The purpose of your team plan and a set of recommended contents are covered in the next chapter, Develop Team Plans.

REVIEW QUESTIONS

Use the questions in Figure 3.10 to review your progress and make sure you are ready to continue on to the next chapter.

☐	Has the team listed all of its outputs?
☐	Has the team listed all of its customers?
☐	Has the team listed all of the requirements its customers have for each of its outputs?
☐	Has the team met with its customers?
☐	Has the team confirmed the requirements it listed?
☐	Has the team received importance and satisfaction ratings for each requirement?

Figure 3.10. Review questions.

NOTES

1. Carl Sewell and Paul B. Brown, *Customers for Life: How to Turn That One-Time Buyer into a Lifetime Customer* (New York: Pocket Books, 1990), 162.

2. *Ibid.*, 167.

DEVELOP TEAM PLANS

The aim of the *plan for customer satisfaction* portion of the continuous process improvement cycle is to develop action plans for every team based upon the customer information learned in the first part of this cycle step. After the voice of the customer has been heard, plans can be developed to document a team's planned activities. Every team should develop its own plan.

Developing plans probably is not new to you, so let me start this chapter with a challenge. Look at the survey in Figure 4.1. How are plans used in your organization?

Plans can be effective management tools when used properly. The purpose of this chapter is to explain how team plans can be developed to be useful tools for managing quality improvement.

PURPOSE OF TEAM PLANS

Team plans provide a road map for the teams to follow in improving their work processes to satisfy customer requirements. Plans provide order and purpose to every team. After the plans have been developed, everyone on every team knows the direction their team is heading and what their responsibilities are.

Team plans also serve as an excellent method for management to communicate its direction and specific activities to lower-level work teams. This way, all of the teams in an organization know the direction of the organization and can plan the activities they need to perform to fit in and support other teams. The team plans provide the means by which everyone in the organization can work together toward the same aims.

How does your organization rate? ☑		
☐ Document specific responsibilities	—or—	☐ Written generically enough to not assign clear responsibility
☐ Prioritize activities	—or—	☐ Ignored when prioritization decisions are made
☐ Document planned resource allocations	—or—	☐ Ignored when resource allocation decisions are made
☐ Identify planned start and completion dates	—or—	☐ Offer broad or vague time frames
☐ Referenced frequently to guide action	—or—	☐ Ignored when decisions are made
☐ Used to status progress	—or—	☐ Forgotten, no baseline used to status against
☐ Updated as frequently as required to be useful	—or—	☐ Considered complete and final as initially prepared
☐ Distributed to communicate organizational direction	—or—	☐ Distribution limited to management

Figure 4.1. "How are plans used?" survey.

RECEIVE AND UNDERSTAND TEAM MISSION

The first step in developing a team plan is for the team to receive and understand its team mission. A team's mission describes its purpose—its unique contribution to the organization. Each team within an organization needs to know the role it is expected to fulfill. To this end, every team (from the overall organization to the lowest level teams within the organization) should have a documented mission.

Developing a Team Mission

One of management's primary duties is assigning responsibilities to its teams, or departments, or units. Since a mission describes the team's purpose, it documents its responsibilities. For this reason, missions are developed by members of management. This section is provided to help management develop mission statements for each of its teams.

Elements of a Mission. Properly written mission statements completely describe why a team exists. To accomplish this aim, certain elements should be included in the mission. Figure 4.2 lists and describes these elements.

These elements should be considered for missions in every level and every part of an organization. Probably the most important element

Figure 4.2. Mission statement elements.

MISSION

A team's purpose—its unique contribution to the organization.

of the mission is the description of the team's products and/or services. What product does the team produce or service does it provide to its customers? Remember, the mission should be written specifically enough to describe the unique contribution of the team. So, for example, describing the product/service of a team within a law firm as legal advice is not specific enough. What kind of advice? What advice does the team provide that is different from other parts of the firm? Real estate or intellectual property advice would probably provide a better description of the service provided by the team.

The markets and/or customers the team serves also help define the unique purpose of the team. This portion of the mission should describe to whom the products/services are provided. Again, make the list as specific as possible. In some cases, it may be helpful to group the markets/customers. Retail stores and all managers are examples of groups of customers.

A team's boundaries, a description of its beginning and ending responsibilities, help define its role by bounding the activities for which it is responsible. A clear description of team boundaries will be helpful later for analyzing missions for overlaps or gaps.

Since the mission should describe the unique purpose of the team, document any traits or special features that differentiate the products or services offered by the team as part of the mission. If nothing unique comes to mind as you are developing the mission, skip this element for now. After you have written the missions for all of your teams, look back at each of them. Are they all unique? If not, identify what should differentiate one team from the other.

Level of Detail.   Each mission statement should be detailed enough to describe the unique purpose of the team, but not so detailed that it describes only a portion of the team's purpose. Sounds complicated, doesn't it? Getting the correct level of detail of a mission can be difficult, but it is important. A mission that is stated too broadly provides little help to the team; after all, a mission is supposed to describe what the team does. If the team cannot tell from its mission what it is expected to do, then what good is having it? A description that is too narrow can confuse a team because it knows it is responsible for more than the boundaries described by the mission. One test is to make sure the mission is worded such that it can describe only one team. If the mission can be interpreted to describe the purpose of more than one team, it is too general.

Organizations have missions, but so do the individual departments within the organization. So, how detailed should the missions be for each level of the organization? The mission for the entire organization should be the most broad—after all, it is describing the purpose for an entire organization. As the missions are written for teams lower in the organization, they should be more detailed because the purpose of the team is more focused and can be stated much more specifically. For example, the mission for an electronics manufacturing company may be

> Design, manufacture, and market wireless home electronic equipment to be sold to large retail stores.

The mission for the engineering department of the same company may be

> Produce product designs that satisfy design requirements, use the latest technology available, and consider the ease of production and maintenance.

Notice the mission for the engineering department is more detailed (it references the type of technology and other design considerations) than that of the entire company. Missions for departments within engineering will be even more specific.

Mission Flowdown.   The only way the organization can accomplish its mission is to have it deployed throughout the organization. This is one time when there certainly is an advantage for small businesses. The smaller the organization, the simpler the flowdown.

An organization's mission should not be its best kept secret—especially from its own employees! The organization's mission actually is accomplished by the many teams throughout the organization. Any team that does not accomplish its mission adversely affects the entire organization's

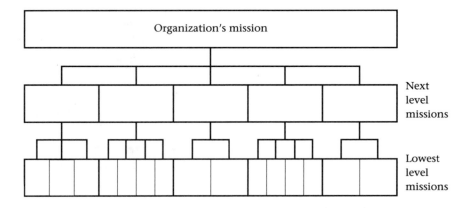

Figure 4.3. Mission flowdown through the organization.

ability to accomplish its mission. Figure 4.3 shows this relationship between the missions of teams at different levels within the organization.

No Overlaps or Gaps. Notice that none of the missions overlap. It is important to make sure each team has its own unique purpose. Overlapping missions mean duplication of work. If an analysis reveals some of your teams do have overlapping missions, decide which team should be responsible for the overlapping activities and rewrite the missions to reflect the changes.

There should be no gaps between the missions of the teams, either. Gaps reveal areas of the organization's mission that have not been deployed to its lower-level teams. Identification of gaps can be difficult; it requires detailed analysis of a team's mission and all of the missions of its reporting teams. If an analysis reveals gaps, decide how the gaps can be eliminated and update team missions as required.

Understanding the Team's Role in the Organization

A team's mission not only describes its purpose, but also helps the members understand their role in the organization. This understanding requires the team to have access to the missions of the teams above it in the organization. Teams need to know their activities are an integral part of producing outputs ultimately provided to the organization's external customers. This understanding helps teams know why they do what they do, and why it is important for them to perform their jobs according to documented requirements.

Missions developed by following this flowdown method offer any team a clear and exact picture of how it fits into the overall organization. Team members can follow the trail of missions from their team all the way to the organization's top-level mission.

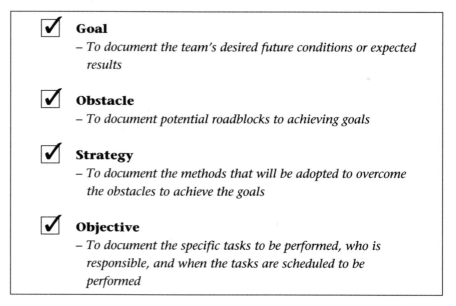

Figure 4.4. Plan elements.

ELEMENTS OF TEAM PLANS

Figure 4.4 lists the elements of a team plan and provides a short purpose for each. The elements, and their corresponding purpose statements, are not provided as the only proper definitions. There are many definitions, in fact, for the elements shown. In some circles, the words *goal, strategy,* and *objective* are used interchangeably. How the individual plan elements are defined is not nearly as important as the fact that a common vocabulary has been established and communicated throughout the organization. Common plan elements, using common definitions, allow everyone in the organization to communicate using the same language. The purpose of this section is to establish such a vocabulary that can be used within teams and between teams in the same organization.

So, if your company already has a set of planning element definitions, do not feel like you need to change them. Use your own vocabulary. (If you have not adopted your own vocabulary yet, the one offered here is recommended.) The key is to develop a set of terms, meaningful to your organization, that fill the purpose of the elements proposed here.

Goals

Goals document desired future conditions or expected results. Notice the emphasis on the future. Goals should not simply be statements of existing conditions. Goals set your team's direction by describing conditions you expect to be true—something to shoot for.

Goals Are Challenging, Yet Attainable. One of the purposes of setting goals is to get your team members to stretch themselves. It is

GOAL

Desired future condition or expected result. Sets the team's direction by describing conditions you expect to occur. Teams should document several goals they plan on achieving in order to fulfill their mission.

easy to get comfortable in a routine and a certain level of performance, but being content does not lead to continuous improvement. Goals are the vehicle that can be used to challenge your team to think beyond your current products, services, methods, and level of performance.

A good example of using challenging yet attainable goals comes from sports. Track and field athletes have long experienced the benefits of setting goals to improve their times and distances. A long jumper, for example, may set a goal of 28 feet. This distance may represent a challenging and attainable goal for a world-class long jumper who has recently jumped around 27 feet. Setting the goal at 32 feet would certainly be challenging, but the athlete would likely recognize the goal as unattainable. Unattainable goals can serve as demotivators rather than motivators. So, your challenge is to walk the fine line between setting challenging and unattainable goals.

Goals Are Associated with the Team's Mission.   Remember the purpose of goals in the overall planning structure. Goals provide direction by setting where your team wants to be at some point in the future. If the direction provided by the goals is not consistent with your mission, then the goals need to be reviewed and rewritten.

Goals May Contain a Time Frame.   Some goals contain a time frame in which they are to be achieved. While not mandatory, it is a good idea to try to document when you are planning to achieve the goal. Each element within the planning structure gets more detailed (as you will see as the other elements are discussed later). For a plan to be beneficial at all, it eventually must contain time-bounded activities. Introducing the expected timing early in the planning process (in the goals) sets the time frame for the remaining plan elements.

The following examples of goals may help your team get started in developing your goals.

- Achieve a market share of 40 percent by the end of the year.
- Win the Malcolm Baldrige National Quality Award in 1996.
- Release version 5.0 of our word processing program by November.
- Introduce our new line of copy machines in September.
- Improve our customer satisfaction ratings by 10 percent this year.
- Reduce our customer response time to 10 minutes by June.
- Meet with all of our internal customers at least once by the end of the year.

Teams should document several goals they plan on achieving in order to fulfill their mission.

Obstacles

Obstacles identify potential roadblocks to reaching team goals. What events, activities, circumstances, issues, situations, or limitations could serve as a roadblock in your path to success?

Be Proactive.   Identifying obstacles early in your team's improvement process allows you to anticipate likely problems that may make it difficult or impossible to accomplish your goals. This proactive approach is an important element of the planning process since it can help you be better prepared for events that may happen down the road.

OBSTACLE

Any event, activity, circumstance, issue, situation, or limitation that may stand in the way of reaching team goals. Several obstacles should be documented for each goal.

Limit Obstacles to Those Over Which You Have Control.   Listing obstacles can sometimes end up as complaint and gripe sessions. It can be tempting to create a long list of obstacles with which your team can do nothing. Remember, the purpose of listing obstacles is to anticipate things that may go wrong and plan activities to overcome the obstacles. If your team has no control, there is nothing for you to plan.

The following types of obstacles may help you identify some of your team's obstacles. Some items on the list may be relevant, others may help spark an idea.

- Schedule conflicts
- Resource limitations
- Lack of relevant experience
- Limited capabilities
- Lack of cooperation from another department
- New or untried technology
- Untrained employees
- Lack of management support or involvement

Document Obstacles for Each Goal.   Several obstacles should be documented for each goal. Try to identify as many obstacles as possible. Remember, the purpose of this listing is to identify things that could keep you from achieving your goals. Think! The time spent now can save a lot of time later.

Strategies

Strategies document specific methods or approaches that will be adopted to overcome the obstacles to achieve the goals. In other words, strategies are how-tos. Teams should consider all of their options before selecting (and then documenting) the strategies they will adopt. Do not jump to conclusions and select the first strategy suggested. Try to identify as many strategies as possible. (You may want to skip ahead to chapter 13 to find some creative-thinking techniques you can use in identifying possible strategies.)

STRATEGY

Specific method or approach that will be adopted to overcome an obstacle to achieve a goal. Each obstacle should have at least one strategy documenting how it will be overcome.

Strategies Have Alternatives.   Each strategy must have at least one viable alternative. Without the alternative, the strategy is just a statement of the obvious. Remember, you want to do whatever you can to make the plans really useful. So ask yourself the following question for each strategy you have written: "What other practical, workable approach could be taken?" If you cannot think of any, you have not identified a strategy. Record all of the ideas generated. After a list of possible strategies has been made, select the strategy that best overcomes the obstacle(s) to achieve the goal.

One company I worked with was experiencing what its management thought was excessive employee turnover. One of its goals was to reduce turnover by 25 percent in a year. After identifying the obstacles, the managers began work on strategies. One strategy mentioned was "to motivate the employees." After some discussion, I asked, "What is the viable alternative to motivating the employees?" They obviously couldn't think of any alternatives (attempting to demotivate the employees is not an option), so they set out to consider methods for motivating the employees. After identifying several alternatives, they selected the best one for them.

Strategies Include a "By" or "Through."   It may be helpful to think of strategies as having two elements: what you are going to do, followed by either "by" or "through," and an explanation.

An example may help. Let's assume you have established the following goal.

- To accumulate $100,000 for your child's college tuition and books

Let's also assume you have identified the following obstacles for the college tuition goal.

- I spend everything I make.
- I have never been able to save money.
- I don't know how to invest money.

There are many possible approaches one could take for this goal/obstacles combination. The following strategies are offered as examples.

- Purchase U.S. Savings Bonds through weekly payroll deductions.

- Invest in the stock market by using a discount broker.
- Win the money by playing the lottery every week.
- Inherit the money by spending a lot of time with an elderly, rich relative.

Notice the wording of the strategies provided. Each statement contains the word "by" or "through" to describe the approach. Since there are many ways one could purchase savings bonds, for example, the strategy should explain the specific approach to be considered. Purchasing savings bonds each year with money from your Christmas bonus is a different strategy than purchasing them each week through payroll deduction.

Document Strategies for Each Obstacle.   Each obstacle should have at least one strategy documenting how it will be overcome. It is possible to have a single strategy that addresses more than one obstacle, but be careful. Trying to economize on the number of strategies almost always results in strategies that do not completely address the obstacles they were selected to overcome.

Objectives

Objectives, the most detailed elements in the plan, answer the following questions.

- What activities need to be performed?
- Who will be responsible for performing each of the activities?
- In what sequence should the activities be performed?
- How long should it take for each of the activities to be performed?

OBJECTIVE
The most detailed element of a plan. Documents specific activities, provides a measure for completion, assigns responsibilities, and documents time frames. Each strategy should have many objectives.

Document Specific Activities.   The first step in developing objectives is to document the specific activities that need to be performed. Since objectives are the most detailed element of a plan, they need to be written specific enough to allow progress against the objectives to be monitored. Broadly worded objectives do not provide the reference required to accurately monitor performance.

Document Measurable Activities.   Measurable objectives provide a means of determining to what level the objective is complete. An objective that reads "Review all customer complaints by January 1" allows one to monitor the progress of the activity. After half of the complaints have been reviewed, the objective is half completed. This information allows you to estimate whether the activity is likely to be completed on schedule or not.

Document Who Is Responsible.   Responsibilities should be clearly documented to ensure everyone knows what their responsibilities are. Responsibilities can be assigned to individuals, a group, or maybe the entire team. Undocumented or vaguely worded objectives lead to confusion that results in incomplete activities.

Document Time Frames.   An important part of a specifically worded objective is a statement of the time frame in which the objective will be implemented. Because the objectives serve as a means to monitor progress, the objectives should include specific start and end dates. The objectives can then serve as an outline of the activities the team is to perform.

Objectives are the part of the plan you will likely reference frequently. You will refer to the plan to verify the activities you have planned to perform and to monitor your progress against your plan. The objectives will allow you to determine if you are on schedule.

Each strategy should have many objectives.

RELATIONSHIP BETWEEN PLAN ELEMENTS

The previous paragraphs have described the relationship between each of the plan elements. The relationships are shown graphically in Figure 4.5.

The figure shows five objectives for just one strategy designed to overcome one obstacle of one goal. Obviously this approach can lead to many objectives. Having many objectives is good; it demonstrates a detailed (and probably well-thought-out) plan.

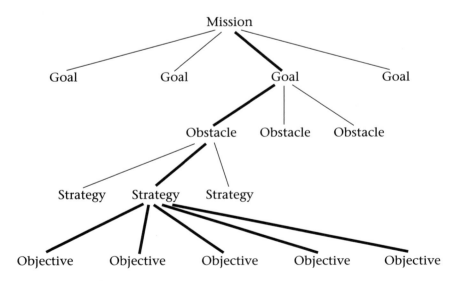

Figure 4.5. The relationship between plan elements.

CASCADING PLAN ELEMENTS

As plans are developed throughout the organization, care must be taken to ensure plans at all levels of the organization are working together. This caution applies to any size company. It is true that this is more of a problem for large companies, but it is such a critical concept that small businesses should also take note.

It is possible for a team to develop a plan that is contradictory to the plan developed by the next higher level team. For this reason, a systematic approach should be adopted to ensure plans developed throughout the organization are not only compatible, but actually work together toward the same aim.

This synergy is accomplished by passing plan elements from one level of the organization to the next. Specifically, a strategy at one level is translated into a goal at the next lower level.

For example, an organization may establish a goal to improve its public image. The strategies would then document how the organization plans to improve its image. Strategies may include the following:

- Demonstrate care for the community by becoming involved in civic activities.
- Publicize the healthful attributes of our products through a new advertising campaign.
- Demonstrate commitment to the environment by switching to environmentally safe packaging materials.

The corresponding objectives would then document details such as who is to make certain decisions and by what date.

To ensure consistency with this plan, lower-level teams should develop some of their goals based upon these strategies. For example, one team may develop the following goal (corresponding to the first strategy mentioned above): the organization is a member of at least one local civic organization by the end of the year. The strategies would then document how the civic organization(s) would be selected.

This method of flowing or cascading plan elements from one team to the next is depicted in Figure 4.6.

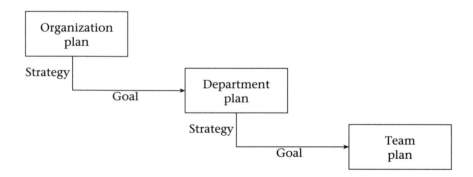

Figure 4.6. Cascading plan elements to ensure compatibility.

USING TEAM PLANS

The plans should be accessed, referenced, and used. They were not developed just to sit on a shelf. Team plans serve many useful purposes. The following discussion describes some of the primary uses of team plans.

Communicate Purpose and Direction

The primary use of team plans is to document the team's purpose and direction. The plans (often for the first time) provide visibility into where the team fits into the overall organization. This visibility leads directly to an understanding of its role. After a team sees how it fits in the organization, the members also can see the role their team is expected to fill. Finally, understanding its role provides a team with the direction it needs to develop the specific activities to be performed (documented throughout the plan).

Document Responsibilities

Another significant benefit of developing and using team plans is the fact that the plans document specific responsibilities for members of the team. The objectives list individual activities that are to be performed, by whom, and when they should be complete. This level of detail is very helpful to teams because the members can always reference the plans and know who is scheduled to be doing what.

The plans also document the interdependencies within the department so individuals can see how the other members of their team may be dependent on them to perform their activities.

UPDATING TEAM PLANS

Plans often are out of date as soon as they come off of the printer. This reality does not mean plans should not be developed. Plans must be continually reviewed and updated to reflect the team's current thinking and direction.

If the team does not maintain its plan, the time spent developing the plan originally is almost completely wasted (maybe not entirely since the planning process itself can be very revealing). Reasons for plan updates include new members added to the team (to document what they will be responsible for performing), new outputs provided (to update all process documentation), and changes in direction provided by management.

Your team notebook is a good place to store your plan. In the notebook, everyone will know where the plan is when they want to reference it.

SUMMARY

A well-written plan serves as an action guide for the team. The plan documents who should do what, and by when. The team's actions documented in the plan should be aimed at satisfying customers by building on the information gained in the previous chapter.

This chapter completes the *plan for customer satisfaction* step of the continuous process improvement cycle. At this point, your team should have documented what they need to do to satisfy their customers. The next step is to examine the work you perform that is passed to your customers. You need to understand your processes.

REVIEW QUESTIONS

Use the questions in Figure 4.7 to review your progress and make sure you are ready to continue on to the next chapter.

☐ Has a mission been written for every team?

☐ Is the mission for each team truly unique?

☐ Does the mission for each team completely describe the purpose of the team?

☐ Has the team developed its plan?

☐ Do the team's goals relate to its mission?

☐ Does the team's plan work together with higher-level plans?

☐ Has the team identified all of the obstacles that may keep it from success?

☐ Have strategies been selected for each obstacle?

☐ Are the objectives specific enough to allow the team to monitor its progress?

Figure 4.7. Review questions.

DEFINE PROCESSES

The processes a team performs must be defined before they can be understood and improved. This sequence means the first step in the *understand processes* step of the continuous process improvement cycle must be to define work processes. This chapter presents a structured method for defining the work processes of any team or organization. Before getting to the specific method of defining work processes, some general information about work processes is necessary.

ALL WORK IS A PROCESS

Processes exist in every part of an organization. Many people mistakenly think of only production or manufacturing operations when process improvement is discussed. Production processes often come to mind because we all can visualize the systematic progression of activities from receiving parts to assembling the parts to produce the product. But every part of an organization performs work that also can be systematically described. All work performed involves receiving input, and adding value to produce the outputs provided to the customers. Administration, billing, sales, human resources, training, and maintenance are all examples of areas in which processes exist.

PROCESS DEFINITIONS

Some processes are obvious, and therefore easy to define. Others are not so obvious. The steps listed in Figure 5.1 are provided as a means to define the processes that any organization performs.

The sequence of these steps, starting by listing outputs, may seem a little unusual, but the reasoning behind the sequence is sound (as you

1. List team outputs
to document the results of the work performed.

2. Group similar outputs
to create an outline of the process.

3. Name the process
to allow it to be easily referenced.

4. Define process boundaries
to establish beginning and ending points.

5. List process activities
to provide examples of the tasks involved.

6. Identify inputs
to determine the resources required.

Figure 5.1. Process definition steps.

will see throughout the explanation that follows). Teams that have previously had trouble defining their processes have been able to clearly define the work they do as specific processes by following these six steps. The completed definitions then serve as the basis for process improvement.

The process definition steps are shown graphically in Figure 5.2 and will be discussed in detail.

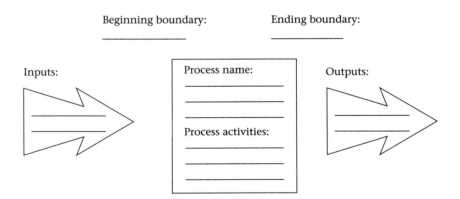

Figure 5.2. The elements of a process definition.

List Team Outputs

The first step in defining your processes is to list all of your team's outputs. The team outputs are the results of the work a team has performed that are provided to its customers. Your team's output list should already be completed from your work in chapter 3. Take a few minutes to evaluate your list to make sure it is complete and accurate.

Group Similar Outputs

The outputs of a single process share common traits. So by grouping similar outputs together, you can define the process that produces each group of outputs.

Teams with several outputs may find it helpful to record each of their outputs on an index card. Randomly spread all of the cards out on a table and have everyone on the team gather around. The cards can then be moved around the table to form logical groupings. In creating the groupings of similar outputs, consider

- The steps involved in producing the output
- The individuals involved
- The inputs required

As two or more outputs seem to fit together, place them next to each other on the table. Everyone on the team should participate in developing the groupings. Make sure everyone has a say. Someone may suggest an alternative output grouping, listen to their reasoning.

Some outputs may be difficult to group or there may be disagreement within the team as to which group the output belongs. Place these cards aside for now—don't get bogged down. Return to these later and give everyone a chance to express their opinions. In some cases, a single output may not be grouped with any others. That's all right; it just means the process has a single output.

For example, all the reports a team produces may be grouped together. This makes sense if the steps involved and information required are somewhat similar. If not, the reports may be further separated into different groupings.

A team responsible for developing an accounting software package may list the following outputs.

- Accounting program(s)
- Installation program
- Data conversion program
- User's guide
- Installation guide
- Flowcharts/technical documentation
- Instructions for technical support
- Time card logs

• Accounting program(s)
• Installation program
• Data conversion program
Grouping 1

• User's guide
• Installation guide
Grouping 2

• Flowcharts
• Instructions for technical support
Grouping 3

• Time card logs
Grouping 4

Figure 5.3. Possible output groupings.

There is no *right* way to group these outputs into processes. One way they could be grouped is shown in Figure 5.3.

This method of grouping places all the programs in grouping 1, documentation for the users in grouping 2, technical documentation in grouping 3, and time card logs are not grouped with any other outputs.

Another possibility is to group the outputs as shown in Figure 5.4.

Teams should use their judgment and experience in grouping similar outputs to define a process.

Name the Process

After the team agrees on the output groupings, assign a name to each of the groupings. The name of the groupings is the name of the process so it should be descriptive of the outputs. Record the process name on another card in large print and with a different color ink (so

• Accounting program(s)
• User's guide
• Flowcharts
• Instruction for technical support
Grouping 1

• Installation program
• Installation guide
Grouping 2

• Data conversion program
Grouping 3

• Time card logs
Grouping 4

Figure 5.4. Alternate output groupings.

they will stand out from the other cards). After everyone agrees on the names, bundle each grouping (with a rubber band or paper clip) with the name card on top.

The Process Definition Worksheet. The process definition worksheet can be used to document the result of each of the process definition steps. See example on page 72.

At this point, record the outputs (in the large arrow on the right) and process name (in the top portion of the center box) for one of the process groupings. Follow the remaining steps to define the process and complete the process definition worksheet for the selected process. You will return to the other card stacks shortly to define your remaining processes.

Define Process Boundaries

Process boundaries must be defined to clearly establish the beginning and ending points of the process. The beginning boundary should describe the state of the process as the team begins its work. The ending boundary should describe the state of the process after the team has completed its work. Boundaries must be set to highlight the interfaces between the process being analyzed and other processes. Process interfaces frequently are the source of process problems stemming from confusion about responsibilities. It rarely matters whether a task is listed as the last step for one process or the first step in the next process. The key is that everyone involved understands what the boundaries are (and therefore where the responsibilities lie).

PROCESS BOUNDARY

A clear description of the state of the process at its beginning and at its end.

Let's look at an example of someone working at a fast food restaurant responsible for making French fries, onion rings, and fried fruit pies (notice that similar outputs have been grouped to define the frying process). What are the boundaries of this process? Is it part of the frying process to get the required food from the freezer, or does the process begin with the appropriate quantity of frozen food delivered to the fryer? Does the process end with the product in its package, or is packaging part of the "deliver food to the customer" process?

Document the beginning and ending boundaries for the process you have selected on the process definition worksheet.

List Process Activities

Next, list the series of activities that are performed as part of the process. What steps does your team perform to produce the outputs listed? The activities will be documented in significant detail later, but an overview of the activities performed helps define the process now. The activities should be listed only after the process boundaries have been established. This way, the activities listed can serve as an overview of the steps involved from the beginning boundary to the ending boundary. Only list activities to the level of detail necessary to help define the process.

Process Definition Worksheet

3
Beginning boundary:

_____

_____

4
Ending boundary:

_____

_____

6
Inputs:

2
Process name:

_____

_____

_____

5
Process activities:

_____

_____

_____

_____

_____

_____

_____

_____

_____

1
Outputs:

A securities broker may list the following activities for the *provide investment advice* process.

- Review existing portfolio.
- Understand investment philosophy of the client.
- Research options.
- Make recommendations.

Obviously, there are many more steps in providing this service, but these four probably provide enough detail to help clarify the process being defined.

Record the process steps in the bottom portion of the center box on the process definition worksheet.

Identify Inputs

The final step in defining a process is to list the inputs required by the process. Review the process activities listed in the previous step to identify the inputs required by the process to produce its outputs. The process input list should include items like the human resources, equipment, materials, and information required by the process to produce its outputs. These inputs are provided by the team's suppliers.

The inputs for someone preparing individual tax returns would include complete income and deduction information from the customer, up-to-date tax laws from the government, and tax preparation software for the current year. It may be easy to envision a computer software vendor as a supplier, but not all customer/supplier relationships are this obvious. Sometimes, your customers serve as suppliers by providing you with information or products you need to do your job. In the tax preparation example, the customer (the one having the taxes prepared) must provide inputs (income and deduction information) to the supplier to allow the function to be performed.

Document the inputs in the large arrow on the left side of the process definition worksheet.

A COMPLETED EXAMPLE

A process definition worksheet has been completed for a fictitious company's paycheck generation process (see page 74). Notice that reviewing the time cards for completeness is part of this process. This is visible from looking at the beginning boundary and the activity list. The beginning boundary does not indicate that the cards have already been reviewed. If the review is considered to be part of another process, the boundary should clearly describe the beginning point of the process after the review. This situation provides a good example of the need for clearly defining the beginning and ending process boundaries. Clearly stated boundaries eliminate many potential problems.

Process Definition Worksheet

COMPLETED

3
Beginning boundary:

Receipt of completed

time cards

4
Ending boundary:

Checks sorted by

department

6
Inputs:

Completed time cards

Blank checks

Computer software

Printer

2
Process name:

Paycheck generation

5
Process activities:

Review time cards

Return incomplete cards

Enter hours worked

Review check amounts

Print checks

Sort checks by department

1
Outputs:

Paychecks

Check stub information

The process activities listed certainly are not all inclusive—there are many other activities the team performs in generating the paychecks. The list, however, does provide enough information to help define the process to everyone involved.

DEFINE ALL OF YOUR TEAM'S PROCESSES

At this point, take the time to define *all* of your team's processes. Return to your card stacks and complete a process definition worksheet for each stack. This completeness will make sure all of your outputs are assigned to a process. The completed list of processes will be used later to prioritize your team's improvement activities. As your team produces new outputs (due to management direction, customer requests, new ideas generated by the team, and so forth), new processes should be defined, or existing process definitions updated to reflect changes caused by the new output. Keep your process definition worksheets up to date.

PREPARE A PROCESS MAP FOR THE ENTIRE ORGANIZATION

Individual process definition worksheets, when grouped with definitions of other surrounding processes, provide useful information to management. The worksheets can be posted on a large wall to display the sequence of processes performed within the organization to transform inputs from external suppliers to the outputs provided to the organization's external customers. Figure 5.5 shows how this arrangement can provide a visual representation of the activities performed and serve as an excellent analysis tool.

PROCESS MAP
A diagram of the sequence of processes performed within the organization to transform inputs from external suppliers to the outputs provided to the organization's external customers.

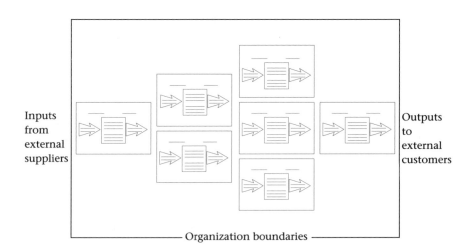

Inputs from external suppliers

Outputs to external customers

Organization boundaries

Figure 5.5. An organizational process map.

Look for Gaps and Overlaps

The process boundaries, as documented on the individual process definition worksheets, should match from one process to the next in the overall flow. For example, if adjoining processes both include transportation, something is wrong. Transportation should be documented as part of one process or the other, not both. Conversely, the analysis may identify some activities that actually take place, but are not documented as part of either process. Most of the time this gap is caused by each team documenting its process assuming that the activity is part of the other process. It probably does not matter in which process the activity is documented, just that it is documented somewhere.

Identify Areas of Duplication

Analysis of the overall process map may reveal some activities or entire processes that are being performed by more than one team in the organization. There is rarely need for this duplication. After areas of duplication are identified, management should analyze the process to determine how (and by whom) the process should be performed.

Verify Output/Input Matches

All of the outputs of a process should serve as inputs to another process or be provided to an external customer. If an output does neither, then why is it produced? It can be very difficult to identify the outputs that are not needed without being able to see the entire process. The organization's process map provides this visibility.

It may be difficult to verify all of the output/input matches because different words and phrases can be used to describe the same output or input. An output identified as "customer list" by one team may be the same as the "labels" input listed by another. The process map can help identify these vocabulary differences. After they are identified, the two teams can work together to develop a common vocabulary.

PRIORITIZE PROCESSES FOR IMPROVEMENT

Process improvement requires systematic analysis, so teams cannot afford to take the time to improve all of its processes at once. The team's processes should be prioritized so process improvement can begin in a logical sequence, working to improve the processes most needing improvement first. This prioritization must be based on inputs from your customers. The processes your customers tell you need improvement are the processes that need improvement! Your customer may not tell you directly which processes need the most improvement, but you already have the information you need. The process that your customers have said is the most important, but has a low satisfaction rating, is the place to begin.

Process priority is determined to provide guidelines for the order in which your improvement efforts should be planned. This certainly is not an exact science, but a method for providing an orderly list of processes for improvement is helpful.

Calculate Process Priority Scores

All the information you need to calculate the priority score for each of your processes has already been collected. All you need to do now is sort, total, and analyze some data.

The total of the Priority column on your output requirements worksheets provide the priority numbers for each of your outputs. The higher the priority number, the more unsatisfied the customer is with an important output requirement, and therefore the higher priority for improvement. Next, use the information from the process definition worksheets to total the priority numbers for each of the outputs of a process to get an overall process priority score. These relationships are shown in Figure 5.6. The process priority scoring worksheet on page 78 may be helpful in calculating these totals.

Identify Priority Groupings

The result of the previous step is a process priority score for each of your processes. The process priority list worksheet can be used to record all of your processes in priority order (see page 80). List all of your processes and their corresponding process priority scores.

This list is meant to assist you in prioritizing your process improvement efforts, not to dictate your actions. This means you should analyze the list to decide the best place to start. The processes at the top of the list should be worked on before those at the very bottom of the list, but you may not choose to start with the top (or even the second) process. You probably will notice groupings or clusters of processes

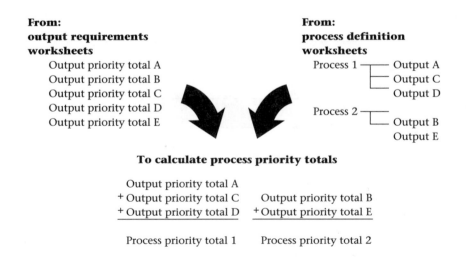

Figure 5.6. Inputs to calculating process priority totals.

Process Priority Scoring Worksheet

Date: _____

Process: _____

Outputs	Output priority total
1. _____	_____
2. _____	_____
3. _____	_____
4. _____	_____
5. _____	_____
6. _____	_____
7. _____	_____
8. _____	_____

Process priority score: [   ]

Process: _____

Outputs	Output priority total
1. _____	_____
2. _____	_____
3. _____	_____
4. _____	_____
5. _____	_____
6. _____	_____
7. _____	_____
8. _____	_____

Process priority score: [   ]

with similar process priority scores. It may be helpful to identify these groupings, then prioritize the process within a grouping. This way, the scores provide the basis for the prioritization, but you use your judgment and experience for processes with similar process scores.

SUMMARY

Defining processes is a prerequisite to process improvement. A complete process definition contains six elements: the process outputs, name, beginning boundary, ending boundary, list of activities, and inputs. This chapter presents a systematic method of clearly defining all work processes and documenting the results on process definition worksheets. The completed process definition worksheets can be used to make a process map of the entire organization.

With a completed process definition and the customer information gained in chapter 3, a team is prepared to provide supplier feedback.

REVIEW QUESTIONS

Use the questions in Figure 5.7 to review your progress and make sure you are ready to continue on to the next chapter.

☐ Has the team defined all of its processes?

☐ Have the process boundaries been clearly stated?

☐ Has the team listed all of its inputs?

☐ What is the result of analyzing the process map?

☐ Has the team developed a process priority list?

Figure 5.7. Review questions.

Process Priority List Worksheet

Date: _____

	Process	Process priority score
1.	_____	_____
2.	_____	_____
3.	_____	_____
4.	_____	_____
5.	_____	_____
6.	_____	_____
7.	_____	_____
8.	_____	_____
9.	_____	_____
10.	_____	_____
11.	_____	_____
12.	_____	_____
13.	_____	_____
14.	_____	_____
15.	_____	_____

PROVIDE SUPPLIER FEEDBACK

A quick review of what has been covered so far will put the steps performed into context and set the stage for the next step, providing supplier feedback. Figure 6.1 provides this review and identifies what needs to be done next.

The next step is to talk to your suppliers. Communication is a critical element of any process improvement initiative. *Never assume that just*

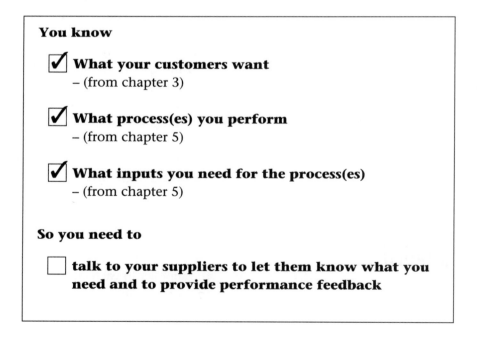

Figure 6.1. The steps leading to providing supplier feedback.

because your team has worked with a supplier for many years that this communication is unnecessary. Do not leave something as important as defining your input requirements to chance.

YOU ARE DEPENDENT ON YOUR SUPPLIERS

Because you rely on your suppliers to provide you with the products and services you need to satisfy your customers, you are dependent on them. If you do not receive what you need from them when you need it, it can be difficult (or even impossible) to provide what your customers need when they need it.

From your customers' point of view, you are the provider. They certainly are not concerned with any problems you have with your suppliers and they don't want to hear any excuses. Your customers look to you, and you alone.

A frustrated friend of mine recently told me a story of his latest experience with the repair shop he takes his car to for maintenance. After explaining the problems he was experiencing with his car to the mechanic, he was assured his car would be fixed and ready to be picked up after work that afternoon. Just before he was ready to go pick up his car, he received a call from the mechanic. The mechanic explained that he had encountered some problems locating a part he needed for the repair and the car would not be ready for another two days. The problem was that all of the local parts supply stores the mechanic purchases parts from were out of the needed part, so he had ordered the part from an out-of-state supplier. The problem was not really the mechanic's fault (he assumed the part would be available locally like it usually was when he promised the repairs would be done that day), but with whom do you think my friend was disappointed? To him, the mechanic was the supplier. Any other relationships were irrelevant to him.

What does this story point out about your relationship with your customers and suppliers? To your customers, *you* are the supplier. All other relationships are irrelevant. This story highlights the need to manage your relationships with your suppliers. You certainly don't want to leave the details to chance.

MEETING WITH YOUR SUPPLIERS

If every team within an organization communicates with its customers (as called for in chapter 3), there is no need for supplier feedback since the supplier in each customer/supplier relationship would be instigating the communication. Reaching this level of maturity takes a long time, if it happens at all (it seems like there are always some teams that do not have time to talk to their customers). So, in the meantime, providing supplier feedback fills a critical need.

The steps involved in meeting with your suppliers, and the purpose of each, are shown in Figure 6.2.

> **1. List input requirements**
> *to ensure the supplier knows what you need and expect from the products/services provided.*
>
> **2. Document level of performance**
> *to inform the supplier which requirements are most important.*
>
> **3. Document level of satisfaction**
> *to provide performance feedback.*

Figure 6.2. The steps in providing supplier feedback.

INPUT REQUIREMENTS

As a customer, you have specific requirements for each of the inputs you receive from your suppliers. Just as it is important to receive important output attributes from your customers, it is important to communicate the requirements you have for your suppliers.

List the Requirements

What requirements do you, as the customer, have for the inputs provided to you by your suppliers? Input requirements answer questions like those listed in Figure 6.3.

These requirements are based on your understanding of your customers' requirements and your knowledge of the process you perform to produce the outputs to their specifications.

What
- What will it be used for?
- What size should it be?
- What color should it be?
- What level of accuracy is needed?

Where
- Where will it be used?
- Where should it be delivered?

When
- When should it be delivered?
- When will it be used?

How
- How often is it needed?
- How should it be packaged?
- How should it be presented?
- How long should it be?
- How much should it cost?
- How much should it weigh?
- How should it be delivered?

Figure 6.3. Identify input requirements.

Many requirements can be classified as either feature, accuracy, or timeliness requirements.

Features. Input features include the format, appearance, design, and layout of the product or service being received. For example, reports are common process inputs. Report features may include its spacing (single or double space), margin spacing, single- or double-sided, software compatibility, and so forth.

Accuracy. Another common input requirement category is accuracy. Many inputs will have some type of accuracy requirements such as: The holes must be drilled to within ±.001 inch, or the data must be accurate to within ±2 percent.

Timeliness.   You probably have requirements for when you need the inputs provided by your suppliers. Make sure your suppliers know when you need the inputs they provide to you.

Be as specific as you can in stating your timeliness requirements. If you need something at a specific time, then state the time. If you need something no later than a specific day or time, then state your requirement accordingly (in this case, also try to document the earliest time in which you could accept the input). In some cases, you may be able to live with a day or time range. For example, your timing requirement may be

- At 4:00 P.M. every Friday afternoon
- Within 30 minutes of the end of each shift
- Before the close of business each day
- Any time after Tuesday morning, but before 3:30 P.M. on Thursday
- Between 11:00 A.M. and 1:30 P.M.

Make sure your timeliness requirements are accurately communicated. Evaluate when you need each of your inputs. If you don't need something until Thursday afternoon, don't say you need it Wednesday morning. This type of hedging may seem harmless, but imagine the impact if everyone hedged their requirements even just a little. Remember, you are going to be asking your suppliers to schedule their work around the requirements you provide them (and those they receive from their other customers), so be honest.

Other. Features, accuracy, and timeliness are helpful categories of input requirements, but they certainly do not encompass every type of input requirement. These categories have been emphasized because of their near-universal application. Other requirements or attributes may include reliability, cost, and accessibility.

Be Willing to Negotiate

In some cases, your suppliers may question a requirement or suggest a different approach. Be willing to listen—your suppliers' experience can help you. Negotiate as necessary; just make sure you both understand the requirements as they are agreed upon.

LEVEL OF IMPORTANCE

Not all of the requirements you have for your inputs are equally important, are they? Some inputs are critical to your process to ensure you can produce outputs that satisfy your customers, others are not nearly as important. Some may just be *nice to haves*. So, how important are each of the attributes of the inputs provided to your team?

Use the following rating categories (already introduced for communicating with your customers) to identify the importance of each input requirement.

- Extremely important or critical
- Very important
- Important
- Somewhat important
- Not important

Remember, this rating scale is absolute, not relative. The idea is not to determine that "compared to this other input requirement I have rated as important, this requirement is extremely important." Select which of the five categories best describes the importance you place on the requirement. This information will be used later to help prioritize your improvement efforts. So, all requirements must be rated on the same, absolute scale.

LEVEL OF SATISFACTION

A critical piece of information to your suppliers is your current level of satisfaction with their performance for each requirement of the inputs they provide to you. If you are not satisfied with their performance, they want to know. They also want to know what you think they could do to improve.

Use the following five categories to describe your levels of satisfaction with each of your requirements.

- Extremely satisfied or delighted
- Very satisfied or pleased
- Satisfied
- Dissatisfied
- Very dissatisfied

USING THE SUPPLIER FEEDBACK WORKSHEET

The worksheet on page 87 may be used to record the requirements for a single input and their levels of importance and satisfaction.

The Priority Column

You already have found that your processes are prioritized based on the levels of importance and customer satisfaction provided by your customers. Your suppliers also should be interested in gathering this type of data to use in prioritizing their process improvement efforts. You can help facilitate their improvement by completing the prioritization portion of the worksheet. The beginning of this prioritization process is to calculate the priority of each input. The priority is calculated by multiplying the weighting factors (in the small check boxes) of the requirement importance and satisfaction. After the priority is calculated for each requirement, add the priorities and record the total in the input priority total box.

CONDUCTING THE MEETING

A selected team representative should meet personally with each supplier to communicate the information on the worksheet. In the discussion of customer meetings in chapter 3, we introduced questionnaires and focus groups as means of getting feedback representative of all customers from only a few. Unfortunately, this type of shortcut is not appropriate for supplier meetings. All of your suppliers need to know exactly what you need from them—telling a representative sample will not do. Remember, you are relying on these suppliers, so give them all the information they need to provide you with the products and services you need from them.

PROVIDE REGULAR SUPPLIER FEEDBACK

Providing feedback to all of your suppliers should become a regular part of your job, it is not a one-time activity. Regular feedback ensures there are no surprises—you know you have communicated your requirements to your suppliers, and they know what you require, what is important to you, and how you think they are doing.

There is no way to recommend the best feedback frequency. All processes are different. Several factors affect the determination of the proper frequency.

- How often is the input received? (Inputs provided frequently need more frequent feedback.)
- How critical is the input in producing an output to the external customer? (Critical inputs call for more frequent feedback.)

Supplier Feedback Worksheet

Date: _____

Input: _____

Supplier(s): _____

Completed by: _____

Requirements	Importance	Satisfaction	Priority

Requirements   **Importance**   **Satisfaction**   **Priority**

A. _____
_____

- [5] Extremely important/critical
- [4] Very important
- [3] Important
- [2] Somewhat important
- [1] Not important

- [1] Extremely satisfied/delighted
- [2] Very satisfied/pleased
- [4] Satisfied
- [6] Dissatisfied
- [10] Very dissatisfied

_____

B. _____
_____

- [5] Extremely important/critical
- [4] Very important
- [3] Important
- [2] Somewhat important
- [1] Not important

- [1] Extremely satisfied/delighted
- [2] Very satisfied/pleased
- [4] Satisfied
- [6] Dissatisfied
- [10] Very dissatisfied

_____

C. _____
_____

- [5] Extremely important/critical
- [4] Very important
- [3] Important
- [2] Somewhat important
- [1] Not important

- [1] Extremely satisfied/delighted
- [2] Very satisfied/pleased
- [4] Satisfied
- [6] Dissatisfied
- [10] Very dissatisfied

_____

D. _____
_____

- [5] Extremely important/critical
- [4] Very important
- [3] Important
- [2] Somewhat important
- [1] Not important

- [1] Extremely satisfied/delighted
- [2] Very satisfied/pleased
- [4] Satisfied
- [6] Dissatisfied
- [10] Very dissatisfied

_____

E. _____
_____

- [5] Extremely important/critical
- [4] Very important
- [3] Important
- [2] Somewhat important
- [1] Not important

- [1] Extremely satisfied/delighted
- [2] Very satisfied/pleased
- [4] Satisfied
- [6] Dissatisfied
- [10] Very dissatisfied

_____

F. _____
_____

- [5] Extremely important/critical
- [4] Very important
- [3] Important
- [2] Somewhat important
- [1] Not important

- [1] Extremely satisfied/delighted
- [2] Very satisfied/pleased
- [4] Satisfied
- [6] Dissatisfied
- [10] Very dissatisfied

_____

G. _____
_____

- [5] Extremely important/critical
- [4] Very important
- [3] Important
- [2] Somewhat important
- [1] Not important

- [1] Extremely satisfied/delighted
- [2] Very satisfied/pleased
- [4] Satisfied
- [6] Dissatisfied
- [10] Very dissatisfied

_____

H. _____
_____

- [5] Extremely important/critical
- [4] Very important
- [3] Important
- [2] Somewhat important
- [1] Not important

- [1] Extremely satisfied/delighted
- [2] Very satisfied/pleased
- [4] Satisfied
- [6] Dissatisfied
- [10] Very dissatisfied

_____

I. _____
_____

- [5] Extremely important/critical
- [4] Very important
- [3] Important
- [2] Somewhat important
- [1] Not important

- [1] Extremely satisfied/delighted
- [2] Very satisfied/pleased
- [4] Satisfied
- [6] Dissatisfied
- [10] Very dissatisfied

_____

Input Priority Total: [ ]

- How consistent is the supplier's performance? (The more inconsistent, the more frequent the feedback should be.)
- Has the supplier made any recent changes to the process that produces the input provided to you? (New or untested methods call for more frequent feedback.)

Regular feedback also helps your suppliers identify a negative trend and react before the problem gets serious. This approach is what TQM is all about: identifying and fixing problems before the customer is affected.

Through these meetings you will develop an increasing level of teamwork with your suppliers. The borders of your team begin to stretch to include your suppliers. This growth is good. The better you can work with your suppliers (and they with you), the better you can satisfy your customers.

SUMMARY

You rely heavily on your suppliers to provide you with the products and services required to satisfy your customers. It is difficult, if not impossible, to satisfy your customers if you are not first satisfied with your suppliers. For this reason, it is important that you provide your suppliers with feedback so they know what is important to you and how you think they are performing.

Defining processes and providing supplier feedback have prepared you for the next step in *understanding processes*—document processes.

REVIEW QUESTIONS

Use the questions in Figure 6.4 to review your progress and make sure you are ready to continue on to the next chapter.

☐	Has the team listed all of its suppliers?
☐	Has the team listed all of the requirements it has for each of the inputs?
☐	Has the team met with all of its suppliers?
☐	Has the team communicated its importance and satisfaction ratings for each input?

Figure 6.4. Review questions.

DOCUMENT PROCESSES

A key step in understanding a process is to be able to document it by listing the steps involved. The document will then serve as a primary process improvement tool. Everyone involved with improving the process will view the process the same since they all will be referencing the same document.

Process flow diagrams (also commonly called flowcharts) provide a means of graphically describing a process by using simple symbols, lines, and words to display sequenced activities. It has been said that "a picture is worth a thousand words." A process flow diagram is a picture of a process.

SELECT PROCESSES TO DOCUMENT

Eventually, your team should document all of your processes to assist in identifying ways to improve them. To get started, select one of your highest priority processes to document. You will return to this part of the cycle later, after the selected process has been analyzed and improved, to document other processes.

USE PROCESS FLOW DIAGRAMS

Process flow diagrams are simple, but effective, process improvement tools. This section documents some guidelines to keep in mind as you develop your process flow diagrams.

Identify Proper Level of Detail

Almost any process can be documented with as few as five process activities, but this level of detail provides little help in clarifying the

PROCESS FLOW DIAGRAM
A means of graphically describing a process by using simple symbols, lines, and words to display sequenced activities. An effective process improvement tool. Also called flowchart.

process flow or identifying process improvements. List the process steps in as much detail as possible—take nothing for granted. Document all of the activities, even if they seem obvious. Do not worry about being too detailed. When in doubt, list the detail steps performed. For example, rather than documenting an activity as "prepare the closing report," list the individual activities (and decisions) that are performed to produce the report.

Remember, these diagrams will be used to analyze the process for improvement. The more detailed the documentation, the more information the document contains, and the more opportunities for improvement will be identified.

Ensure Process Definition Compatibility

The start and stop points documented on the process flow diagram should correlate to the beginning and ending boundaries documented on the process definition worksheet. The process inputs and outputs also should match. Update the process definition worksheet as required to make sure it is accurate and matches the detail information shown on the process flow diagram.

PROCESS FLOW DIAGRAM SYMBOLS

Some process flow diagrams look complicated because they use a very specialized set of symbols, each depicting a specific type of action. This complexity is not necessary for documenting processes for identifying improvement opportunities. The set of simple symbols shown in Figure 7.1 are all that are required.

Several software packages are now available for producing flow diagrams. If you are comfortable using your computer, consider getting one of these packages. The software makes it easy to make changes to the diagrams and produces attractive charts. Hand-drawn charts, however, can serve the purpose just as well. Don't feel you need to buy new software.

TYPES OF PROCESS FLOW DIAGRAMS

There are three primary types of flow diagrams used to document processes—each emphasizing a different type of flow and providing different information for use in process improvement. You will need to decide which type(s) to use for each process you analyze.

Operations Process Flow Diagrams

The most common type of process flow diagram, an operations process flow diagram, documents the series of activities performed and decisions made as part of the process. These diagrams are the primary tool for process improvements. Figure 7.2 is an example of a simple operations process flow diagram.

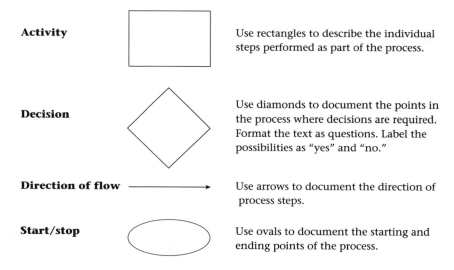

Activity		Use rectangles to describe the individual steps performed as part of the process.
Decision		Use diamonds to document the points in the process where decisions are required. Format the text as questions. Label the possibilities as "yes" and "no."
Direction of flow		Use arrows to document the direction of process steps.
Start/stop		Use ovals to document the starting and ending points of the process.

Figure 7.1. Process flow diagram symbols.

OPERATIONS PROCESS FLOW DIAGRAM

Most common process flow diagram. Documents the series of activities performed and decisions made.

Functional Process Flow Diagrams

Notice that the diagram begins and ends with an oval. The first oval signals the start of the process and the last oval signals the end of the process (the words "start" and "stop" should be written in the ovals). The diagram then shows the sequence of steps to be performed. The diamond depicts a decision to be made. Depending on the result of the decision/question one of two different activities is performed.

Functional process flow diagrams are a special type of operations process flow diagram. Sometimes, teams may want to document who does what as part of a process flow diagram. A functional process flow diagram is a means of not only documenting the sequence of activities, but also recording who is responsible for performing each of the activities.

The first step in developing a functional process flow diagram is to divide the page the process is to be documented on with horizontal lines to create sections on the page for each of the people or teams involved in the process. The process flow diagram symbols are then drawn in the

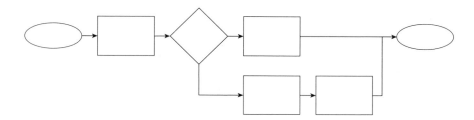

Figure 7.2. Operations process flow diagram.

FUNCTIONAL PROCESS FLOW DIAGRAM

Documents who is responsible for performing each activity, as well as the sequence of the activities.

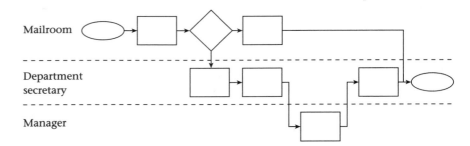

Figure 7.3. Functional process flow diagram.

appropriate section of the page with the process flow generally shown from left to right. An example of a simple functional process flow diagram is shown in Figure 7.3.

In this example, the process begins in the mailroom. The department secretary and eventually the manager are involved, depending on the result of the decision.

Layout Process Flow Diagrams

A layout or geographic flow diagram depicts the floor plan of an area. The diagram then shows the flow of paperwork or other materials and products, and the location of work areas, equipment, file cabinets, storage areas, etc. Figure 7.4 is an example of a layout process flow diagram.

USES OF PROCESS FLOW DIAGRAMS

Process flow diagrams serve many purposes in process improvement. Methods for analyzing processes for improvement are covered in chapter 8. Even before this analysis, there are other uses of the diagrams. Some of the primary uses of the diagrams are shown in Figure 7.5.

LAYOUT PROCESS FLOW DIAGRAM

Depicts the floor plan of an area and shows the flow of paperwork or other materials through that area.

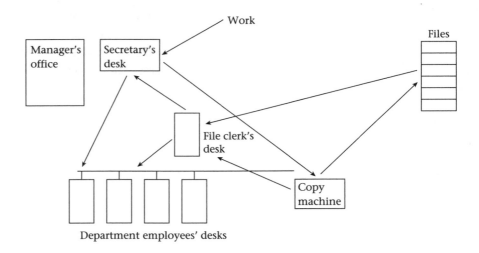

Figure 7.4. Layout process flow diagram.

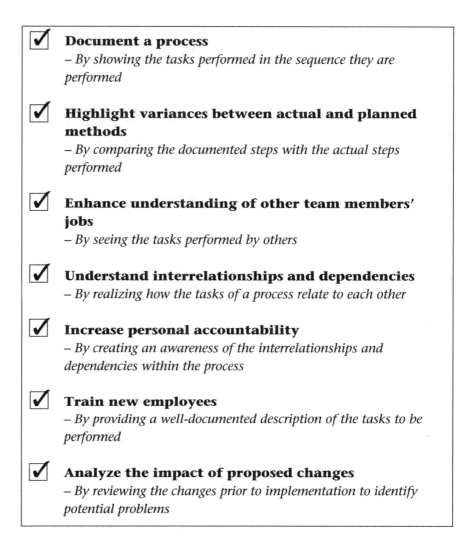

Figure 7.5. Process flow diagram uses.

Document a Process

The primary benefit of using process flow diagrams is to provide a record of a process that enables anyone to examine and understand the process. The process should be documented the way the process actually is being performed. Resist the temptation to document the process the way you wish the process was performed. The next two chapters will rely heavily on the flow diagrams for process improvement identification and measurement development, so they must be accurate.

Attempts to document a process often will highlight misunderstanding and different methods used in performing the process. At this point, the team should work together to decide how the process will be performed, and document it accordingly. After the diagram is completed, everyone can see the process the same way. The completed process flow diagram is then the basis for the process improvement techniques discussed in later chapters.

Highlight Variances Between Actual and Planned Methods

Comparing a flow diagram to the actual process activities being performed will highlight the differences, if any, between the way an activity is supposed to be conducted and the way it actually is conducted. Where there is a difference, either the process or the documentation needs to be updated. The documentation cannot be helpful unless it is an accurate representation of how the process is performed. If the documented process steps are not followed because a better method has been identified, the better process should be documented. In some cases, the current method used will need to be changed to match the documentation because the documented method must be followed to comply with customer (internal or external) or regulatory requirements.

Enhance Understanding of Other Team Members' Jobs

Everyone involved with the process being documented should participate in developing the process flow diagram to ensure the process is accurately documented. A pleasant side effect of this teamwork in developing the diagrams is an enhanced understanding of other team members' role in the process. This understanding helps cross-train the members of the team to perform each other's job when required.

Understand Interrelationships and Dependencies

Process flow diagrams document how the activities of a process relate to each other. This awareness helps everyone understand how their job fits into the team's bigger picture and why they do what they do. As a result, team members are better prepared to support other team members later in the process. Understanding how their output is used later in the process also allows team members to suggest improvements to their portion of the process. They may be able to identify tasks they perform that are not needed, are redone later, or could make someone else's job easier (for example, they could perform a task while the checks are sorted so someone else doesn't have to sort the checks again later to do their part of the process).

Increase Personal Accountability

Awareness of these dependencies also leads to individuals accepting personal accountability for their portion of the process. Process reviews will result in everyone knowing that others depend on them to completely and accurately perform their part of the process. The team can only be successful when everyone does their part.

Train New Employees

Process flow diagrams serve as excellent tools in training new employees. A well-documented process will greatly assist an employee's efforts to study and understand their new job. If they are accurate representations of the process, the diagrams provide a link from the employees(s) currently performing a job to the new employee(s). You no longer have to worry what knowledge of the process will be lost during employee changes. The process flow diagram will list all of the process steps, identify the proper sequence, document the necessary decisions, and list the appropriate actions to take for each decision possibility. This type of documentation speeds training time and leads to more consistent performance.

At a break in a recent workshop, the owner of a small print shop came up to talk to me. Her question was a common one: "All these ideas you are talking about sound good, but what can I do?" Since we had just been talking about process flow diagrams, I asked her if she spent much time training her employees. She looked at me like I had read her mind and admitted that she had experienced quite a bit of employee turnover recently. As a result, she spent a significant amount of time training new employees. As we talked, she realized that not only could process flow diagrams be helpful in training her new employees, they would help her be consistent in how she taught everyone.

Analyze the Impact of Proposed Changes

Process flow diagrams are used primarily to analyze current process performance, but they also are effective tools for analyzing the impact of proposed changes. A team using a process flow diagram to document proposed changes to a process can analyze the *to be* process before actually implementing the change. This method allows potential problems with the proposed changes to be identified and eliminated before they are experienced firsthand.

The *to be* process flow diagram also can be shown to the team's customers or other informed parties to determine if they can identify any potential problems. They may be able to see ways the proposed change could adversely affect them. By recognizing the potential problem in advance, a solution to the problem may be identified and implemented allowing the change to take place without consequence to the customer.

UPDATING PROCESS FLOW DIAGRAMS

In order for the process flow diagrams to continue to be helpful, they must be updated as process changes are made. The benefits described earlier can be achieved only if the diagrams are updated with every process change. This type of updating ensures the diagrams are always accurate representations of the actual process. Store your process flow diagrams in your team notebook.

Management Must Encourage Updates

Members of management can help ensure the flow diagrams are up to date by encouraging and reminding employees to modify the diagrams as necessary. In many cases, managers will be aware of the changes to a process. They should immediately encourage the appropriate diagram(s) to be updated.

Schedule Periodic Reviews

Even with the best intentions, some process changes may not be reflected on the diagrams. Periodic process reviews are a good habit to get into. In most cases, annual process reviews are sufficient. New processes or companies in rapid-pace industries may need to schedule reviews more frequently. These reviews not only provide opportunities to identify changes required to the diagrams, but also often result in the identification of additional improvement opportunities. You may find that just by reviewing the diagram to ensure it is up to date you think of an improvement to be made.

SUMMARY

Process flow diagrams are excellent process documentation tools. The diagrams allow everyone involved to view the process in the same way. This chapter describes the different types of process flow diagrams and explains their uses.

A key reason for documenting a process is to allow it to be analyzed for improvement opportunities. Specific process analysis methods are documented in the next chapter.

REVIEW QUESTIONS

Use the questions in Figure 7.6 to review your progress and make sure you are ready to continue on to the next chapter.

☐ Has the team selected a process to document?

☐ Has the process flow diagram been completed?

☐ Do the start and stop points on the process flow diagram correlate to the beginning and ending boundaries documented?

☐ Is there any need for a functional or layout process flow diagram?

☐ Does the diagram accurately reflect how the process is currently being performed?

Figure 7.6. Review questions.

IMPROVE PROCESSES

Process flow diagrams serve as excellent process analysis tools. Many times, a quick review of a process flow diagram reveals simple, immediate improvements that can be made to the process. These types of relatively easy and obvious improvements are the focus of this chapter. Other, more involved and significant improvements will be made in the *take action to improve* portion of the continuous process improvement cycle. The methods discussed in this section are shown in the tree diagram in Figure 8.1.

WASTE REDUCTION

The first step in improving a process is to eliminate the waste associated with the process. Everyone knows waste must be eliminated, but the question is: How? The following techniques of waste reduction will be discussed in more detail.

- Value-added assessment
- Minimize checks and inspections
- Minimize administrative tasks
- Minimize storage and transportation activities
- Optimize internally required activities

Assess the Value-Added for Each Activity

The starting point for reducing waste is to assess the value each activity adds to the overall process. Every activity, or step of a process, involves a cost to the organization. The aim of assessing the value-added for each activity is to ensure every activity contributes real value to the process.

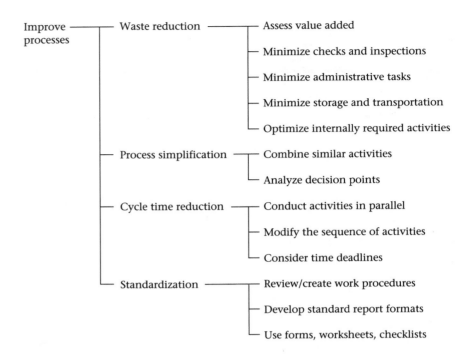

Figure 8.1. Process improvement methods.

Figure 8.2 presents several questions to ask in assessing the value an activity adds.

As the checklist suggests, value must be defined from two points of view: value to the customer and value to the business.

Value to the Customer. First, the customer's point of view should be considered. All the customers care about is receiving a product or service that satisfies their requirements. Activities that must be performed to meet customer requirements are definitely value-added activities.

To help determine if an activity adds value to the customer, ask: "Would any of your customers notice if the activity was not performed?" If the answer is no, the activity is nonvalue-added to the customer. Even if the customers notice, do they really care that the activity was not performed? Would they offer any objections?

Value to the Business. Activities other than those required to produce the product or service for the customer may need to be performed. There are some activities required internally that add no value from the customer's vantage point. Attending meetings, developing plans, writing procedures, and complying with company or

---

1. Does the activity add value to the *customer?*

Yes   **No**

☐ Would any customers notice if the activity was not performed? ☐

☐ Would any customers care if the activity was not performed? ☐

☐ Would any customers object if the activity was not performed? ☐

☐ Do the customers appreciate the results of the activity? ☐

2. Does the activity add value to the *business?*

Yes   **No**

☐ Is the purpose of the activity known and necessary? ☐

☐ Would anyone in the business notice if the activity was not performed? ☐

☐ Would anyone in the business care if the activity was not performed? ☐

☐ Would anyone in the business object if the activity was not performed? ☐

Figure 8.2. Value-added assessment checklist.

regulatory guidelines are all examples of activities that may add value to the organization. Each of these activities should also be examined to determine if they add value to the business.

The first question to consider in determining if an activity adds value to the business is: "Is the purpose of the activity known?" Many of the tasks are performed just because "we've always done it that way." What is the purpose? Is the activity really necessary? Next, ask the questions raised in the figure to verify value to the customer. "Would anyone in the business notice/care/object if the activity was not performed?" This analysis may result in the identification of some nonvalue-added activities.

Nonvalue-Added Activities.   Unfortunately, in many processes there are activities that add no value at all. For example, inspections, administrative tasks, and storage and transportation activities add no value to a process.

Value-added assessment is an analysis of every activity in the process to determine its contribution to meeting end-customer expectations. The object of the assessment is to optimize the activities that add value to the customer or business and minimize or eliminate nonvalue-added activities. The organization should ensure every activity within the process contributes value to the process. Does this activity add value to the customer or the business?

One way to test whether an activity adds value to the process is to ask: "Would I want to increase the number of times I perform the activity, if possible?" If the answer is no, then the activity does not add value (because if it did, you would want to increase the number of times the activity is performed to add even more value to the process). Checks and inspections are good examples. Some people may think checks and inspections are value-adding activities. Would you want to increase the number of checks and inspections in a process? If one inspection activity is good, is 50 better? Anyone would obviously want to minimize the number of checks and inspections in a process because, although they may be necessary, they add no value to the process.

Minimize Checks and Inspections

Checks and inspections may be necessary in a process. As has already been pointed out, however, they add no value to the process. Each inspection point should be identified and challenged.

Identify All Checks and Inspections.   Checks and inspections are often documented on process flow diagrams as decisions (such as, did the report pass the check?). Review the process flow diagram to identify all of the checks and inspections performed as part of the process.

Challenge the Checks and Inspections.   After all the checks and inspections have been identified, they should be challenged to determine if they are necessary. Figure 8.3 lists some questions to use in this challenge.

First, decide if the inspection could be eliminated. If you decide the inspection is necessary, see if you could delay the inspection to a point

---

1. What if the inspection was *deleted?*
  - *Would the inspection be missed?*
  - *What is the potential impact of eliminating the inspection?*
  - *What potential consequences exist if the inspection is eliminated?*
  - *What is the likelihood that the inspection would have revealed a problem?*

2. What if the inspection was *delayed?*
  - *What is the potential impact of delaying the inspection?*
  - *What potential consequences exist if the inspection is delayed?*
  - *What is the likelihood that the inspection, in its previous point in time, would have revealed a problem that should have been addressed prior to the new inspection point?*

Figure 8.3. Inspection challenge questions.

later in the process. You may be able to combine inspection activities by sliding one of the inspections to a point later in the process.

Minimize Administrative Tasks

In some organizations, administrative tasks have taken on a life of their own. They can strangle the ability of the organization to respond and focus on the needs of its customers. Administrative tasks often result in delays in process time due to excessive paperwork, levels of reviews, and multiple signatures (mostly by people who, it seems, are never available when needed).

Identify All Administrative Tasks.   Review your process flow diagram to identify any administrative tasks. If these activities are not necessary, eliminate them, but be careful. Sometimes an activity may not have an obvious purpose, but is valuable to some other process in the organization or required by some sort of regulation. Do not be too quick in your judgment; make sure you know the original purpose of the activity before eliminating it.

Administrative tasks can be identified by looking for the following types of activities documented on the process flow diagram.

- Reviews
- Approvals
- Signatures
- Preparing written documentation
- Making copies
- Filing copies
- Distributing copies

Assess the Value of the Administrative Tasks.   Some administrative reviews are created in response to a one-time problem or event. In order to fix the problem so it never happens again, someone in management may have established a new policy, such as: "From now on, I will sign all travel reimbursement forms." Now is the time to analyze the need for reviews like this one.

The value of each of the administrative activities should be assessed. Consider answering questions such as those listed in Figure 8.4 to assess the need of each administrative task.

Use these questions to challenge the administrative tasks you have identified. You may find that there is little or no value added by some of the signature and review steps. If no new information is ever requested or no new problems are ever identified, why is the signature or review needed? It may have served a purpose at some point, but what about now? Are they necessary? Are file copies ever referenced? You may be able to identify copies that are currently made that can be eliminated.

☐ **Is new information requested by the person providing the second (or subsequent) signature?**
– How often?

☐ **Are new problems found by the person providing the second (or subsequent) signature?**
– How often?

☐ **Are items rejected as a result of each review?**
– How many?

☐ **Do all of the copies serve a specific, necessary purpose?**
– What?

☐ **Are file copies used?**
– For what purpose?
– How often?

☐ **Does everyone currently receiving a copy need a copy?**
– For what purpose?
– Could copies be shared?

☐ **Is the current report generation and distribution frequency necessary?**
– For what purpose?

Figure 8.4. Administrative task assessment checklist.

Minimize Storage and Transportation Activities

Sometimes, storage and transportation activities are necessary evils, but because they are both nonvalue-adding, they should be minimized. The purpose of just-in-time inventory systems is to minimize the amount of inventory stored.

Think of the impact of having a warehouse full of new cellular phones you have just produced, when a technical problem is discovered or a new regulatory requirement mandates a design modification. Every one of the phones must be reworked or thrown away. On the other hand, imagine a process with minimal storage requirements. Technical problems or regulatory changes will not require significant rework to completed products.

A true story may also help highlight the need to minimize storage. I am on the mailing list for several organizations. After a job change, I called to notify them of my new address. I was politely informed by one of the organizations that I would begin receiving their mailings at my new address in several weeks. They had already prepared, printed, and labeled (with my old address) their next two months of mailings! They were stacked in a warehouse waiting for distribution. Not only did I miss out on some of the mailings, but the organization lost sales opportunities that could have resulted from my receipt of the mailings.

Transportation activities are also nonvalue-adding. Analysis of layout process flow diagrams often reveals excess transportation activities. What can be done to reduce the number of transportation activities? Often, the relocation of a single activity can significantly reduce the transportation requirements.

Optimize Internally Required Activities

Some activities are required by internal, customer, or regulatory requirements. This reality does not mean they should not be challenged. Why do the requirements exist? Whose requirements are they? Would they listen to reasons why the requirement is not needed?

PROCESS SIMPLIFICATION

Simplification means reducing the complexity of a process. Simplification can lead to fewer activities and fewer things to go wrong. The simpler a process is, the easier it is to learn and perform consistently (more on standardization later). The steps to perform in simplifying processes are listed in Figure 8.5.

---

1. Combine similar activities
- *Is this activity similar to any others?*
- *What would happen if the similar activities were combined?*
- *What impact would the changes have on the process?*
- *Would this change affect anyone else? How?*

2. Analyze decision points
- *What is the real purpose for the decision?*
- *Does the question really need to be asked?*
- *Are the "yes" and "no" actions taken significantly different? Do they need to be?*
- *Does the decision need to be made at the point where it is currently documented?*
- *What if the question was not asked?*
- *Could the process be redesigned to eliminate the need for the question?*

Figure 8.5. Process simplification steps/checklist.

Combine Similar Activities

The first step to take in simplifying a process is to analyze its process flow diagram for similar activities. Analysis of the diagram may reveal similar process activities performed in different parts of the process. Look at each of the activities documented to identify ones that could be performed together.

For example, frequently the same or very similar information is generated at different parts of a process. The information may even be generated by different organizations. Not only does this add to the overall cost of the process, it provides the possibility of generating conflicting data. No organization can afford duplicate data sources to check on each other. What if the two sources do not agree? Which one is right? If one source is relied upon more than the other, why not eliminate the second?

In some cases, these similar activities can be combined. Make sure the combination would not adversely affect the process, but at the same time, challenge each activity.

Make sure the combinations decided upon actually are made in the way the process is performed. The purpose of this step is to change the process, not to eliminate detail from the process flow diagram by combining activities. This combination should result in fewer activities, a more streamlined method, and a simpler process.

Analyze Decision Points

Many decision points (diamonds) complicate a process flow diagram. Anyone looking at a process flow diagram would agree that a process with many decision points looks more complicated than one with a few decision points. These processes not only look more complicated, they are more complicated to perform.

A process can be simplified by analyzing each of the decisions documented on the process flow diagram. The need for the decision should be carefully evaluated. One way to evaluate the need for the decision is to compare the actions taken for the "yes" branch of the process with the "no" branch. Are the actions taken significantly different? Do they need to be? Many process steps, including decisions, are part of the process because "that's the way we've always done it."

This is not to say all decision points should be eliminated from a process. The process flow diagram must accurately reflect the process steps performed. The point is to analyze the decisions to determine if they are really needed, or to redesign the process so the decisions are no longer needed. A process that does not require the person performing the process to make decisions is a simpler process to perform, and one that relies less on the expertise of the person performing the process.

One team I worked with spent several hours each week sorting cards identifying inspection results by type. (Sorting functions often are shown as diamonds on process flow diagrams since decisions are made to perform the sort.) Analysis of their process flow diagram revealed that, regardless of the type, all cards were treated the same. In other words, the sort was not needed. This team was able to simplify its process by eliminating the sort. This example may seem simple, like the team should have realized how unnecessary the sort was. They probably should have, but they were simply performing the process the way they had been told it was to be performed. Do your processes contain any unnecessary sorts?

CYCLE TIME REDUCTION

Cycle time is the time (in minutes, hours, days, weeks) required to deliver a product or service to a customer. Cycle time includes delays, processing time, time required to check and redo tasks, and so on. Long cycle times not only prevent prompt product deliveries to your customers, but also increase costs. Some techniques for reducing cycle time are shown in Figure 8.6.

Analyze Queues

Do you want to get an idea of how much your cycle times could potentially be reduced? Perform this simple test. Physically walk through the process being performed by accompanying the work product (such as a part or report) through every step of the process. At each step, ask the person performing the task to put aside whatever they are doing and process the product you are accompanying. The person should not do anything else differently from what they otherwise would do. Follow the product providing these instructions to everyone involved in the process. Keep track of the actual time required to perform the process from start to finish. Compare this time with the time it regularly takes to complete the process. The difference represents the potential opportunity for cycle time reduction just by eliminating the time the product waits to be processed. What could be done to eliminate or reduce these queue times?

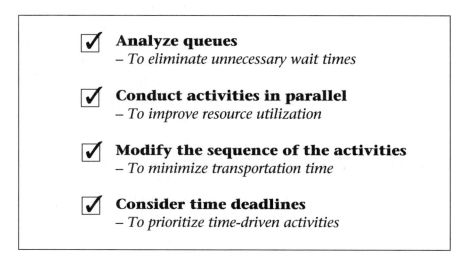

Figure 8.6. Cycle time reduction methods.

Activities performed in serial

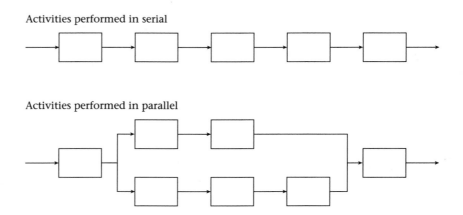

Activities performed in parallel

Figure 8.7. Serial vs. parallel process activities.

Conduct Activities in Parallel

In many cases, activities that are performed serially (sequentially) can be performed in parallel (at the same time). (See Figure 8.7.) This technique results in reduced cycle time by better utilizing resources. Identify activities with delays. Is there anything that could be done during the delay? Identify automated activities that require little attention once started. What could be done while the automated activity is being performed?

Modify the Sequence of Activities

Some organizations are surprised to find out some of their outputs move from one location to another, only to return to the original location for additional processing. Much of this movement may be unnecessary. The layout process flow diagrams introduced earlier serve as an excellent tool for documenting the geographic flow of process outputs. In many cases, organizations are not aware of the enormous journeys their products take in their production process. Examination of the activity sequence often results in recommendations for changes that can reduce cycle time. By performing all activities that must be performed in a certain location while the product is there, the transportation time can be significantly reduced. Getting all of the required signatures on a document before it is forwarded to another location is a familiar example of how cycle time can be reduced by modifying the activity sequence.

Consider Time Deadlines

Some activities are especially time-driven. Mail pickup and delivery is a good example. If you know your outgoing mail is picked up between 11:00 and 11:45 each morning, you try to have everything that needs to be mailed out complete and in the out basket by 11:00. A letter that is completed five minutes after the mail goes out will wait 24 hours (adding 24 hours to the cycle time, even though you are through processing it now). Look at your process flow diagrams to identify your time-driven activities. How can you prioritize your work, maybe even change the sequence of the activities, to ensure your time deadlines are met?

STANDARDIZATION

After process improvements have been made based upon the previous methods, means to standardize the process should be pursued. When each person is performing the process differently, it is difficult, if not impossible, to make major improvements in the process. Standardization is aided by documentation showing how the process is to be performed. This documentation may be in the form of work procedures, report formats, forms, or worksheets.

Review/Create Work Procedures

Work procedures provide a means to ensure all current and future employees use the best methods to perform process activities. Because the procedures document how a process is to be performed, it must be based on careful analysis to make sure the best method is documented. The procedures must be written simply to make sure everyone can understand them and that they cannot be misunderstood. Procedures should

- Describe accepted methods
- Identify responsibilities
- Establish limits of authority

Make sure all affected employees have access to the procedures. They serve no purpose locked in someone's desk or office.

Consider including process flow diagrams as part of your procedures. As previously discussed, the diagrams are an excellent way to document the steps and responsibilities of a process.

Develop Standard Report Formats

Meet with the customers who receive your reports to find out what sections of the report they use and how they use them. Use this information to develop a set of standard report formats. Customers will become familiar with the report format and will be able to reduce the time required to read the reports or look for specific information in a report. This familiarity will also lead to fewer errors in interpretation of the information contained in the reports.

Use Forms, Worksheets, and Checklists

Develop forms, worksheets, and checklists whenever possible to help standardize activities. Forms and worksheets help to remind everyone of the important information required in a data gathering process. Checklists are great for reminding someone of the steps involved in performing a task. They also can serve later as a verification that all the necessary steps were performed, when, and by whom.

Be careful not to allow the use of forms, worksheets, and checklists to become bureaucratic. If you are not careful, your standardization efforts can end up being nonvalue-adding activities. In other words, make sure your efforts to standardize processes are performed for a specific purpose. Review your activities periodically to ensure they are having the desired effect.

SUMMARY

Some individuals may be satisfied with the process improvements made so far. This is just the beginning. Remember that this step, improve processes, is part of the *understand processes* step of the continuous process improvement cycle. Most significant and lasting changes are made in the *taking action to improve* portion of the cycle. Before we can get to that portion of the cycle, we need to visit the *measure performance* portion. How will you know your processes are improving without a means to measure process performance? Measuring process performance is the next step in the cycle.

REVIEW QUESTIONS

Use the questions in Figure 8.8 to review your progress and make sure you are ready to continue on to the next chapter.

☐ What improvements has the team identified?

☐ What improvements has the team implemented?

☐ How has waste been reduced in processes?

☐ What actions have been taken to simplify processes?

☐ How has process cycle time been reduced?

☐ How have processes been standardized?

Figure 8.8. Review questions.

DEVELOP PROCESS MEASURES

After a team truly understands its processes, the next step in the continuous process improvement cycle is to measure the performance of its processes. Before getting into the techniques of developing process measurements, we need to cover the focus of measurements, why process measurements are important, and the effects of process variation.

MEASURE PROCESSES, NOT PEOPLE

The focus of this chapter is measuring work processes, not people. Are the processes able to satisfy customer requirements? Are the processes improving?

Throughout this book, emphasis is placed on the need for accurate information from the measurements. In order to get this accurate information, it must be stressed that the measurements are designed to reflect process performance. If people think they are being measured (rather than the process), they may be tempted to report only the positive data. You don't want this filtered version of performance, accurate information is needed to manage the processes! You need to know when things are not going as you would like, so you know when something needs to be changed. This point is critical. Everyone must be convinced the data being collected, analyzed, and eventually acted upon are measuring process performance.

This point has significant meaning for management. Management must never use process performance data to judge the performance of an individual (positive or negative). The first time this evaluation is done, no matter how many times you say the emphasis is on measuring process performance, the employees will think you really are using the data to judge them. From this point on, management can expect to receive filtered data.

WHY MEASURE?

Process measurements serve as a means to listen to a process. When appropriately analyzed and interpreted, the measurements provide accurate, meaningful, and timely process performance feedback. The measurements can tell you a lot about the process. Process measurements are useful for many purposes including those listed in Figure 9.1.

Each of these purposes will be discussed.

Understand What Is Happening

How can you really understand what is happening to a process without having a way to accurately monitor its performance? Monitoring the performance of a process is accomplished through the use of process performance measurements. Whoever is managing the process needs to know whether the process is improving, staying the same, or getting worse.

Provide Objective Performance Feedback

It is not enough to *think* you know what is happening, you must *know* what is happening to your processes! This assurance comes only from reliable process measurements, even if you have been performing the

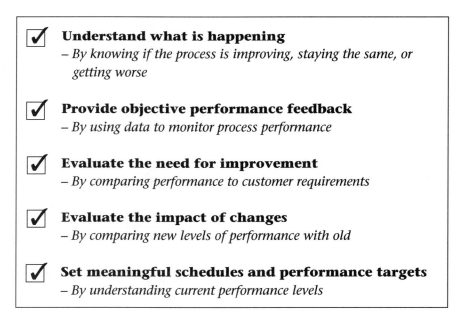

☑ **Understand what is happening**
  – *By knowing if the process is improving, staying the same, or getting worse*

☑ **Provide objective performance feedback**
  – *By using data to monitor process performance*

☑ **Evaluate the need for improvement**
  – *By comparing performance to customer requirements*

☑ **Evaluate the impact of changes**
  – *By comparing new levels of performance with old*

☑ **Set meaningful schedules and performance targets**
  – *By understanding current performance levels*

Figure 9.1. Process measurement purposes.

process for many years. Being responsible for performing a process day-in and day-out places you almost too close to objectively monitor performance. It is easy to feel like the process is performing as required, but feelings are not enough. Meaningful process performance measurements report just the facts.

Evaluate the Need for Improvement

How can you know whether a process needs to be improved? In general, there are two drivers for improvement: customer satisfaction and continuous improvement. A process not satisfying customer requirements and expectations obviously needs improvement. The problem with relying on this approach is it is often too late once you find out the customer requirement has not been satisfied. Process performance measurements provide a means of looking upstream to measure critical performance points in the process. Reliable data from these points help evaluate the need for improvement.

The concept of continuous improvement implies that all processes can be improved. Process performance measurements reveal whether a process is improving or not. This data can then be used to evaluate the need for improvement.

Evaluate the Impact of Changes

Have your process improvements had the desired effects? The only way to know for sure is to have process data describing the performance of the process before and after implementation of the process improvement. So, don't wait until you have improved a process to begin measuring it—you will need this baseline data to compare against. Do the data reflect the change expected from the improvement? (Be sure to read on—improvement trends need to be statistically analyzed to ensure a significant change has occurred.)

Set Meaningful Schedules and Performance Targets

Reliable process performance data are required to set meaningful schedules and performance targets. Schedules and targets established without an understanding of what the process can perform are useless (or worse yet, harmful). Management can encourage, exhort, demand, threaten, and punish all it wants to get employees to perform to this month's quota without lasting success. The process must be understood before meaningful schedule and performance targets can be established. This understanding comes from proper analysis of the process. Methods for analyzing process performance data are discussed later.

Have you ever had an impossible schedule thrust upon you? (Most of us have, I think, at one time or another.) How did you feel? Unrealistic schedules and performance targets have a negative and even demoralizing effect. These problems can be avoided by using information from process measurements to set meaningful schedules and performance targets.

UNDERSTAND PROCESS VARIATION

Process variation must be understood to accurately interpret process performance data. Misunderstanding process variation can result in improper conclusions drawn from data analysis.

What Is Process Variation?

The best way to describe process variation is through some examples. Consider the following:

- Do you arrive at work the same time each day?
- Do all two-liter bottles of a soft drink contain exactly two liters?
- Do all Quarter-pounders™ weigh $\frac{1}{4}$ of a pound (before cooking)?
- Does the steam press always operate at the same temperature?
- Does the 10:30 train always arrive at the same time?
- Is your mail delivered to your home or office at the same time each day?

PROCESS VARIATION

Fluctuations in the level of process performance. Exists in all processes. Undesirable because it causes uncertainty.

The answer to all of these questions is no. These examples demonstrate that variation exists in the processes represented by these questions. In fact, all processes demonstrate variation.

Since we are all customers of the U.S. Post Office (at home and work), it provides an example to which we can all relate. This universal example will be used throughout this chapter to discuss the effects of variation on any process.

One day the mail may be delivered at 10:45 A.M. and the next it may not come until 2:30 P.M. The mail delivery process obviously exhibits some variation. The table on page 113 shows the time mail was received at our office over an eight-week period.

Figure 9.2 shows how the mail delivery time data are distributed. (The figure is an example of a histogram. Histograms and other data collection and analysis tools are covered in chapter 10.)

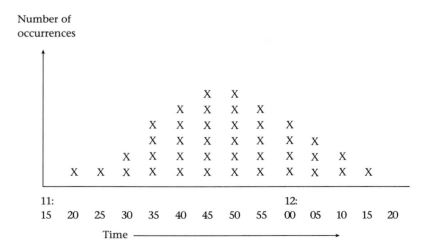

Figure 9.2.   Mail receipt distribution.

Day of the week	Mail delivery time	Day of the week	Mail delivery time
Monday	12:00	Monday	12:05
Tuesday	11:40	Tuesday	11:45
Wednesday	11:45	Wednesday	11:50
Thursday	11:35	Thursday	11:45
Friday	11:50	Friday	12:00
Monday	11:55	Monday	12:10
Tuesday	11:55	Tuesday	11:35
Wednesday	11:40	Wednesday	11:35
Thursday	11:50	Thursday	11:40
Friday	11:40	Friday	11:55
Monday	12:15	Monday	12:00
Tuesday	11:30	Tuesday	11:55
Wednesday	11:35	Wednesday	12:05
Thursday	11:20	Thursday	11:45
Friday	11:25	Friday	11:45
Monday	12:00	Monday	12:05
Tuesday	11:45	Tuesday	11:50
Wednesday	11:30	Wednesday	11:40
Thursday	11:50	Thursday	12:10
Friday	11:55	Friday	11:50

Many process performance measurements, when the number of occurrences of some event are counted and charted, look like the shape in the figure with many of the points clustered around the middle. The shape may look familiar; it is commonly called a *bell curve*. The bell curve is a graphical representation of what statisticians call a natural distribution. Most processes can be accurately modeled by a natural distribution.

Process Variation Is Undesirable

Variation causes uncertainty, which means you cannot predict process outcomes. An example may help.

Would you like to know when (within just a few minutes) your mail is going to be delivered and picked up each day? Consider a couple of situations.

Imagine you are at home on a rainy day and expecting an important letter in the mail. Because of the rain, you want to avoid multiple trips to the mailbox, so you wait until 2:00 P.M. thinking that surely the mail has been delivered. Your mad dash results in finding an empty mailbox.

Another day at the office, you are working on an important letter that needs to be mailed today. Much to your surprise, the mail is delivered at 10:45 A.M., but your letter is not even close to being ready. If only the mail had not come until 12:00, like it often does, you would have been ready.

In both of these situations (and probably many more) you certainly would like to know when you can expect the mail to be delivered and picked up. If the mail comes at 10:45 A.M. some days and not until 2:30 P.M. other days it is difficult to plan. This is an example of process variation—too much variation. On the other hand, if you knew the mail was always delivered and picked up between 11:30 and 12:00 you could plan your activities much easier because the process would have much less variation. (Knowing the delivery is always between 11:30 and 11:45 is even better!)

Variation in any process is bad. The more you know what to expect from a process (the smaller the amount of variation), the better you can manage the process.

Variation Causes Loss

With the knowledge that variation is undesirable, a way of looking at the loss associated with variation in your processes is needed. This section introduces and analyzes two different ways this loss can be viewed.

The Traditional View of Loss.   Traditionally, "good" and "bad" products and services have been determined by comparing the product against specification limits or customer requirements. The traditional view of loss treats all points within the customer requirements as good.

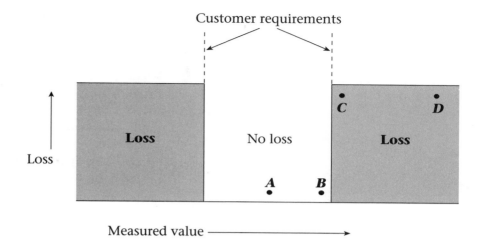

Figure 9.3. The traditional view of loss.

This concept can be shown graphically. Figure 9.3 shows what is called the traditional view of loss.

Several questions could be asked about the points plotted in the figure.

- Is point *B* a good point?
- Is point *C* a bad point?
- Is point *D* worse than point *C*?
- Are points *A* and *B* equally desirable?

In this example, points *A* and *B* are treated the same; they are both good since they fall between the customer requirements. Points *C* and *D*, on the other hand, are both bad because they fall outside the customer requirements. For example, if the customer has said a report is needed between 2:00 P.M. and 4:00 P.M. (these are the customer requirements), anywhere within that range must be acceptable and equally desirable, right? Continuing this thought process, any time before 2:00 P.M. or after 4:00 P.M. must be unacceptable and equally undesirable.

Let's take a further look. What is the difference between point *B* and point *C*? The difference is small, yet point *C* is considered bad. Continuing the report example, should the report received at 4:10 P.M. be rejected? If this was a manufacturing example, the part just over the limit would be rejected. What about point *D*? It is obviously bad, no one wants to receive something one hour late. Is point *D* worse than point *C*?

This subject has been discussed as a view of loss. This title is used because the traditional view assumes no loss is experienced within the range of customer requirements meaning that all of the points within the limits are equally desirable. However, any point outside of the limits immediately incurs loss. In fact, all points outside the specification limits are assumed to incur the same amount of loss.

This view is sometimes called *goal post* thinking. It is so described because of the analogy to kicking a field goal in football. The team kicking the ball is awarded three points if the ball passes anywhere between the goal posts. The ball may pass just one inch inside the left goal post and still be worth three points. But, if the ball is just one inch outside the left goal post, the kick is no good—zero points.

The traditional view of loss generates many questions.

- Is a point just inside the customer requirements good?
- Is a point just outside the customer requirements really bad?
- Is a point significantly outside of the customer requirements worse than one just barely outside the range?
- Are all points within the customer requirements equally good or desirable?

These questions can be answered with discussion of the realistic view of loss that follows.

The Realistic View of Loss.   The realistic view of loss shows that loss results from any deviation from the desired level. The realistic view of loss graphically shows, in Figure 9.4, what we have already discovered, process variation is bad—it causes loss.

Point *C* is what the customer really wants from this process. At point *C* there is no loss, but as the points vary from this ideal point, loss is incurred (shown by the curve). The farther from the desired level, the more loss. Point *B*, while within the range of customer requirements, has loss associated with it. There is little difference between points *D* and *E,* they both have about the same amount of loss, but point *D* is good and *E* is bad according to traditional thinking.

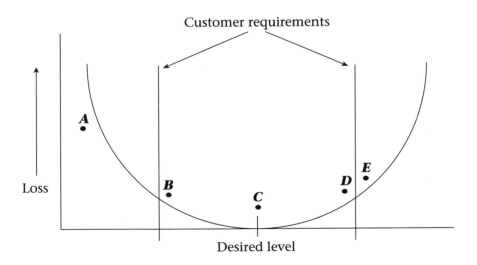

Figure 9.4. The realistic view of loss.

Causes of Variation

Now that we know variation exists, and that it is bad, what can be done about it? The first step is to understand the causes of the variation.

There are two causes of variation: common and special causes. Common and special causes are very different and must be handled differently. Each of the causes will be discussed.

COMMON CAUSES OF VARIATION

The many sources of variation that produce chance or normal variation. The small differences that always exist in a process. Also called nonassignable causes.

Common Causes.   Common causes (also called nonassignable causes) of variation are built into the process, they are a normal part of the way the process functions. Common variation is the result of all the small differences that always exist in a process. These differences cause the data collected to vary in a normal manner. The random variation that we have already seen exists in all processes is the result of common causes.

Common causes cannot be tied directly to a specific problem, they are more general. Common causes of variation are part of the process.

SPECIAL CAUSE OF VARIATION

A large or unusual difference in the process caused by some unnatural, unique, or out-of-the-ordinary event. Causes the data collected to vary in an abnormal manner. Also called assignable causes.

Special Causes.   Occasionally, however, there is a large or unusual difference. This type of difference may be more important than all the normal differences described earlier. These differences cause the data collected to vary in an abnormal manner.

Variation created by special (or assignable) causes are not part of the process. These variations are caused by some unnatural, unique, out-of-the-ordinary event.

Examples of special causes include

- New or untrained employees
- Supplies received from a new vendor
- Extreme weather conditions (very hot, cold, or humid)
- Installation of a new version of a software package
- Contaminated chemicals
- Change in procedures

Let's return to the mail delivery example. What could cause the variation in the mail delivery and pickup process? Are these causes common or special causes? By their very nature, special causes are identifiable while common causes are much more difficult to pinpoint since they are built into the process. What would happen if, even after all of these causes had been identified and eliminated, unacceptable variation still existed? The process must be changed.

If the performance of a process is not acceptable, and only common causes exist, the process must be changed to get different results. This type of change is almost always the responsibility of management. Management has created the systems the process operates within. This means management should not hold the workers responsible for such problems. The system is management's responsibility. If management is not satisfied with the amount of common variation in a system, it must act to remove it.

Because special causes are due to an unusual event, the source of special causes frequently can be detected and removed by the people directly involved with the process. This does not mean, however, that management has no role in dealing with special causes. Management's role is to set policy to ensure the causes will not happen again (assuming the effect is undesirable). It is possible for a special cause to improve the performance of a process. In these cases, management should establish policy to repeat the action.

Common and Special Causes Must Be Treated Differently.   Dealing with each type of cause requires entirely different approaches. Reacting to common-cause variation as if it were due to special causes will only make matters worse and increase variation. So, you will need a method of determining whether the cause is part of the system (common) or something unique or different (special). Control charts provide this information. Techniques for preparing and analyzing control charts are described in chapter 11. First, we need to take a step back to develop the measurements that will require this analysis.

DEVELOP MEASURES

What good are data collection and analysis if it is not clear what is being measured? The mistake of many quality improvement efforts is that the company starts with data collection and analysis. What characteristic are they going to measure? What process is the characteristic part of? What processes do they perform? Who are their customers? This approach creates more questions than answers.

All of the activities described so far have been building up to this step—developing process performance measures. Process performance measures provide the information required to monitor the performance of a process. How is the process performing? Is its performance predictable? Does it satisfy customer requirements?

Types of Process Performance Measurements

There are two primary classes of process performance measurements: effectiveness and efficiency measurements. For reasons that will be explained, it is important to achieve the proper balance between effectiveness and efficiency measurements. You will need information from both types of measurements to manage your processes.

EFFECTIVENESS
The ability of a process to satisfy customer requirements and expectations.

Effectiveness.   Effectiveness measurements are used to monitor the performance of a process from the customer's point of view. They measure process characteristics important to the customer (such as, accuracy, timeliness, and dependability).

Examples of effectiveness measurements include

- Typos or spelling errors per page
- Errors reported/statement mailed
- Prescriptions filled per day
- Patient compliments received per month
- Engineering change orders/drawings produced
- Invoicing errors/invoices produced
- Percent of calls put on hold before talking to a service representative
- Trouble calls received per day
- Maintenance calls received per day
- Correctly addressed envelopes prepared per day
- Deliveries made before 10:30 A.M.
- Percent of statements mailed before the 30th
- Customer inquiry response time
- Bid or proposal preparation time

EFFICIENCY

The ability of a process to produce its product with minimal resources. Used primarily to monitor internal operations.

Efficiency.   Efficiency measurements are used primarily to monitor internal operations. It is not enough to measure only the effectiveness of a process. Without regard to resource utilization, you could be driven out of business with very effective processes. It is important to monitor the resources required to produce the products and services that satisfy customer requirements and expectations. Efficiency measurements provide information on the resource utilization and cost of producing your products and services.

Examples of efficiency measurements include

- Hours spent to prepare a bid
- Hours required to produce the engineering design
- Hours to prepare customer statements per statement mailed
- Time required to prepare proper paint mix
- Cost to maintain office equipment per month

Identify Critical Process Performance Characteristics

The key step in developing meaningful process performance measurements is the identification of critical process performance characteristics. For example, it may be simple to gather accurate outside temperature data every hour on the hour. However, what good is this data if you are interested in analyzing your shelf-stocking or statement preparation process?

This example may seem ridiculous, but think back over your business career. Can you think of data you (or someone you know) collected that had little or no relevance to what you were trying to do? Data are sometimes collected just because collection is easy.

Don't Let Measurement Activity Become Nonvalue-Added.   The activity of selecting measurements, collecting data, and analyzing the resulting information can become a nonvalue-added task if the data are not used.

Data collected on irrelevant process characteristics can not only be wasted time, but can take time away from what otherwise might have been meaningful data analysis. Members of a chemical processing department once proudly showed me all of the data they were collecting (some of which were mandated by a multitude of governing regulations). The pure volume of data was impressive. When I asked what they did with the data, the answer was surprising. They had no time to perform any kind of data analysis (even if they had known how). They spent all of their available time collecting the data. Together, we were able to select the process characteristics that were meaningful to their processes and significantly reduce the amount of time spent collecting data. The remaining time was converted to properly analyzing the data and implementing process improvements.

The identification of critical process characteristics to measure is best accomplished by involving everyone associated with the process being analyzed. Figure 9.5 suggests two methods for identifying critical process performance characteristics to measure. The ideas are provided to help your team think of as many measurements as possible. List all of the ideas suggested. You can review the completed list later to select the actual measurements you will analyze.

Think from the Customers' Point of View.   One of the primary benefits of having meaningful process performance measurements is the

---

1. Think from the customers' point of view
- *Who are the customers of this process?*
- *What characteristics of the process are important to the customers?*
- *How could I know if the process is satisfying the requirements and expectations my customers have for the outputs of the process?*
- *How could I know if the process is improving?*

2. Review process flow diagrams
- *What do I need to know about the process at this point?*
- *If I measured the process here, what information would I gain?*
- *What information do I need here to avoid a problem later?*
- *If I knew this information, would I do anything differently?*
- *How could I use this information?*

Figure 9.5. Critical process performance characteristics identification methods.

ability to identify problems before they occur—before the customer even knows about them. In order to accomplish this aim, the process must be analyzed from the customers' point of view.

Ask the questions from the top part of Figure 9.5 for the process being analyzed. These questions may spark some ideas of what could be measured about the process. You already know what characteristics are important to your customers from conducting the customer requirements analysis earlier. This is important information. What could you measure in your process to ensure the customers' critical process characteristics are satisfied? Record all of the ideas suggested.

Review Process Flow Diagrams.   Process flow diagrams are excellent process analysis tools. They also are helpful in identifying important process characteristics to measure. Review each activity (rectangle) or decision (diamond) recorded on the flow diagram. At each point documented for the process, ask the questions from the bottom part of Figure 9.5.

These questions probably will help you decide if there are any possible measurements to take at this point. Suggest anything you can think of, you can select the specific measurements you will use later. Review every task documented on the process flow diagram. This may sound time-consuming, but, with just a little practice, you will be able to ask these questions very quickly and identify several possible measurements. Avoid the temptation to skip around the flow diagram. Quickly and systematically, look at each activity and decision.

Review and Combine Lists.   Now, review the list of all possible measurements to select the ones that reveal the information needed to manage the process. Some ideas may duplicate or be similar to another. In these cases, try to identify a way to combine the ideas. Reducing the list may be difficult, but it is worth your time to carefully consider each measurement possibility. What information do you need to manage the process, know how the process is performing, and know where improvements are needed?

It may seem like the more measurements, the better, but consider a practical point: Measurement data collection and analysis takes time. Make your selections based on the cost and benefits associated with each measurement.

DOCUMENT MEASUREMENT DECISIONS

The final step in developing measurements is to document the measurement decisions made. This step is crucial. A significant amount of time has been spent to this point developing the measurements, complete the process by recording all of the necessary information. Document your decisions to make sure everyone understands what has been agreed upon. For each measurement, record the following information:

- The measurement itself
- The source of the data
- The person responsible for collecting the data
- The frequency the data are to be collected

The Measurement Decision Documentation Worksheet. This information provides clarity to the team by documenting exactly what is being measured and by whom. The measurement decision documentation worksheet is provided as a means of recording this information. (See page 123.) It is formatted so information for five measurements can be recorded for a single process. Based on experience, this quantity is sufficient for most processes. If you decide you want to measure more than five characteristics for a process, just use another worksheet.

SUMMARY

Meaningful process measurements provide the performance information necessary to properly manage a process. This chapter presents the need for process measurements, the evils of process variation, the types of process performance measurements, and a means of identifying and selecting the critical process performance characteristics to measure. After the characteristics to measure have been selected, the next step is to collect and analyze the data called for by the measurements.

REVIEW QUESTIONS

Use the questions in Figure 9.6 to review your progress and make sure you are ready to continue on to the next chapter.

☐ How were the process characteristics selected for measurement?

☐ Has the team selected characteristics critical to the performance of the process?

☐ Has the team selected enough measurements to adequately monitor the performance of the process?

☐ Has the team used a good balance of effectiveness and efficiency measures?

☐ Have the team's measurement decisions been documented?

Figure 9.6. Review questions.

Measurement Decision Documentation Worksheet

Date: _____

Process name: _____

1.
Process measurement: _____

Source of data: _____

Person responsible for data: _____

Frequency of data collection: _____

2.
Process measurement: _____

Source of data: _____

Person responsible for data: _____

Frequency of data collection: _____

3.
Process measurement: _____

Source of data: _____

Person responsible for data: _____

Frequency of data collection: _____

4.
Process measurement: _____

Source of data: _____

Person responsible for data: _____

Frequency of data collection: _____

5.
Process measurement: _____

Source of data: _____

Person responsible for data: _____

Frequency of data collection: _____

COLLECT AND ANALYZE DATA

The next step is to collect the data required for the process performance measurements. Collecting process performance data help answer questions such as:

- What is happening?
- How is the process performing?
- Is the process improving?
- Is the process satisfying customer requirements?

This chapter introduces and explains several tools that can be used to collect and begin analyzing the data.

TYPES OF DATA

There are two types of data: attributes and variables. Each type will be discussed.

Attributes Data

Attributes data are counted, not measured. They are collected when all you need to know is yes or no, pass or fail, accept or reject. Examples of attributes data include

ATTRIBUTES DATA
Data collected by counting when all you need to know is yes or no, pass or fail, or accept or reject.

- Did the clerk give the cash register receipt to the customer?
- Is the department staying within their budget?
- Was the report turned in on schedule?
- Did the bank teller ask the customers if they would like to know their current balance?

Variables Data

VARIABLES DATA

Result from measurements. Provide a more detailed history of the process than attributes data. Report on the frequency and severity of the situation.

Variables data provide a more detailed history of the process. Rather than just reporting whether or not an event occurred, variables data also provide information about the frequency or severity of the situation. Examples of variables data include

- Number of errors on a typed page
- Cost to send a package overnight mail
- Number of complaint calls received

Comparing Attributes and Variables Data

The differences between attributes and variables data can be demonstrated through an example. Consider the following questions.

- Did we receive any complaint calls today? (attributes data)
- How many complaint calls did we receive today? (variables data)

Which of these questions would lead to an answer with the most information?

Many process characteristics can be measured using either attributes or variables data. It usually takes longer to collect variables data (because you take measurements rather than just observe), but often the picture provided is much more revealing. You get much more information about the output when you collect variables data.

DATA COLLECTION AND ANALYSIS TOOLS

The remainder of this chapter is devoted to the introduction to and instruction in tools to be used to collect and analyze the data necessary to objectively assess process performance. The tools are summarized in Figure 10.1.

CHECK SHEETS

Understanding how often certain events happen is a common starting point in collecting data. Check sheets provide a simple, organized way to collect data on the frequency certain events occur. (See Figure 10.2.)

Decide What Data Will Be Collected

This point may seem obvious, but the first step in preparing a check sheet is to decide what data you will be collecting. Think about what you are trying to learn by collecting the data. Identify the possible categories that exist (the types of errors found on a report, for example, include: spelling, typos, punctuation.) Be as specific as possible so it is always obvious into which category each event should fit. Use your experience to identify what categories should be used.

Check Sheets

Defect	April					Total
	10	11	12	13	14	
Spelling	Ⅲ̄Ⅱ	Ⅲ̄Ⅱ I	II	IIII	IIII	21
Typos	II		IIII	I		7
Punctuation	I	III	IIII	Ⅲ̄Ⅱ I	Ⅲ̄Ⅱ II	21
Total	8	9	10	11	11	49

Provide a simple, organized way to collect data on the frequency with which certain events occur. Tick marks are used to record the occurrence of individual events. The data is totaled.

Pareto Charts

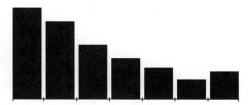

Are a form of a vertical bar graph, sorted to help prioritize problems or problem causes. They focus attention on the vital few versus the trivial many.

Histograms

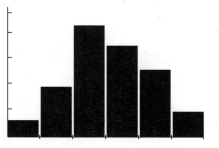

Display the frequency of occurrence of process measurements and reveal the amount of variation within the process.

Scatter Diagrams

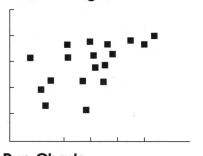

Analyze the possible relationship between two variables. The pattern formed by the points on the diagram reveals whether the relationship is positive, negative, or nonexistent.

Run Charts

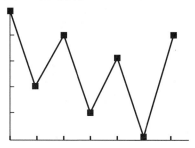

Monitor the performance of a process over time. They allow patterns in the data to be seen.

Figure 10.1. Data collection and analysis tools.

Select the Time Period

The next decision is to select the time period over which the data will be collected. Consider how often the process is performed in selecting the best time period. For a process completed in just minutes, you may want to record the number of occurrences each hour. For processes performed just once a month, on the other hand, you may want to record the data by month. The example in Figure 10.2 lists the occurrences per day.

Create a Data Collection Form

The next step is to create a simple data collection form based on the results of the first two steps. Record the time period across the top of the form and the data to be collected down the left column. Add a total column on the right and across the bottom of the form.

Record the Data

The only thing left to do now is collect and record the data. Be honest in recording the data. Remember, the purpose of collecting data (with a check sheet or any other tool) is to be able to analyze the data to make proper decisions. Proper decisions cannot be made based upon faulty data.

CHECK SHEET

A simple, organized way to collect data using tick marks to report on the frequency of certain events.

Purpose

To collect data on the frequency with which certain events occur.

Defect	April					Total
	10	11	12	13	14	
Spelling	ⅢⅢ	ⅢⅢ I	II	IIII	IIII	21
Typos	II		IIII	I		7
Punctuation	I	III	IIII	ⅢⅢ I	ⅢⅢ II	21
Total	8	9	10	11	11	49

Steps
1. Decide what data will be collected.
2. Select the time period.
3. Create a data collection form.
4. Record the data.

Figure 10.2. Check sheet.

Resist the temptation to only record favorable data or fudge the readings to make things look better. Accurately capture all of the data. This need for complete, accurate data is the reason process performance (rather than personal performance) has been stressed.

To record the data, just make a tick mark for each occurrence. Cross each fifth tick across the previous four. This format, while certainly not the only way to record the data, allows for easy totaling later.

Uses

Check sheets are used to record the number of occurrences of any event. Common applications of check sheets include recording types of errors (such as, spelling, math, pagination), types of phone calls received (orders, complaints, information request, sales calls), and times of phone calls received (8:00–9:00, 9:01–10:00).

Location Check Sheets.   A specialized type of check sheet, called a location check sheet, can be used to help record the physical location of the event being analyzed. The example in Figure 10.3 is a drawing of my front yard, with the locations marked where I found my morning paper delivered over 21 consecutive days. (I collected the data just after having seeded my new lawn. Each morning, I had to walk across my muddy yard to retrieve the paper.)

This example provides a lot of information about where my paper is delivered and even something about the person who delivers my paper. The clump of symbols in the lawn shows the delivery is relatively consistent. Most of the points in the lawn are together, and all of the points are about the same distance from the street. Sometimes, the paper even ended

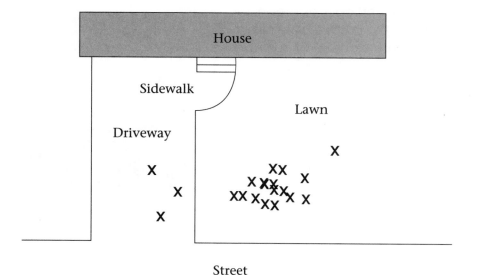

Figure 10.3. Location check sheet.

up on the driveway! (After talking to the man who delivers my paper, I found that he was purposefully doing what he was told to do—put the paper on the lawn. Since our conversation, he consistently places my paper on the drive where I want it.)

Applications for location check sheets include documenting the locations of defects on a part, potholes in a road, and damaged areas on shipping cartons.

Activity

Use the mail delivery data from the previous chapter to complete the check sheet activity that follows on page 131. Take the time to do this now, the resulting data will be used in another activity.

PARETO CHARTS

Pareto charts (named after the Italian economist Vilfredo Pareto) are a form of a vertical bar graph, sorted to help prioritize problems or problem causes. (See Figure 10.4.) Pareto charts focus attention on the *vital few* vs. the *trivial many*. The vital few are the few factors that account for the largest part of the total. The trivial many are the multitude of factors that account for the small remainder.

Collect the Data to Be Analyzed

Data should be collected by categories such as defect types, product types, size, and so forth. A check sheet (described earlier) is a helpful tool for collecting data for the different categories. The categories used on the checklist will be the same ones listed across the bottom of the Pareto chart.

PARETO CHART

A form of vertical bar graph, sorted to help prioritize problems or problem causes. Focuses attention on the vital few vs. the trivial many.

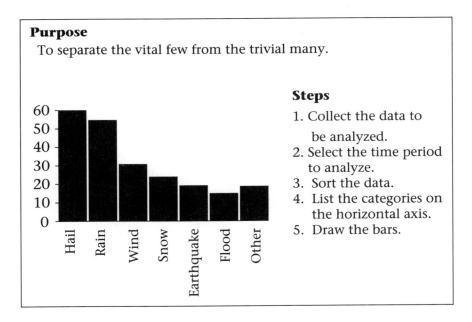

Purpose

To separate the vital few from the trivial many.

Steps

1. Collect the data to be analyzed.
2. Select the time period to analyze.
3. Sort the data.
4. List the categories on the horizontal axis.
5. Draw the bars.

Figure 10.4. Pareto chart.

Check Sheet Activity

Time	Number of occurrences					
	Monday	Tuesday	Wednesday	Thursday	Friday	Total
11:15						
11:20						
11:25						
11:30						
11:35						
11:40						
11:45						
11:50						
11:55						
12:00						
12:05						
12:10						
12:15						
12:20						

Select the Time Period to Analyze

The time period selected varies depending on the situation being analyzed. Make sure the time period selected is convenient for you in collecting the data. If you select a time that is not convenient, the data may not be collected as frequently as necessary. Also, take into account any other diagrams that may be compared against the one being developed. You may want to select the same time periods to make comparisons possible.

Sort the Data

Sort the data recorded on the check sheets. Identify the category that has occurred the most frequently, the next most frequently, and so on, until all categories have been listed.

List the Categories on the Horizontal Axis

List the elements from the most frequent to the least. You may find you have some elements with a small number of occurrences relative to the other elements. Because the purpose of a Pareto chart is to focus attention on the elements that occur frequently, you may want to use an *other* category to group several infrequent elements. If you do use an other category, put it at the end of the list.

Draw the Bars

Draw a rectangle above each category whose height represents the number of times the event occurred.

Uses

Because resources are limited, it is important to concentrate on the most important problems and issues. Pareto charts are good at highlighting the most important problems. They often result in focusing a team's attention on a common problem. The most important problems are represented by the tallest bars on the Pareto chart.

STRATIFICATION

A technique by which the elements of individual categories are further analyzed for additional information. Commonly used with Pareto charts.

Stratified Pareto Chart. In some cases, more information on a specific category shown on a Pareto chart may be needed. Stratification is a technique by which the elements of individual categories are further analyzed for additional information.

In the example in Figure 10.5, two elements are prominent in the first Pareto chart, so more information was requested for each of them. Additional research resulted in the two lower Pareto charts. The 60 observations of the primary element were divided into six additional elements, one of which is obviously the primary element. Focusing on this one element first will result in significant improvement.

For example, let's assume the top Pareto chart in Figure 10.5 depicts the types of errors found on a sales proposal. The tallest bar (with 60 observations) represents the number of typing errors. Further analysis of the situation (the stratified Pareto chart on the lower left) has revealed that of the 60 typing errors, 40 were spelling errors. Implementing a solution to help

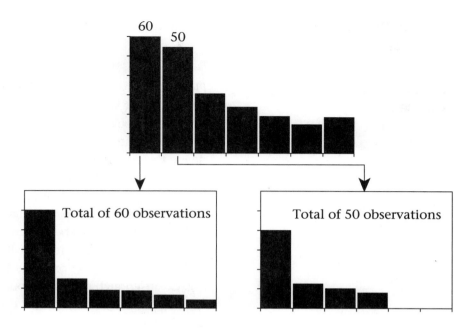

Figure 10.5. Stratified Pareto chart.

reduce or eliminate the spelling errors (installing a spelling checker, hiring a proofreader, and so on) will improve the sales proposals significantly.

HISTOGRAMS

Histograms provide a picture of the distribution of a process by displaying the frequency of occurrence of process measurements and revealing the amount of variation within the process. (See Figure 10.6.)

HISTOGRAM

A bar graph displaying the frequency of occurrence of process measurements and revealing the amount of variation within the process.

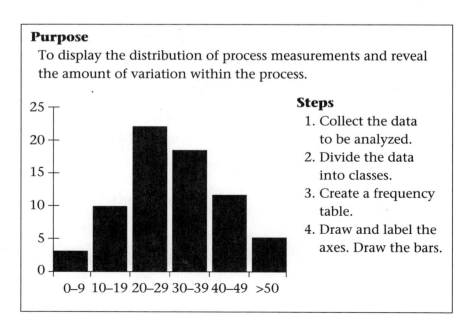

Figure 10.6. Histogram.

Collect the Data to Be Analyzed

Record the data to be analyzed.

Divide the Data Into Classes

Plotting every individual value on the horizontal axis of a histogram would almost surely cause the chart to go off the side of the paper. To avoid this problem, the data on the horizontal axis of a histogram probably will need to be grouped into classes. There is no right or best way to divide the data into classes. A rule of thumb for the number of classes is the square root of the number of data points. (So, if you have collected 50 data points, you may consider using about seven classes.) In most cases, the best guide is your own judgment and experience. Using few classes will result in each class being very broad. Broad classes may end up covering over significant differences within a class. Using too many classes may make your data collection unnecessarily cumbersome and time consuming. Create enough classes for your subsequent analysis to be meaningful.

Make sure the data classes do not overlap. For example, if the first class includes the points 0 to 9, the next class should start at 10.

Create a Frequency Table

The next step is to count the number of occurrences of the event within each class. The easiest way to get this data is to create a frequency table. List the data classes in a column down the left side of a piece of paper. Record a tally mark for each observance beside the correct class. Similar to the check sheets, I recommend you mark each fifth tally across the previous four to make the final counting easier. Once all of the observances have been tallied, calculate and record the count for each class.

Draw and Label the Axes

Record the classes across the bottom of the histogram (the horizontal axis) in ascending order. Prepare the vertical axis by analyzing the data in the frequency table to determine the appropriate scale.

Draw the Bars

Draw a rectangle above each class whose height represents the number recorded in the frequency table.

Uses

Descriptions of several of the uses of histograms follow.

Variation Identification. The primary uses of histograms are to identify the amount of variation within the process and to view the shape of the distribution (Figure 10.7).

Processes demonstrating a small amount of variation are shown on histograms with a few number of relatively tall bars. This means the

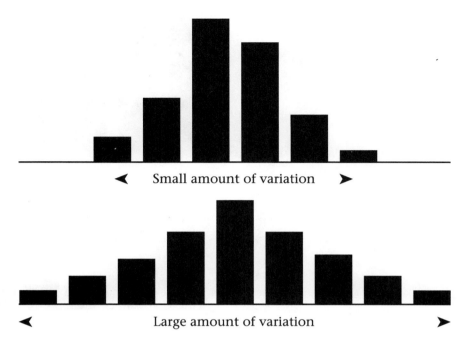

Figure 10.7. Using histograms to view variation.

occurrences of the event being counted cover only a small range—a small amount of variation. Processes with more variation have more, shorter bars. This is caused by the total number of observances being spread over a larger range—more variation.

Degree of Skewness.   Histograms also help identify the degree of skewness of a process. (See Figure 10.8.)

Obviously, not all distributions are symmetrical. The distribution may be skewed to either the right or left (the distribution is said to be skewed toward the side with the tail). This will be important information later when you begin to analyze the performance of the process for customer satisfaction.

Stratified Histogram.   Data on a histogram can be stratified like the Pareto chart example earlier. Histogram data can be stratified to reveal hidden information. It may be helpful to look at the distribution of data for just a piece of the total. Common stratification categories include days of the week, internal departments, and different vendors. This type of analysis can reveal if a certain situation is more common on a specific day of the week, within a specific department, or unique to a specific vendor.

In the example shown in Figure 10.9, the maintenance department is skewed to the left. This situation should be analyzed to determine why its distribution is different from that of the other departments'. If the charac-

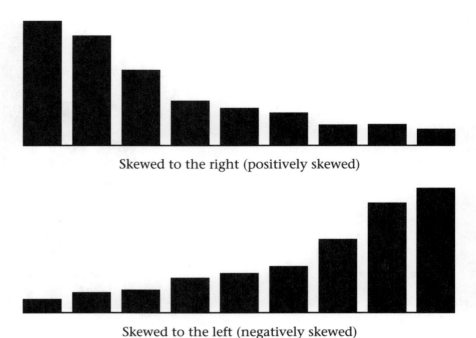

Figure 10.8. Using histograms to view process skewness.

teristic being measured is a *higher is better* measurement, then you would want to find out what the maintenance department is doing right that the other departments could benefit from.

The shape of a histogram can show that a process is not normal—leading you to the conclusion that a special cause is present. It cannot pinpoint the time when the special cause was acting on the process. Tools introduced later provide this type of information.

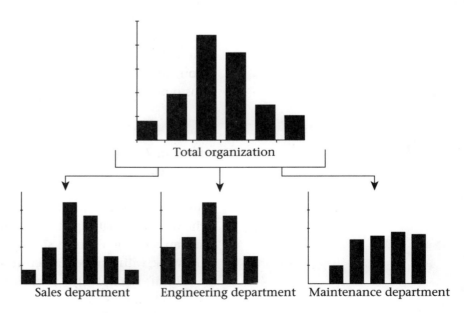

Figure 10.9. Stratified histogram.

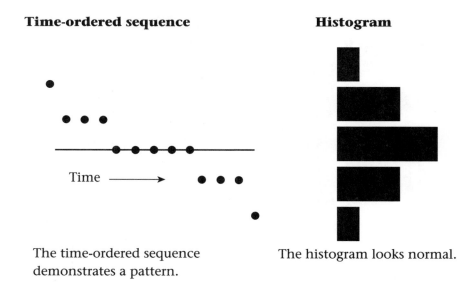

Time-ordered sequence

Time ⟶

The time-ordered sequence
demonstrates a pattern.

Histogram

The histogram looks normal.

Figure 10.10. Histogram caution.

Histogram Caution.   It is possible for the information provided by analyzing a histogram to be misleading. Because histograms do not reflect data taken in time order, a pattern like the one shown in Figure 10.10 may be present but not visible on the histogram.

Analysis of histograms can provide very useful information, but be careful. It is always a good idea to look at the data charted on a histogram in time order sequence also by using a run chart as described later in this chapter. (There will be more about why you should be interested in data patterns later.)

Activity

Refer back to the check sheet for the mail delivery times earlier in this chapter and prepare a histogram with this data. Does the histogram look normal?

Next, stratify the data by days of the week on the activity sheet on page 138 (prepare five smaller histograms). Analyze the stratified histograms. Do these charts reveal any information hidden in the overall histogram?

The data for Monday appear to be centered later than the other days. This shift means the mail is delivered later in the day than the other days of the week. This information is not obvious from the initial, overall histogram. This type of information often is available only after the data have been stratified.

SCATTER DIAGRAMS

Scatter diagrams are used to analyze the possible relationship between two variables. (See Figure 10.11.) They let you test your assumptions about the relationship between two variables.

Histogram Activity

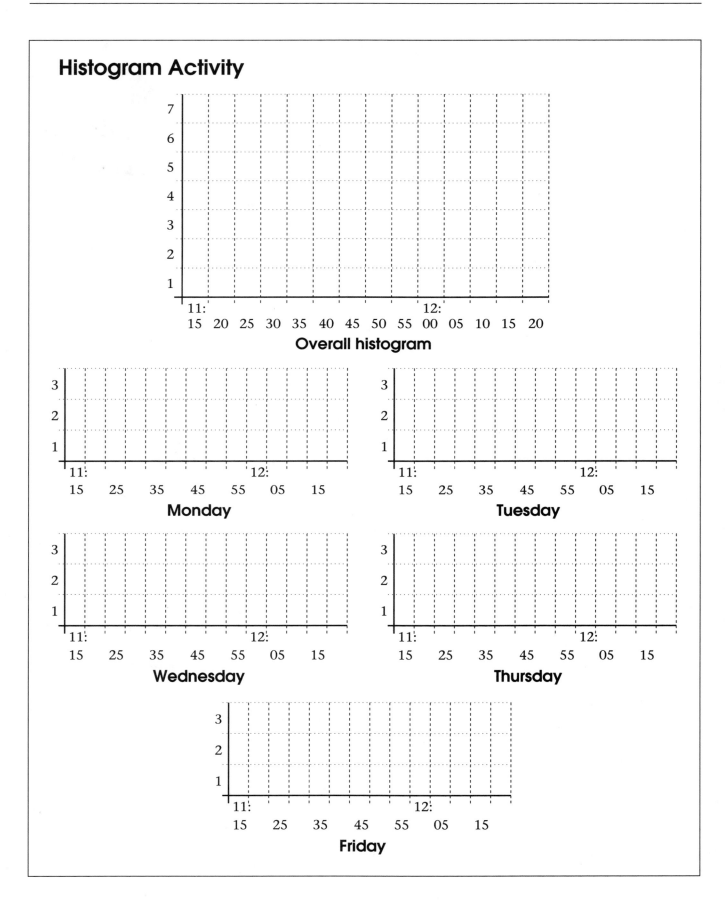

Overall histogram

Monday

Tuesday

Wednesday

Thursday

Friday

SCATTER DIAGRAM

A graphical display used to analyze the possible relationship between two variables. The compactness of the points gives an indication of the relationship's strength.

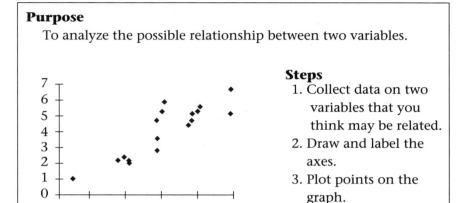

Purpose

To analyze the possible relationship between two variables.

Steps
1. Collect data on two variables that you think may be related.
2. Draw and label the axes.
3. Plot points on the graph.
4. Analyze the data for possible correlations.

Figure 10.11. Scatter diagram.

Collect Data on Variables That May Be Related

The first step is to collect data on two variables you suspect are related. Scatter diagrams can be used to help verify your suspicions. Note that each point on the plot requires two pieces of data. For example, if you want to analyze the relationship between the number of overtime hours worked and the number of errors made, data for both variables must be collected for the same time period.

Draw and Label the Axes

The values on the axes should get larger as you move up and to the right. Following this standard will be important later when you begin to look for possible correlations.

Plot Points on the Graph

Draw a simple symbol (such as a small point, circle, or square) at the point on the diagram where the two variables intersect. Some intersection points may need to have more than one symbol, just plot the symbol as close to the intersection point as possible.

Analyze the Data for Possible Correlations

A correlation means a complementary relationship exists between two factors. Our interest is in finding out if there is a relationship between two variables, and if there is, the strength of the relationship. There are different types of correlations. Figure 10.12 shows examples of a positive correlation, no correlation, and a negative correlation.

Uses

Scatter diagrams can be used to test suspected cause and effect relationships. If there is a relationship, controlling one variable may allow you

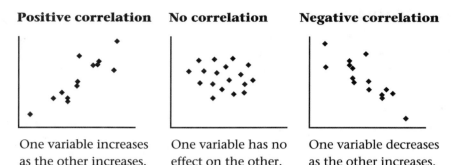

Figure 10.12. Types of correlations visible on scatter diagrams.

to control the other. This information can also be used to predict one variable when you know the other.

The compactness of the bunch of points gives an indication of the relationship's strength (there are mathematical equations for calculating the strength of the relationship, but a visual analysis is sufficient for most purposes). The more the points are bunched together to look like a straight diagonal line, the stronger the relationship. The more random and spread out the points are, the weaker the relationship.

POSITIVE CORRELATION

The condition that exists when one variable increases as the other increases. Visible on a scatter diagram as a positively-sloped diagonal line (see Figure 10.12).

Positive Correlations.   A positive correlation means one variable increases as the other increases. A common example of a positive correlation is the comparison of men's height and weight (women's height and weight comparisons should be conducted separately since they are different from men's). In general, taller men weigh more than shorter men. In other words, as height increases, so does weight. There are obviously some exceptions to this generalization, but the scatter diagram would show a tight collection of points along the diagonal line.

Some interesting business-related situations that may show positive correlations follow.

- Overtime hours worked vs. number of errors made
- Time spent waiting in line vs. customer complaints
- Time to prepare and issue a check vs. the check amount

NEGATIVE CORRELATION

The condition that exists when one variable decreases as the other increases. Visible on a scatter diagram as a negatively-sloped diagonal line (see Figure 10.12).

Negative Correlations.   Conversely, negative correlations mean one variable decreases as the other increases. Examples of variables that may have negative correlations include the following:

- Hours spent on preventive maintenance vs. downtime hours
- Time spent in design vs. number of errors reported by customers
- Tool speed vs. tool life

RUN CHART

A graphical tool used to monitor the performance of a process over a period of time.

Purpose

To monitor the performance of a process over time.

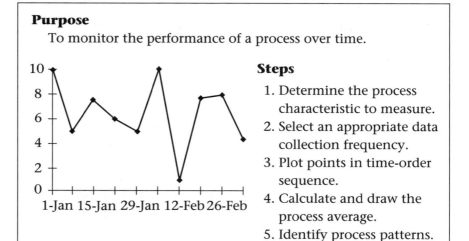

Steps

1. Determine the process characteristic to measure.
2. Select an appropriate data collection frequency.
3. Plot points in time-order sequence.
4. Calculate and draw the process average.
5. Identify process patterns.

Figure 10.13. Run chart.

RUN CHARTS

Run charts (sometimes called time plots) are used to monitor the performance of a process over time (see Figure 10.13). This may be the most common tool introduced so far, everyone probably has seen run charts before. While run charts may be common, some of the analysis techniques discussed herein may be new.

Determine the Process Characteristic to Measure

The first step in developing a run chart is to decide what process characteristic will be measured. As just discussed, the selection of the process characteristic is critical. Selection of the wrong characteristic will not only be a waste of time, but may result in reacting to improper signals.

Select an Appropriate Data Collection Frequency

How often should the data be collected? The answer to this question depends on the process. The primary factor is the frequency the process is performed. A process that is performed many times per day should obviously have data collected much more frequently than one that is performed once a month. Also consider how critical the process is and how predictable its performance is. The more critical or unpredictable, the more frequently the data should be collected.

Plot Points in Time-Order Sequence

Since the purpose of a run chart is to monitor the performance of a process over time, the points must be plotted in time-order sequence. This means the points are plotted in the sequence they actually occur. *The sequence of the data points does matter.* Data collected at 8:00 A.M. are plotted before the 10:00 A.M. point, Monday's data point is plotted before Tuesday's, and so on. The reason for plotting in time order sequence will be explained later. For now, remember it is important.

Calculate and Draw the Process Average

The process average provides an interesting and helpful reference point. Before you calculate the process average, wait until you have collected approximately 20 to 25 data points (to get a statistically valid sample size). Then total all of the data points and divide by the number of points to calculate the average.

Draw a solid horizontal line on the chart at the point of the process average.

Expect Points Above and Below the Process Average.   Don't be concerned with points above or below the process average, this is to be expected. I once read a magazine article that had analyzed the accomplishments of all United States presidents up to that point in time. The article's startling conclusion: about half of the presidents had performed below average. What else would you expect? By definition, about half of any population will be below average. About half of the people in a room will be shorter than the average of the heights of everyone present. (I say "about" because it is possible for a professional basketball player to walk into a small room and raise the average for the group. In this case, more than half of the people may be shorter than the average.) In any classroom, about half of the class will score below the class average. In any data set, you should expect about half of the points to be below the average (the other half above).

Identify Process Patterns

In some cases, patterns become visible on a run chart. Remember from the discussion on variation in chapter 9 that one expects data points to be distributed randomly, so any nonrandom pattern of points signals that something unusual is happening within the process. Different types of patterns reveal different information about a process.

The most common types of patterns are shown in Figure 10.14.

Begin to ask yourself: "What could have caused this pattern to exist?" Seeing a pattern may immediately identify a problem to you. More information on how to determine the causes is provided in chapter 12.

Uses

Run charts are excellent for monitoring the performance of a process over time, but caution should be taken to ensure the data are interpreted correctly. A natural tendency is to view every fluctuation in the data as something significant. This is not the case. Chapter 11 will discuss how simple statistical methods can be used to identify data points that are significant and should be acted upon.

SUMMARY

Collecting and analyzing data are key steps in process improvement. This chapter introduces check sheets, Pareto charts, histograms, scatter diagrams, and run charts as tools for collecting and analyzing process performance

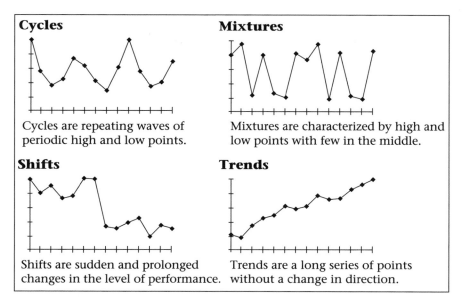

Figure 10.14. Run chart patterns.

data. The techniques discussed in chapter 11 build upon the analysis tools introduced in this chapter to provide additional performance information.

REVIEW QUESTIONS

Use the questions in Figure 10.15 to review your progress and make sure you are ready to continue on to the next chapter.

☐ Have check sheets been established to record findings?

☐ What vital few components have been identified from the Pareto Analysis?

☐ What hidden information was brought to light by stratifying the Pareto chart?

☐ What does the histogram reveal about the amount of variation present in the process?

☐ What hidden information was brought to light by stratifying the histogram?

☐ Did the scatter diagram reveal a relationship?

☐ Are the data on the run chart plotted in time-order sequence?

☐ What patterns are visible on the run chart?

☐ Are the team's recommendations supported by data?

Figure 10.15. Review questions.

USE STATISTICAL METHODS

Run charts provide a lot of information about the performance of a process. But, proper interpretation of time-sequenced data requires statistical data analysis. Without proper analysis, every fluctuation in the data may seem significant. Remember, every process exhibits variation. Some of the variation is caused by common causes, some by special causes. The statistical methods that will be described (specifically process control charts) will be used to distinguish between these causes and inform you when to act.

This chapter contains several activities. I recommend that every reader take the time to do the activities. The best way to learn to use statistical methods, just like anything else, is to do it. The activities are designed to help reinforce the concepts introduced in the text. Solutions are provided for your assistance as necessary.

INTRODUCTION TO CONTROL CHARTS

This chapter is not meant to be a complete text on control charts. Many complete books have been written on the subject (see *SPC Simplified: Practical Steps to Quality*[1], and *Tools and Methods for the Improvement of Quality*[2]). This chapter will, however, introduce the important concepts and offer a practical approach to their application to the analysis of process performance data.

Uses

A control chart provides a running record of a process—it helps you decide when the process is running smoothly and when it needs attention. We

CONTROL CHART

A graphical tool that serves as a running record of a process. Aids in determining whether a cause is part of the system or something unique or different.

IN CONTROL

The condition of a process when no special causes are present—when a process is performing consistently. A process that is in control is also referred to as being stable.

SIGMA

A measure of variation depicted by the Greek symbol σ (see Figure 11.1).

decided earlier that you need a method of determining whether a cause is part of the system (common) or something unique or different (special). Control charts provide this information. A process is said to be in-control if no special causes are present. "Control" does not mean the process is performing the way you want it to, it just means it is performing consistently—you know what to expect from the process (even if it is consistently performing at a level less than you want).

To explain how a control chart works (in a simplistic manner), we need to briefly return to a discussion about the bell curve and a means to measure the variability present in a system. Figure 11.1 shows three bell curves to introduce a means of measuring process variation.

Sigma (depicted by the Greek symbol σ) is a measure of variation. Figure 11.1 shows the portion of the bell curve included within one, two, and three sigma of the average $(\overline{X})$. The area covered by three sigma from each side of the average covers 99.73 percent of the possibilities. If a point occurs outside of the three sigma range, there is a very good chance something different or unusual is happening (since we would expect that to happen normally only 27 times out of 10,000 opportunities). Control charts use this logic to help identify the points that are not part of the system.

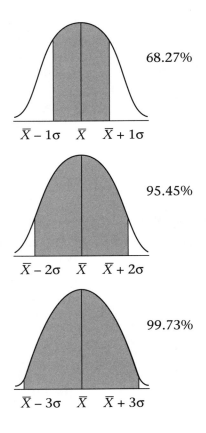

Figure 11.1. Measurement of process variation.

Control Limits

CONTROL LIMIT

A statistically determined boundary of expected process performance based on past performance. Each control chart has two control limits—an upper and a lower. A process can be monitored by comparing the results of a measurement to the control limits.

Control charts are run charts with some additional information—control limits. An upper control limit (UCL) is calculated and drawn at a distance of 3σ above the process average and a lower control limit (LCL) is calculated and drawn 3σ below the process average. Control limits are calculated based on past performance so they show you what to expect from the process as long as nothing is changed. A process can be monitored by comparing the results of a measurement to the control limits. If a point falls beyond the control limits (above the UCL or below the LCL), you can be pretty sure something has changed. This signal points to the need for action. More information on identifying out-of-control conditions is presented later in this chapter.

Types of Control Charts

There are two categories of control charts corresponding to the two types of data introduced before: variables and attributes. The uses and elements of control charts just described are true for all types of control charts. Different situations require different types of control charts. Each chart has its own method of calculating its control limits.

ATTRIBUTES CONTROL CHARTS

Attributes control charts are used when the information is not measured in numbers, but are counts or reflect qualitative characteristics like pass/fail, good/bad, or yes/no.

Since important decisions are going to be made based on the information gained from analyzing control charts, every care should be taken to make sure the control charts provide an accurate picture of the process being analyzed. To make sure the data on the chart are an accurate representation of the total process, wait until you have about 25 data points to calculate the process average and control limits that will be discussed. This sample size is required to ensure you have collected enough data for your analysis to be statistically valid.

There are many different types of attributes control charts. Two will be discussed. These two should provide the tools that almost all teams will need to analyze their processes.

p Charts

The *p* chart is used to monitor and control the percentage of defective pieces in a group. Before we get started, two definitions are important.

- A *defective* piece or event is any piece or event with one or more defects.
- A *defect* is an individual failure to meet a single requirement.

For example, if you visited the automated teller machine (ATM) at your local grocery store and the machine did not give you a receipt (because it was out of paper) and it kept your card (because it got jammed in the reader), you had a *defective* visit. In fact, you experienced two *defects*.

DEFECTIVE

Any piece or event with one or more defects.

DEFECT

An individual failure to meet a single requirement.

The *p* chart is not interested in the number of defects present, just whether any defects exist (in other words, if there are any defective pieces). To prepare a *p* chart, follow these steps.

1. Determine the event to be analyzed.

2. Determine the proper sample size. Consider the following guidelines in selecting the sample size.
   - Use a sample size large enough to give an average of four or more defectives per sample.
   - Use a sample size of at least 50.
   - Use a sample size that makes calculating the percent easy (such as 50 or 100).

3. Count and record the number of defective units on the bottom of the chart.

4. Calculate the percent defective *(p)*. Divide the number of defective units by the sample size times 100 percent.
For example, if you count 8 units to be defective out of a sample size of 50,

$$p = (\tfrac{8}{50}) \times 100\%$$
$$= 0.16 \times 100\%$$
$$= 16\%$$

5. Calculate the average percent defective for the process ($\bar{p}$, pronounced: "p bar").

$$\bar{p} = \text{average percent defective}$$

$$= \frac{\text{total number of defective units in all samples}}{\text{total number checked in all samples}} \times 100\%$$

6. Calculate the upper and lower control limits. The control limits are calculated using the following equations.

$$UCL_p = \bar{p} + 3\sqrt{\frac{\bar{p} \times (100\% - \bar{p})}{n}}$$

$$LCL_p = \bar{p} - 3\sqrt{\frac{\bar{p} \times (100\% - \bar{p})}{n}}$$

where $\bar{p}$ is the average percent defective and *n* is the sample size.
Set LCL_p to 0 if the calculation results in a negative number.

7. Determine the appropriate scale for the chart and label the vertical axis.

8. Draw the process average percent defective (solid line) and upper and lower control limits (dotted lines) on the chart.

9. Plot the data on the chart and connect the points with straight lines (make a run chart).

10. Analyze the chart.

An example using a p chart will help explain the steps. The data on the p chart activity were collected by the claims department of an insurance company (see page 150). This department receives and processes claim forms from their customers. The members of the department have become frustrated with the customers because it seems like they never fill in their claim forms correctly. Often there are parts of the form not filled in, and other parts completed incorrectly. The department has decided to analyze the forms by monitoring the percent of forms with any type of error. The department members have gone back over their records for the last several weeks and randomly selected 50 forms from each week. The data on the p chart activity are what they found.

After the control limits have been calculated and drawn on a control chart, the next step is to analyze the chart. Before we introduce the methods for proper interpretation and analysis of the information on a control chart, we need to introduce a few other types of control charts. The next section of this chapter discusses the methods you need to apply to properly interpret and analyze control chart information.

p Chart Activity

Situation: The following data were collected by the claims processing department of an insurance company. The data reflect the number of claim forms not correctly completed.

Week	Sample size	Number of incorrect forms
05/03–05/07	50	18
05/10–05/14	50	13
05/17–05/21	50	7
05/24–05/28	50	18
05/31–06/04	50	21
06/07–06/11	50	9
06/14–06/18	50	5
06/21–06/25	50	18
06/28–07/02	50	14
07/05–07/09	50	10
07/12–07/16	50	11
07/19–07/23	50	7
07/26–07/30	50	8
08/02–08/06	50	16
08/09–08/13	50	6
08/16–08/20	50	11
08/23–08/27	50	25
08/30–09/03	50	9
09/06–09/10	50	16
09/13–09/17	50	6
09/20–09/24	50	23
09/27–10/01	50	7
10/04–10/08	50	12
10/11–10/15	50	8
10/18–10/22	50	14
10/25–10/29	50	19
11/01–11/05	50	8
11/08–11/12	50	22
11/15–11/19	50	4
11/22–11/26	50	11
	1500	376

Activity: Prepare and analyze a p chart from this data.

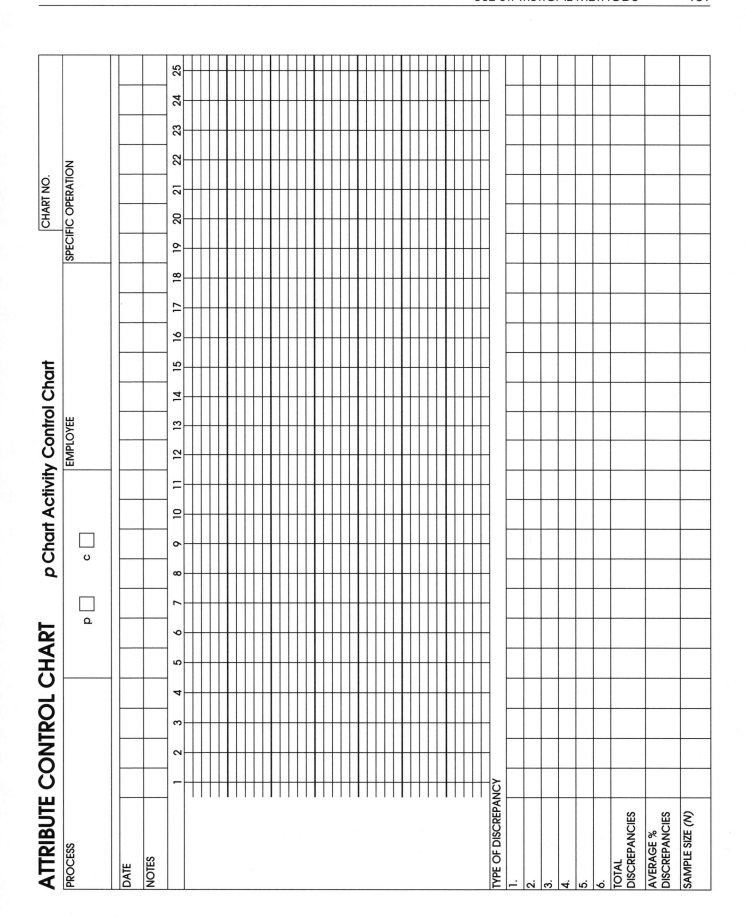

ATTRIBUTE CONTROL CHART   *p* Chart Activity Control Chart

PROCESS		EMPLOYEE		SPECIFIC OPERATION	CHART NO.

p ☐   c ☐

	1	2	3	4	5	6	7	8	9	10	11	12	13	14	15	16	17	18	19	20	21	22	23	24	25
DATE																									
NOTES																									

TYPE OF DISCREPANCY

1.
2.
3.
4.
5.
6.

TOTAL DISCREPANCIES

AVERAGE % DISCREPANCIES

SAMPLE SIZE (N)

The calculations for the centerline and upper and lower control limits follow.

$$\bar{p} = \frac{\text{total number of defective units in all samples}}{\text{total number checked in all samples}} \times 100\%$$

$$= \frac{376}{1500} \times 100\%$$

$$= 25.1\%$$

$$UCL_p = \bar{p} + 3\sqrt{\frac{\bar{p} \times (100\% - \bar{p})}{n}}$$

$$= 25.1 + 3\sqrt{\frac{25.1 \times (100\% - 25.1)}{50}}$$

$$= 25.1 + 3\sqrt{\frac{25.1 \times 74.9}{50}}$$

$$= 25.1 + 3\sqrt{37.6}$$

$$= 25.1 + 18.4$$

$$= 43.5$$

$$LCL_p = \bar{p} - 3\sqrt{\frac{\bar{p} \times (100\% - \bar{p})}{n}}$$

$$= 25.1 - 3\sqrt{\frac{25.1 \times (100\% - 25.1)}{50}}$$

$$= 25.1 - 18.4$$

$$= 6.7$$

The control limits calculated above are based upon the 30 data points for the activity. The control chart on page 153 shows a plot of only the first 25 points (since that is all that fit on the page). The next five (and subsequent) points should be plotted on another chart.

ATTRIBUTE CONTROL CHART p Chart Activity Control Chart (Solution)

PROCESS		EMPLOYEE	SPECIFIC OPERATION	CHART NO. 1
Claims Processing	p ☑ c ☐		# of incorrect claim forms	

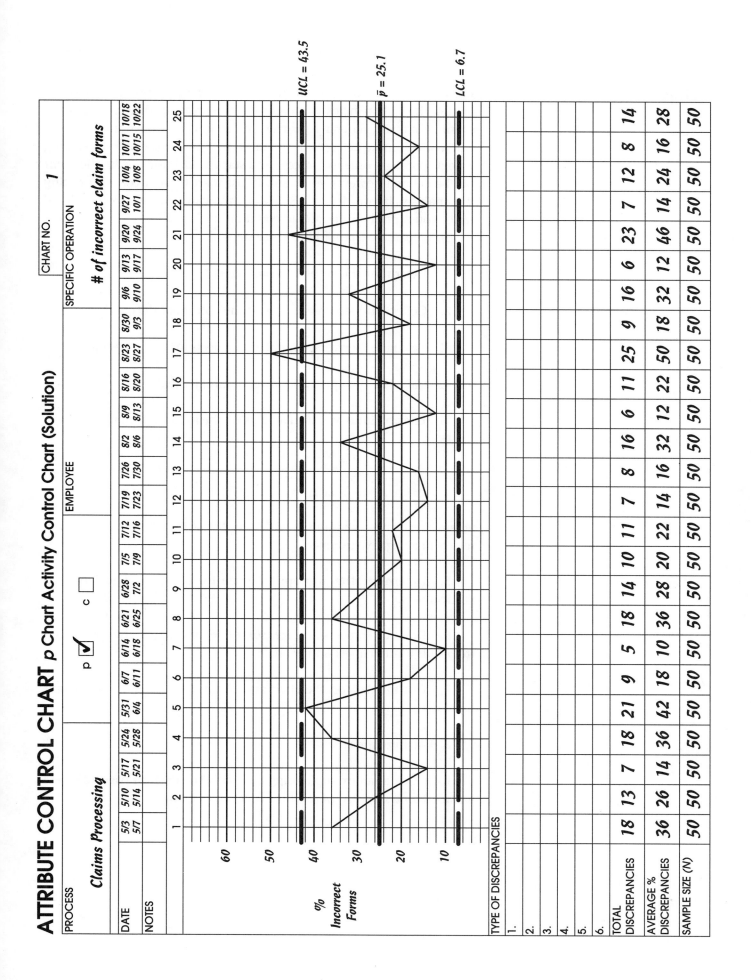

UCL = 43.5

$\bar{p}$ = 25.1

LCL = 6.7

% Incorrect Forms

DATE	1	2	3	4	5	6	7	8	9	10	11	12	13	14	15	16	17	18	19	20	21	22	23	24	25
	5/3 5/7	5/10 5/14	5/17 5/21	5/24 5/28	5/31 6/4	6/7 6/11	6/14 6/18	6/21 6/25	6/28 7/2	7/5 7/9	7/12 7/16	7/19 7/23	7/26 7/30	8/2 8/6	8/9 8/13	8/16 8/20	8/23 8/27	8/30 9/3	9/6 9/10	9/13 9/17	9/20 9/24	9/27 10/1	10/4 10/8	10/11 10/15	10/18 10/22
NOTES																									

TYPE OF DISCREPANCIES

1.
2.
3.
4.
5.
6.

	1	2	3	4	5	6	7	8	9	10	11	12	13	14	15	16	17	18	19	20	21	22	23	24	25
TOTAL DISCREPANCIES	18	13	7	18	21	9	5	18	14	10	11	7	8	16	6	11	25	9	16	6	23	7	12	8	14
AVERAGE % DISCREPANCIES	36	26	14	36	42	18	10	36	28	20	22	14	16	32	12	22	50	18	32	12	46	14	24	16	28
SAMPLE SIZE (N)	50	50	50	50	50	50	50	50	50	50	50	50	50	50	50	50	50	50	50	50	50	50	50	50	50

c Charts

The *p* chart was introduced to help control the percentage of defective pieces. The *c* chart helps you control the number of defects in a single event. A *c* chart generally provides more information than a *p* chart when one or more defects exist in an event. The event may be preparing a single purchase order or processing a stack of 125 time cards. The event can be defined however you want, it just must be kept constant during the analysis. If you define a stack of time cards to be 125 individual cards, you cannot decide later to count only 85 cards.

To prepare a *c* chart, follow these steps.

1. Determine the event to be analyzed.

2. Collect and record the data on the bottom of the chart.

3. Calculate the average number of defects for the process *(c̄)*.

4. Calculate the upper and lower control limits.

The control limits are calculated using the following equations.

$$UCL_c = \bar{c} + 3\sqrt{\bar{c}}$$

$$LCL_c = \bar{c} - 3\sqrt{\bar{c}}$$

where $\bar{c}$ is the average number of defects. Set LCL_c to 0 if the calculation results in a negative number.

5. Determine the appropriate scale for the chart and label the vertical axis.

6. Draw the process average (solid line) and upper and lower control limits (dotted lines) on the chart.

7. Plot the data on the chart and connect the points with straight lines.

8. Analyze the chart.

Let's look at an example using a *c* chart. The data on page 155 were recorded for a single ATM machine in a bank's lobby.

c Chart Activity

Situation: The following data have been collected from an ATM machine in your bank's lobby over the last 25 weeks.

Date	Type of defect				
	Money out	Receipt paper out	Card jam	Keypad problem	Other
02/28–03/06	2	1	0	0	1
03/07–03/13	2	0	0	0	1
03/14–03/20	2	2	0	0	1
03/21–03/27	1	2	1	0	1
03/28–04/03	2	2	0	1	1
04/04–04/10	2	2	2	0	1
04/11–04/17	0	1	1	1	1
04/18–04/24	1	0	1	0	0
04/25–05/01	0	0	0	0	0
05/02–05/08	1	1	1	0	0
05/09–05/15	1	0	1	0	0
05/16–05/22	2	0	2	0	1
05/23–05/29	1	0	0	1	0
05/30–06/05	1	1	3	1	1
06/06–06/12	0	0	3	0	3
06/13–06/19	0	1	0	0	0
06/20–06/26	0	2	1	0	1
06/27–07/03	1	1	1	1	0
07/04–07/10	0	2	0	0	1
07/11–07/17	3	1	0	0	1
07/18–07/24	2	1	1	0	2
07/25–07/31	0	0	0	0	0
08/01–08/07	1	0	0	0	1
08/08–08/14	2	0	2	2	0
08/15–08/21	1	0	0	1	2

Activity: Prepare and analyze a c chart from this data.

ATTRIBUTE CONTROL CHART

c Chart Activity Control Chart

CHART NO.

PROCESS

SPECIFIC OPERATION

EMPLOYEE

p ☐   c ☐

DATE

NOTES

	1	2	3	4	5	6	7	8	9	10	11	12	13	14	15	16	17	18	19	20	21	22	23	24	25

TYPE OF DISCREPANCY

1.

2.

3.

4.

5.

6.

TOTAL DISCREPANCIES

AVERAGE % DISCREPANCIES

SAMPLE SIZE (N)

The calculations for a c chart are somewhat simpler than those for a p chart. The calculations for the centerline and upper and lower control limits follow.

$\bar{c}$ = average number of defects for the process

$$= \frac{96}{25}$$

$$= 3.8$$

$$UCL_c = \bar{c} + 3\sqrt{\bar{c}}$$

$$= 3.8 + 3\sqrt{3.8}$$

$$= 3.8 + 5.8$$

$$= 9.6$$

$$LCL_c = \bar{c} - 3\sqrt{\bar{c}}$$

$$= 3.8 - 5.8$$

$$= -2.0 \text{ (change to 0 since it is a negative number)}$$

ATTRIBUTE CONTROL CHART c Chart Activity Control Chart (Solution)

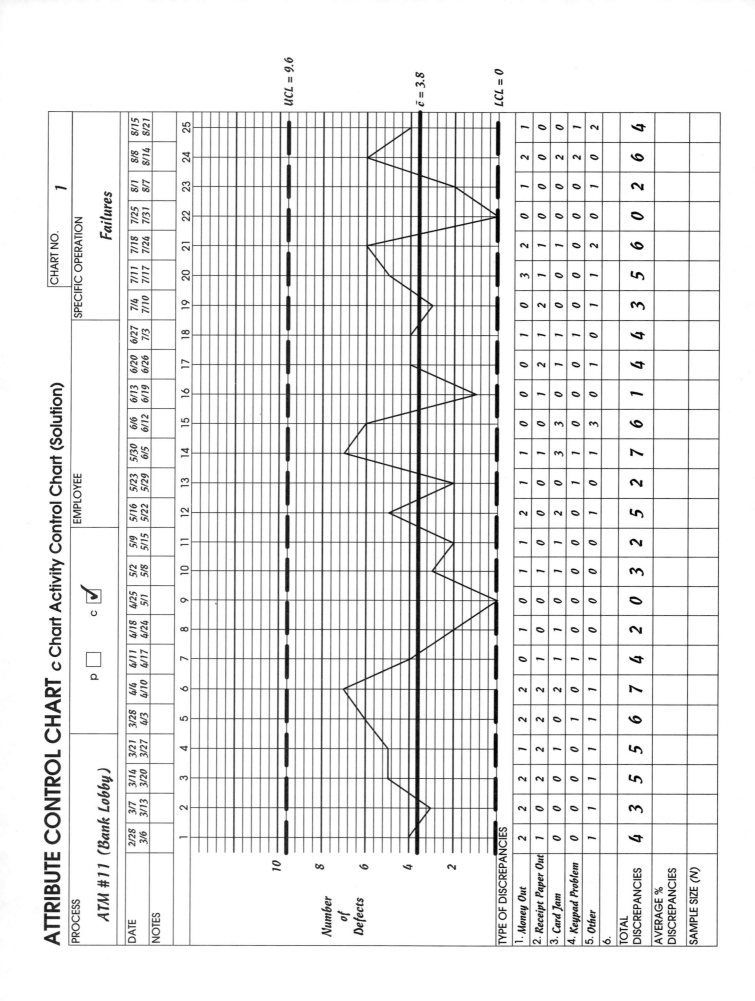

PROCESS: ATM #11 (Bank Lobby)
SPECIFIC OPERATION: Failures
EMPLOYEE:
CHART NO.: 1
p ☐ **c** ☑

UCL = 9.6
c̄ = 3.8
LCL = 0

DATE	2/28 3/6	3/7 3/13	3/14 3/20	3/21 3/27	3/28 4/3	4/4 4/10	4/11 4/17	4/18 4/24	4/25 5/1	5/2 5/8	5/9 5/15	5/16 5/22	5/23 5/29	5/30 6/5	6/6 6/12	6/13 6/19	6/20 6/26	6/27 7/3	7/4 7/10	7/11 7/17	7/18 7/24	7/25 7/31	8/1 8/7	8/8 8/14	8/15 8/21
NOTES	1	2	3	4	5	6	7	8	9	10	11	12	13	14	15	16	17	18	19	20	21	22	23	24	25

TYPE OF DISCREPANCIES

	1	2	3	4	5	6	7	8	9	10	11	12	13	14	15	16	17	18	19	20	21	22	23	24	25
1. Money Out	2	2	2	1	2	2	0	1	0	1	1	2	1	1	0	0	0	1	0	3	2	0	1	2	1
2. Receipt Paper Out	1	0	2	2	2	2	2	0	0	1	0	0	0	1	0	1	2	1	2	1	1	0	0	0	0
3. Card Jam	0	0	0	1	0	2	1	1	0	1	1	2	0	3	3	0	1	1	0	0	1	0	0	2	0
4. Keypad Problem	0	0	0	0	1	0	0	0	0	0	0	0	1	1	0	0	0	0	0	0	0	0	0	2	1
5. Other	1	1	1	1	1	1	1	0	0	0	0	1	0	1	3	0	1	0	1	1	2	0	1	0	2
6.																									
TOTAL DISCREPANCIES	4	3	5	5	6	7	4	2	0	3	2	5	2	7	6	1	4	4	3	5	6	0	2	6	4
AVERAGE % DISCREPANCIES																									
SAMPLE SIZE (N)																									

Number of Defects (y-axis scale): 2, 4, 6, 8, 10

VARIABLES CONTROL CHARTS

Variables control charts are used when the data being analyzed are the result of some type of measurement. The data used in variables control charts are expressed in quantitative units of measurement like time, weight, and length.

There are two primary types of variables control charts (average and range charts, and individuals charts). Each of these charts really consist of two charts: one chart to plot the process location, and the other to chart the process variation.

Average and Range Charts

Average and range ($\overline{X}$–R) charts are used to monitor processes where variables data are collected and the analysis is based upon small sample sizes (individuals charts introduced next are used for single measurements).

To prepare an $\overline{X}$–R chart, follow these steps.

1. Determine the process characteristic to monitor.

2. Decide on the sample size *(n)*. The sample size should be selected to minimize the variation within the sample. This approach allows isolation of special variation between samples while identifying variation within the sample. Sample sizes of 4 or 5 are commonly used. The larger the sample size, the more time required to collect the data, but larger sample sizes result in tighter control limits.

3. Collect the samples and record the data on the top of the chart.

4. Calculate and record the average ($\overline{X}$, pronounced: "x bar") for each sample by totaling the numbers in the sample and dividing by the sample size *(n)*.

5. Calculate the overall average ($\overline{\overline{X}}$, pronounced: "x double bar") by totaling all of the sample averages *($\overline{X}$)* and dividing by the number of samples. Record for $\overline{\overline{X}}$ future use.

6. Determine and record the range *(R)* for each of the samples. The range is defined as the difference between the largest observation and the smallest observation. To determine the range, it may be helpful to circle the largest number and box-in the smallest number in each sample. Then, subtract the boxed-in number from the circled number.

7. Calculate the average range *($\overline{R}$)* by totaling all of the sample ranges *(R)* and dividing by the number of ranges. Record $\overline{R}$ for future use.

RANGE

The difference between the largest observation and the smallest observation.

8. Calculate the upper and lower control limits for ranges.

The control limits are calculated using the following equations.

$$UCL_R = D_4\bar{R}$$

$$LCL_R = 0 \text{ (for sample sizes} < 7)$$

where D_4 is a factor from the following table.

Sample size (n)	D_4
2	3.27
3	2.57
4	2.28
5	2.11

9. Determine the appropriate scale for the R chart and label the vertical axis.

10. Draw the average (solid line) and upper and lower control limits (dotted lines) on the R chart.

11. Plot the data on the R chart and connect the points with straight lines.

12. Analyze the R chart. (Methods for analyzing the chart are discussed in the next section of this chapter.) Do not continue with the $\bar{X}$ chart if the R chart is out of control.

13. After you have determined that the R chart is in control, calculate the upper and lower control limits for averages.

The control limits are calculated using the following equations.

$$UCL_{\bar{X}} = \bar{\bar{X}} + A_2\bar{R}$$

$$LCL_{\bar{X}} = \bar{\bar{X}} - A_2\bar{R}$$

where A_2 is a factor from the following table.

Sample size (n)	A_2
2	1.88
3	1.02
4	0.73
5	0.58

14. Determine the appropriate scale for the $\overline{X}$ chart and label the vertical axis.

15. Draw the average (solid line) and upper and lower control limits (dotted lines) on the $\overline{X}$ chart.

16. Plot the data on the $\overline{X}$ chart and connect the points with straight lines.

17. Analyze the $\overline{X}$ chart.

An example using an $\overline{X}$–R chart may help you understand the steps. The customer service department of a mail order company wants to know how long it takes their representatives to take orders called in from their customers. Every day this week, each representative has recorded the length of their first four calls every two hours. The numbers in the $\overline{X}$–R chart activity on page 162 are the data that one of the representatives recorded.

$\overline{X}$-R Chart Activity

Situation: The following data have been collected from the customer support department of a mail order company. The data reflect the time spent on customer calls.

Date	Time				
	8:00	10:00	12:00	2:00	4:00
March 1	3.5	5.2	10.6	5.7	6.9
	8.1	21.3	16.7	13.5	19.1
	13.9	11.2	18.4	18.6	23.6
	13.8	9.0	9.8	20.4	16.2
March 2	15.0	5.3	18.6	22.2	5.8
	9.4	14.1	5.3	19.9	17.2
	9.2	11.5	13.5	14.0	7.8
	1.8	8.4	17.6	4.6	9.7
March 3	14.7	13.1	19.6	13.8	12.1
	11.6	20.3	19.7	22.6	8.3
	8.7	16.7	14.6	16.4	13.6
	15.1	9.7	5.1	17.8	5.0
March 4	14.1	13.8	4.4	15.5	9.6
	11.8	4.2	12.9	18.2	11.5
	15.8	23.9	6.3	4.5	5.6
	13.6	17.4	9.9	12.6	9.1
March 5	24.1	17.3	7.9	5.1	9.6
	10.9	13.2	10.8	6.8	18.7
	10.4	6.6	8.5	8.2	10.6
	8.5	8.2	18.0	13.2	20.9

Activity: Prepare and analyze an $\overline{X}$-R chart from this data.

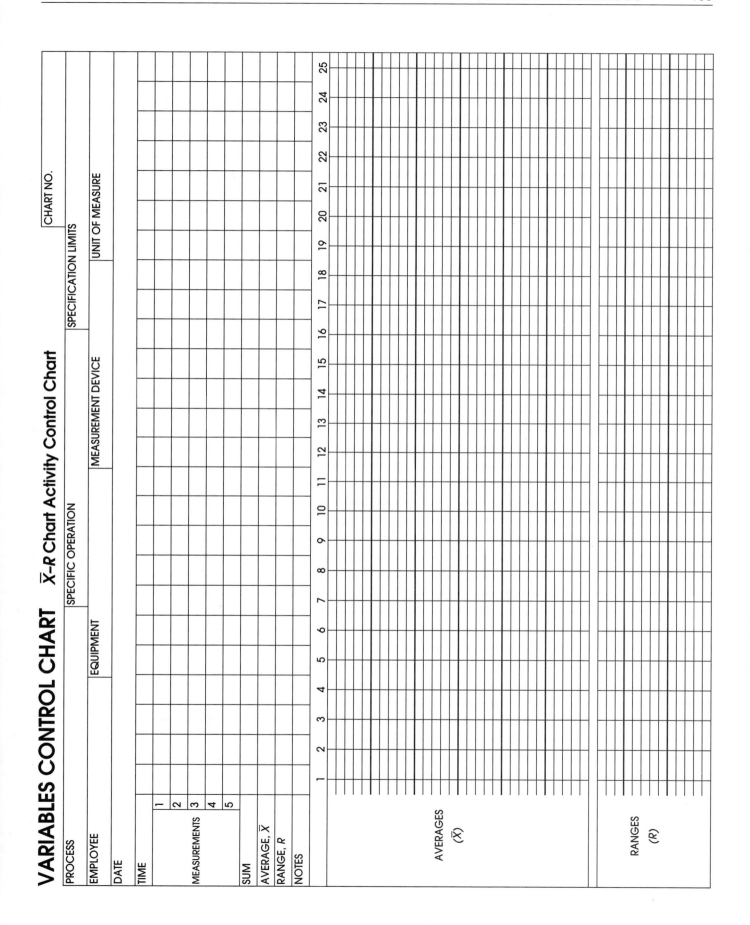

The calculations for the centerlines and upper and lower control limits follow.

$$\bar{\bar{X}} = \text{overall average}$$

$$= \frac{311.8}{25}$$

$$= 12.5$$

$$\bar{R} = \text{average range}$$

$$= \frac{287.4}{25}$$

$$= 11.5$$

$$UCL_R = D_4\bar{R}$$
$$= 2.28 \times 11.5$$
$$= 26.2$$

$$LCL_R = 0 \ (\text{for sample sizes} < 7)$$

$$UCL_{\bar{X}} = \bar{\bar{X}} + A_2\bar{R}$$
$$= 12.5 + (0.73 \times 11.5)$$
$$= 12.5 + 8.4$$
$$= 20.9$$

$$LCL_{\bar{X}} = \bar{\bar{X}} - A_2\bar{R}$$
$$= 12.5 - 8.4$$
$$= 4.1$$

Action should be taken whenever possible to minimize sources of variation in data collection. In this example, the data should come from a single operator to minimize the variation due to differences between operators.

VARIABLES CONTROL CHART $\bar{X}$-R Chart Activity Control Chart (Solution)

PROCESS	Customer support calls	SPECIFIC OPERATION	Mary's calls	SPECIFICATION LIMITS	CHART NO. 1
EMPLOYEE	Mary	EQUIPMENT		MEASUREMENT DEVICE Stop watch #1	UNIT OF MEASURE Minutes

DATE		3/1					3/2					3/3					3/4					3/5				
TIME		8:00	10:00	12:00	2:00	4:00	8:00	10:00	12:00	2:00	4:00	8:00	10:00	12:00	2:00	4:00	8:00	10:00	12:00	2:00	4:00	8:00	10:00	12:00	2:00	4:00
MEASUREMENTS	1	3.5	5.2	10.6	5.7	6.9	15.0	5.3	18.6	22.2	5.8	14.7	13.1	19.6	13.8	12.1	14.1	13.8	4.4	15.5	9.6	24.1	17.3	7.9	5.1	9.6
	2	8.1	21.3	16.7	13.5	19.1	9.4	14.1	5.3	19.9	17.2	11.6	20.3	19.7	22.6	8.3	11.8	4.2	12.9	18.2	11.5	10.9	13.2	10.8	6.8	18.7
	3	13.9	11.2	18.4	18.6	23.6	9.2	11.5	13.5	14.0	7.8	8.7	16.7	14.6	16.4	13.6	15.8	23.9	6.3	4.5	5.6	10.4	6.6	8.5	8.2	10.6
	4	13.8	9.0	9.8	20.4	16.2	1.8	8.4	17.6	4.6	9.7	15.1	9.7	5.1	17.8	5.0	13.6	17.4	9.9	12.6	9.1	8.5	8.2	18.0	13.2	20.9
	5																									
SUM		39.3	46.7	55.5	58.2	65.8	35.4	39.3	55.0	60.7	40.5	50.1	59.8	59.0	70.6	39.0	55.3	59.3	33.5	50.8	35.8	53.9	45.3	45.2	33.3	59.8
AVERAGE, $\bar{X}$		9.8	11.7	13.9	14.6	16.5	8.9	9.8	13.8	15.2	10.1	12.5	15.0	14.8	17.7	9.8	13.8	14.8	8.4	12.7	9.0	13.5	11.3	11.3	8.3	15.0
RANGE, R		10.4	16.1	8.6	14.7	16.7	13.2	8.8	13.3	17.6	11.4	6.4	10.6	14.6	8.8	8.6	4.0	19.7	8.5	13.7	5.9	15.6	10.7	10.1	8.1	11.3
NOTES																										

AVERAGES ($\bar{X}$)

UCL = 20.9
$\bar{\bar{X}}$ = 12.5
LCL = 4.1

RANGES (R)

UCL = 26.2
$\bar{R}$ = 11.5
LCL = 0

Individuals Charts

Variables data also can occur as single measurements. In some situations only a single data point (rather than small samples) is observed and plotted on a control chart. This is when individuals control charts (*X–R* charts) are used.

The single data points taken for individuals charts are considered to have a sample size of one. Since a sample size of one makes it impossible to calculate the range within a sample, the range for an *X–R* chart is calculated as the moving average between points.

To prepare an *X–R* chart, follow these steps.

1. Determine the process characteristic to monitor.

2. Collect the data and record it on the top of the chart.

3. Calculate the range *(R)* by figuring the difference between the current point and the point immediately proceeding the current point (the very first point documented cannot have a range figure). Record the range on the chart. Do not be concerned about negative numbers resulting from the subtraction, record all of the numbers as positive numbers.

4. Calculate and record the process average ($\overline{X}$, pronounced: "x bar") by totaling all the numbers and dividing by the number of data points recorded. Record $\overline{X}$ for future use.

5. Calculate the average range *(R̄)* by totaling all of the ranges *(R)* and dividing by the number of ranges. Record $\overline{R}$ for future use.

6. Calculate the upper and lower control limits for ranges.

The control limits are calculated using the following equations.

$$UCL_R = 3.27 \times \overline{R}$$
$$LCL_R = 0$$

7. Calculate the upper and lower control limits for individuals.

The control limits are calculated using the following equations.

$$UCL_X = \overline{X} + (2.66 \times \overline{R})$$
$$LCL_X = \overline{X} - (2.66 \times \overline{R})$$

8. Determine the appropriate scale for both of the charts (individual and range) and label the vertical axes.

9. Draw the averages (solid lines) and upper and lower control limits (dotted lines) on both charts.

10. Plot the data on the charts and connect the points with straight lines.

11. Analyze the chart.

An example using an *X–R* chart will help understand the steps. In the example on page 168, an individual wants to monitor the mileage of the family car. The owner thinks decisions about regular maintenance (oil change, filter changes, and so on) could be made based upon the information from a control chart.

X–R Chart Activity

Situation: The following data have been collected from an individual monitoring the mileage of the family car. The data reflect the miles/gallon achieved between each fill-up.

Date	Miles/Gallon
February 3	28.5
February 11	25.5
February 15	28.1
February 24	28.7
March 2	29.4
March 13	28.3
March 22	25.8
April 1	27.4
April 6	27.1
April 10	24.9
April 19	29.1
April 28	31.2
May 3	28.1
May 11	28.5
May 18	25.7
May 24	28.7
May 31	28.9
June 3	27.4
June 12	31.5
June 17	30.0
June 22	27.5
June 30	29.2
July 4	26.4
July 6	28.4
July 11	29.6

Activity: Prepare and analyze an *X–R* chart from this data.

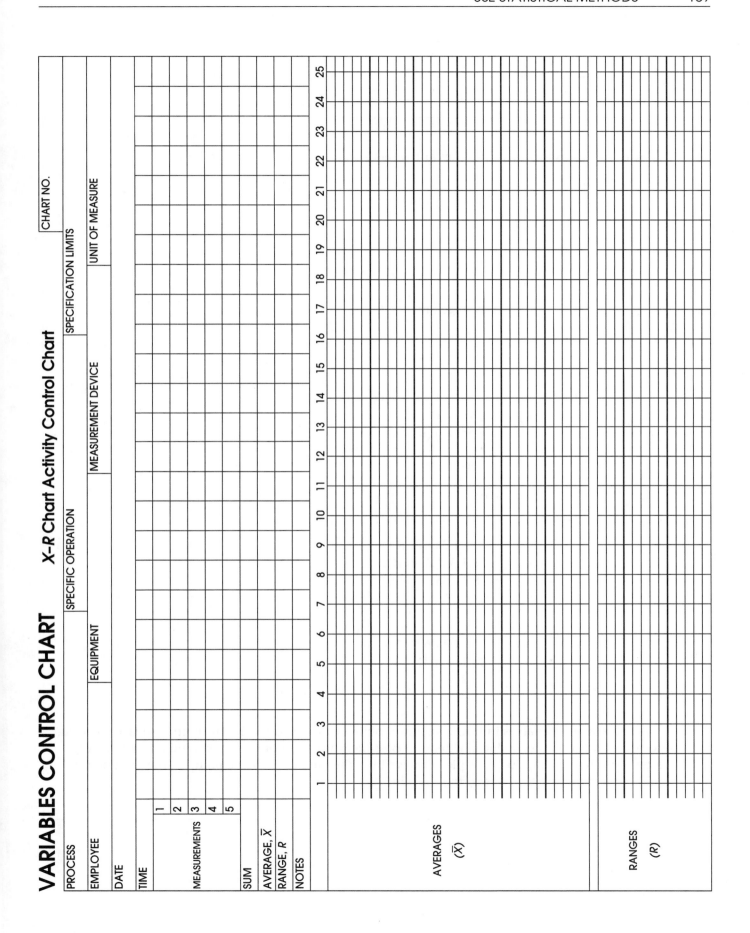

The calculations for the centerlines and upper and lower control limits follow.

$$\bar{X} = \text{process average}$$
$$= \frac{703.9}{25}$$
$$= 28.1$$

$$\bar{R} = \text{average range}$$
$$= \frac{47.7}{24}$$
$$= 2.0$$

$$UCL_R = 3.27 \times \bar{R}$$
$$= 3.27 \times 2.0$$
$$= 6.5$$

$$LCL_R = 0$$

$$UCL_X = \bar{X} + (2.66 \times \bar{R})$$
$$= 28.1 + (2.66 \times 2.0)$$
$$= 28.1 + 5.3$$
$$= 33.4$$

$$LCL_X = \bar{X} - (2.66 \times \bar{R})$$
$$= 28.1 - 5.3$$
$$= 22.8$$

There are many variables in filling an automobile's gas tank and calculating the mileage received. Since variation should be reduced whenever possible, the owner of this car should take whatever precautions are possible. For example, always filling the tank at the same pump at the same station would reduce the variation due to the gas pumps.

VARIABLES CONTROL CHART (INDIVIDUAL & RANGE)

X-R Chart Activity Control Chart (Solution)

CHART NO. 1

PROCESS		
SPECIFICATION LIMITS		
SPECIFIC OPERATION: Gasoline use	UNIT OF MEASURE: *Miles/Gallon*	
EMPLOYEE	EQUIPMENT: *Ford Escort*	MEASUREMENT DEVICE

DATE	2/3	2/11	2/15	2/24	3/2	3/13	3/22	4/1	4/6	4/10	4/19	4/28	5/3	5/11	5/18	5/24	5/31	6/3	6/12	6/17	6/22	6/30	7/4	7/6	7/11
TIME																									
1 (MEASUREMENTS)	28.5	25.5	28.1	28.7	29.4	28.3	25.8	27.4	27.1	24.9	29.1	31.2	28.1	28.5	25.7	28.7	28.9	27.4	31.5	30.0	27.5	29.2	26.4	28.4	29.6
2																									
3																									
4																									
5																									
SUM																									
AVERAGE, x̄																									
RANGE, R		3.0	2.6	0.6	0.7	1.1	2.5	1.6	0.3	2.2	4.2	2.1	3.1	0.4	2.8	3.0	0.2	1.5	4.1	1.5	2.5	1.7	2.8	2.0	1.2
NOTES																									

INDIVIDUALS (X)

ULC = 33.4
$\bar{X} = 28.1$
LCL = 22.8

RANGES (R)

UCL = 6.5
$\bar{R} = 2.0$
LCL = 0

SELECTING THE MOST APPROPRIATE CHART

Selecting the most appropriate chart to use for a given situation is an important, and sometimes confusing, decision. The more you use control charts for your own applications, the more examples you have in your mind to pull from, the easier this selection will become. Figure 11.2 provides some guidelines to follow in selecting the most appropriate chart.

Some practice at selecting the most appropriate control chart will help. Read the situations documented in the control chart selection activity on page 173. Use the guidelines already provided to select the most appropriate type of control chart for each situation. Document your reasons.

IDENTIFYING OUT-OF-CONTROL CONDITIONS

The purpose of generating process control charts is to be able to identify when a special cause is present. The presence of special causes is identified by out-of-control conditions on the control charts. Out-of-control conditions signal something different is happening and the process should be analyzed to determine the source. There are two methods for identifying out-of-control conditions: the presence of nonrandom patterns, and a violation of any of the out-of-control rules.

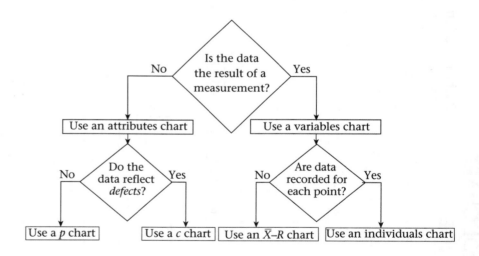

Figure 11.2. Control chart selection flowchart.

Control Chart Selection Activity

Instructions: Select the most appropriate type of control chart for each of the situations presented below.

Situation	Type of Chart/Reason
A. The owner of a small busines wants to analyze the amount of mail received at the office each business day.	☐ p ☐ $\bar{X}$–R ☐ c ☐ X–R Reason: _____ _____ _____
B. The manager of the transportation department of a manufacturing company wants to analyze the mileage (miles/gallon) of each automobile in the fleet.	☐ p ☐ $\bar{X}$–R ☐ c ☐ X–R Reason: _____ _____ _____
C. The members of the customer support department of a bank want to analyze the number of incoming calls that are placed on hold before a representative can talk to the customer.	☐ p ☐ $\bar{X}$–R ☐ c ☐ X–R Reason: _____ _____ _____
D. A pharmacist wants to analyze the number of prescriptions filled per day.	☐ p ☐ $\bar{X}$–R ☐ c ☐ X–R Reason: _____ _____ _____
E. The manager of customer returns in a retail store wants to analyze the time required to complete the paperwork required to return an unwanted item.	☐ p ☐ $\bar{X}$–R ☐ c ☐ X–R Reason: _____ _____ _____

Control Chart Selection Activity (Solution)

Instructions: Select the most appropriate type of control chart for each of the situations presented below.

Situation	Type of Chart/Reason
A. The owner of a small busines wants to analyze the amount of mail received at the office each business day.	☐ p ☐ $\bar{X}$–R ☑ c ☐ X–R Reason: **Counted data**
B. The manager of the transportation department of a manufacturing company wants to analyze the mileage (miles/gallon) of each automobile in the fleet.	☐ p ☐ $\bar{X}$–R ☐ c ☑ X–R Reason: **Measured data, no samples**
C. The members of the customer support department of a bank want to analyze the number of incoming calls that are placed on hold before a representative can talk to the customer.	☑ p ☐ $\bar{X}$–R ☐ c ☐ X–R Reason: **Counted data, interested in defective events (calls on hold)**
D. A pharmacist wants to analyze the number of prescriptions filled per day.	☐ p ☐ $\bar{X}$–R ☑ c ☐ X–R Reason: **Counted data**
E. The manager of customer returns in a retail store wants to analyze the time required to complete the paperwork required to return an unwanted item.	☐ p ☑ $\bar{X}$–R ☐ c ☐ X–R Reason: **Measured data (minutes or seconds), data samples used.**

Nonrandom patterns

As we have discussed, we expect the data points resulting from measuring a process to be randomly distributed due to the natural variation that exists in all processes. So, any time a nonrandom pattern is visible in the data (by analyzing run charts or control charts), you can tell something unusual is happening within the process—the process is out of control.

(Note: This is one of the reasons why it is so important that the points be plotted in time-order sequence. If the points are not plotted in time-order sequence, you could not identify and react to the presence of non-random patterns.)

Identifying the presence of nonrandom patterns is one of the easiest ways to identify an out-of-control condition. No detailed analysis is required. Just look at the charts and see if any type of nonrandom pattern exists.

The patterns introduced in the previous chapter are shown again in Figure 11.3.

Each of the nonrandom patterns reveal something different about a process.

Cycles. Cycles are caused by special disturbances that appear and disappear with some degree of regularity. Cycles can be caused by events like temperature changes and rotation of employees or machines.

Mixtures. Mixtures indicate the presence of two or more distributions. Mixtures can be recognized by the unusually long lines joining the

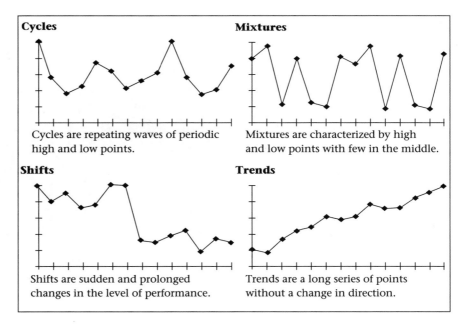

Figure 11.3. Nonrandom patterns.

points. Mixtures can be caused by events like receiving materials from two or more vendors.

Shifts. A shift is one of the most easily detectable control chart patterns. Sudden shifts frequently result from a special cause which moves the process average to a new level, then has no further effect on the process. Shifts can be caused by events like a new untrained worker, using a new kind of equipment or material, purchasing required supplies from a new vendor, and implementing a new approach.

Trends. Trends are gradual shifts that do not settle down. Trends may result from any causes which work on a process gradually such as operator fatigue and inadequate maintenance.

Out-of-Control Rules

A set of four rules exists to help identify when a process is out of control. The rules, based on the laws of statistics and probability, are designed to identify situations we would not expect to normally happen. So, when one of the rules is violated, we know something unusual must be happening.

In order to use the tests, the area between the centerline and the control limits of a control chart must be divided into three zones on each side of the centerline as shown in Figure 11.4.

The rules are explained in Figures 11.5 through 11.8.

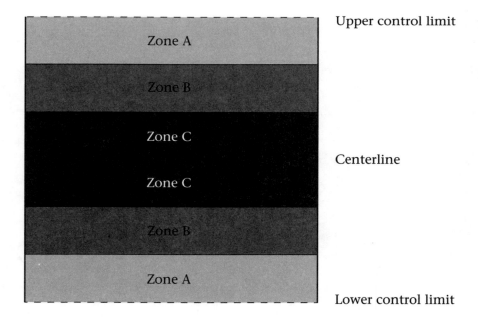

Figure 11.4. Control chart zones.

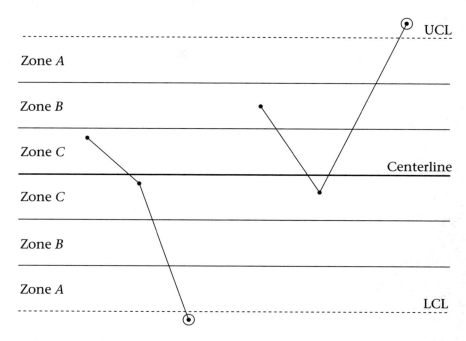

Rule 1: A single point falls outside the control limits.

Figure 11.5. Out-of-control rule 1.

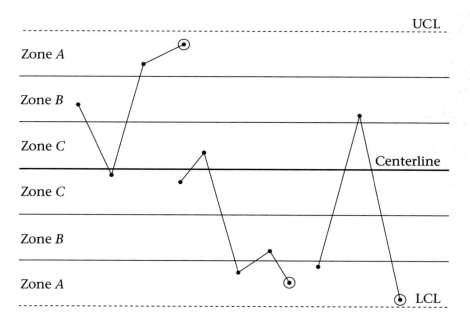

Rule 2: Any 2 out of 3 consecutive points fall in Zone *A* or beyond.

Figure 11.6. Out-of-control rule 2.

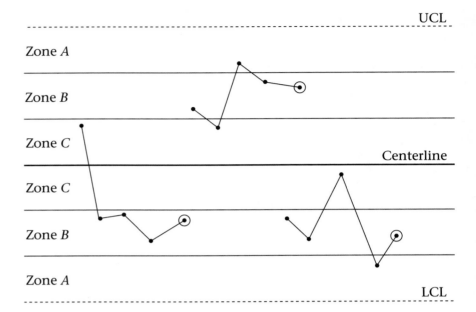

Rule 3: Any 4 out of 5 consecutive points fall in Zone *B* or beyond.

Figure 11.7. Out-of-control rule 3.

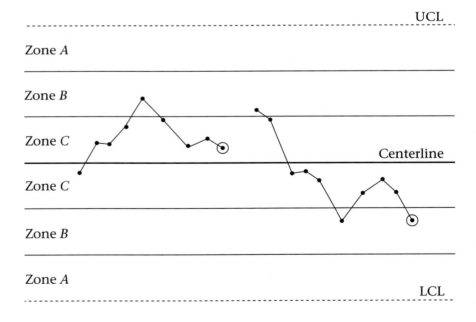

Rule 4: Any 8 or more consecutive points fall on one side of the
centerline.

Figure 11.8. Out-of-control rule 4.

Identifying the condition described by rule 1 is the easiest of the rules. Because the control limits show the bounds of expected process performance (based on past performance), any point outside the control limits is unexpected. Remember, however, that this is not the only rule. A process can be out of control even if all of the points fall within the control limits.

All of these rules are based on the same logic, one would not expect the conditions called for in the rules to occur unless something special was present.

Activity

Analyze each of the control charts on pages 180–182 to determine whether they are in control or out of control. Document the reasons for your conclusions.

Preparing control charts is useless unless you can analyze the charts properly. Chart analysis requires you to be able to determine if the process is in control or out of control. Identifying out of control conditions becomes easier with experience. Use these activities to begin creating your experience with control chart analysis.

The solutions follow. Make sure you understand the rationale used for each chart before continuing.

Control Chart Activity

Instructions: Identify whether the processes documented below are in
control or out of control. Document your reasons.

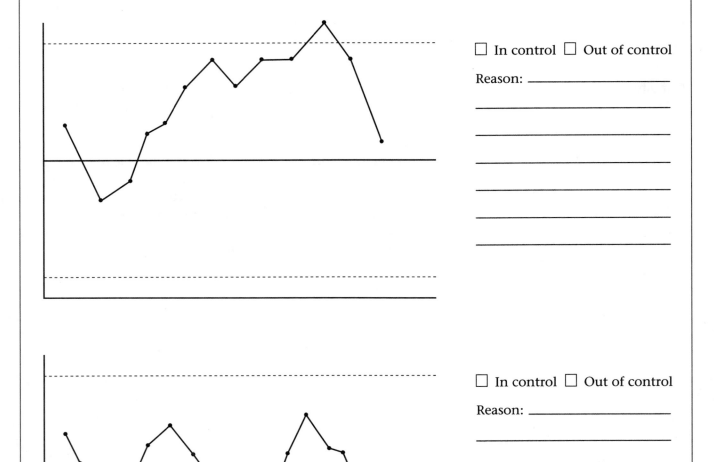

☐ In control ☐ Out of control

Reason: _____

_____

_____

_____

_____

_____

_____

☐ In control ☐ Out of control

Reason: _____

_____

_____

_____

_____

_____

_____

Control Chart Activity–page 2

Instructions: Identify whether the processes documented below are in control or out of control. Document your reasons.

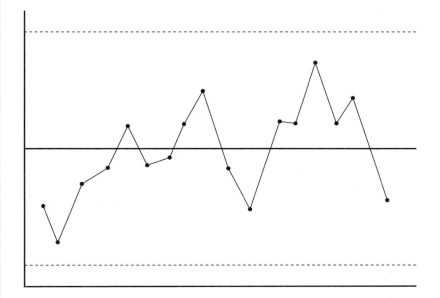

☐ In control ☐ Out of control

Reason: _____

_____

_____

_____

_____

_____

_____

☐ In control ☐ Out of control

Reason: _____

_____

_____

_____

_____

_____

_____

Control Chart Activity–page 3

Instructions: Identify whether the processes documented below are in
control or out of control. Document your reasons.

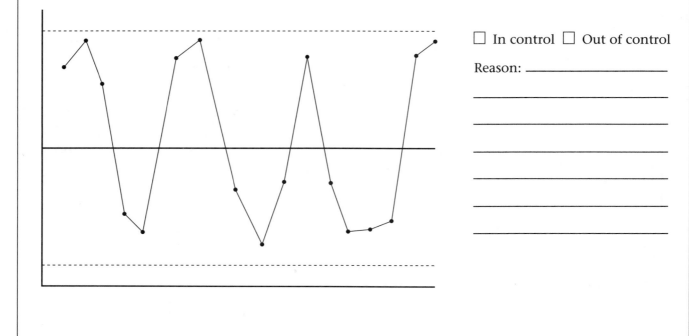

☐ In control ☐ Out of control

Reason: _____

_____

_____

_____

_____

_____

_____

☐ In control ☐ Out of control

Reason: _____

_____

_____

_____

_____

_____

_____

Control Chart Activity (Solution)

Instructions: Identify whether the processes documented below are in control or out of control. Document your reasons.

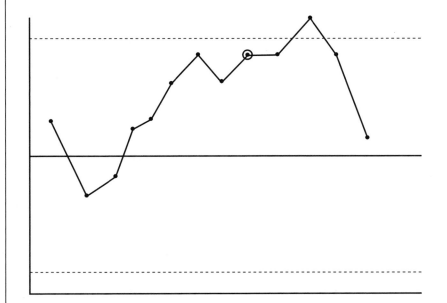

☐ In control ☑ Out of control

Reason: *Rule 2. Two out of three points in Zone A or beyond. A Rule 1 violation exists later, but the process is first out of control because of the Rule 2 violation.*

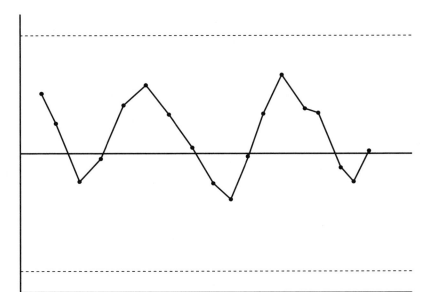

☐ In control ☑ Out of control

Reason: *Cycle.*

Control Chart Activity (Solution)–page 2

Instructions: Identify whether the processes documented below are in
control or out of control. Document your reasons.

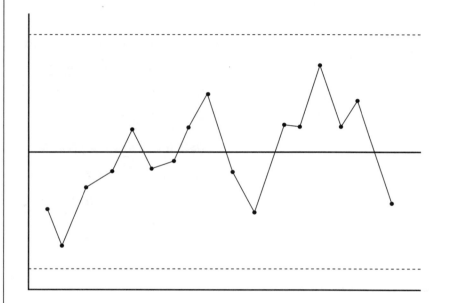

☑ In control ☐ Out of control

Reason: _____

_____

_____

_____

_____

_____

_____

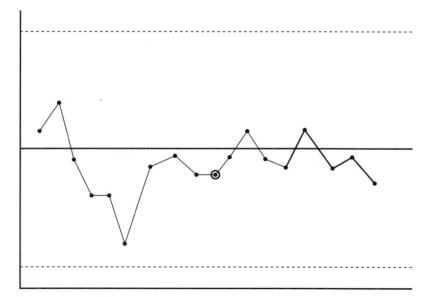

☐ In control ☑ Out of control

Reason: ___*Rule 4. Eight or*___

___*more consecutive points fall*___

___*below the centerline.*___

_____

_____

_____

_____

Control Chart Activity (Solution)–page 3

Instructions: Identify whether the processes documented below are in
control or out of control. Document your reasons.

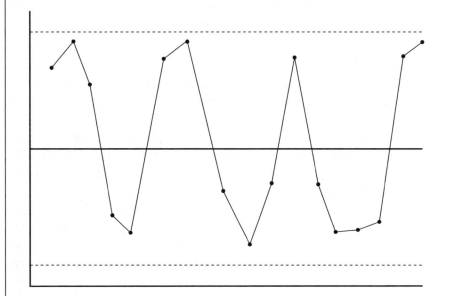

☐ In control ☑ Out of control

Reason: _Mixture_ _____

_____

_____

_____

_____

_____

_____

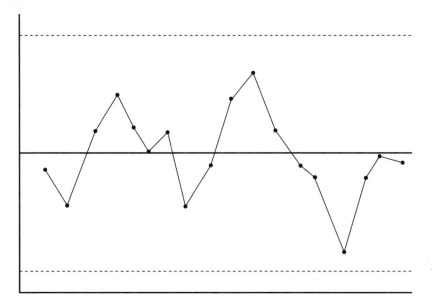

☑ In control ☐ Out of control

Reason: _____

_____

_____

_____

_____

_____

_____

Working with Out-of-Control Processes

At this point, you may be wondering, "What should I do when I have determined that a process is out-of-control?" You need to take action to identify and eliminate the special cause. What is different now that has caused the process to behave the way it is?

The purpose of chapter 12 is to provide a structured approach to problem solving. Since an out-of-control process is a problem, refer to the next chapter for specific techniques that can be used to identify and eliminate the special cause.

Before getting into the specific problem-solving techniques, there is one more important concept to introduce: process capability.

DETERMINING PROCESS CAPABILITY

PROCESS CAPABILITY

A measure of how well a process is performing compared to customer requirements. A process is said to be capable when its expected level of performance satisfies customer requirements.

Once a process is in control, you can predict how it will perform over time. Next, you would probably like to know if it can produce products and services that satisfy customer requirements.

A process is said to be capable if its expected level of performance satisfies customer requirements. Another way of saying a process is capable is that its control limits are within (inside) the customer requirements or specification limits. Refer to Figure 11.9.

In determining process capability, the first step is always determining if the process is in control. Look at the process shown in Figure 11.9, is the process in control? (It is in control since a nonrandom pattern is not present and none of the out-of-control rules have been violated.)

The next step is to look at the location of the control limits with respect to the customer requirements or specification limits. If the control limits are within the specification limits (as is the case in Figure 11.9), the

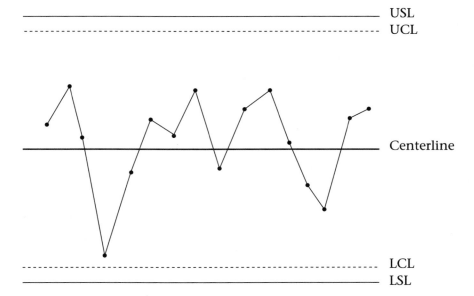

Figure 11.9. Process capability.

process is capable—you can expect the process to produce parts and services that satisfy customer requirements.

Different processes exhibit different levels of capability. Statisticians have developed methods to measure the capability of a process. For our purposes, we will rely on a visual analysis of the control charts. Figure 11.10 provides some examples of process capability.

The first process in the figure is not capable since the range of expected process performance (defined by the control limits) is outside of the specification limits (USL and LSL). In this process, you should expect the process to produce unsatisfactory products and services. Management must be made aware of such processes since removing common causes of variation almost always is management's responsibility.

The second process is capable of satisfying customer requirements. This is the state you have been working toward. In this case, you can expect the process to satisfy customer requirements. If a point exists beyond the customer's specification limits, you know it is due to a special cause—something unusual is happening.

The last process is very capable. Even if an out-of-control condition exists, the process will likely still satisfy the customer's requirements. In other words, you have not produced a bad part.

The benefits of achieving this state are somewhat controversial. Why should a process perform so much better than it needs to? The answer to this question lies in comparing the costs associated with achieving this

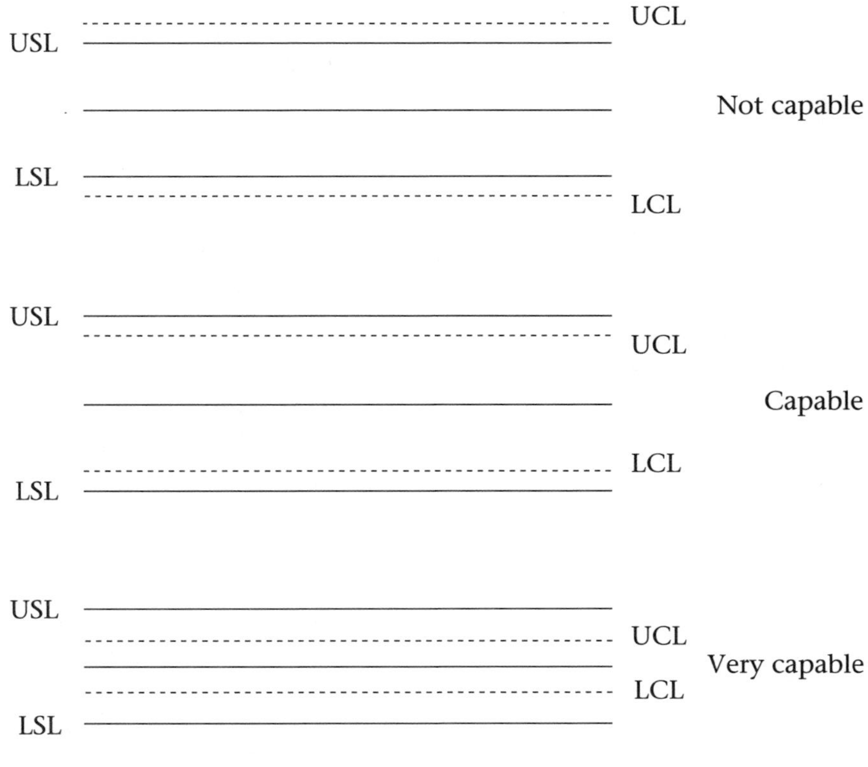

Figure 11.10. Process capability examples.

level of performance (minimal variation) and the associated benefits (remember, variation causes loss). Most companies answer this dilemma by deciding to focus their attention on other processes once the process being analyzed is in control and capable. Generally, it does not make much sense to continue improving a single process when many others are not even in control.

USING PROCESS MEASUREMENTS

Be careful. Developing measurements, collecting data, and analyzing results can all be nonvalue-added tasks if this is all that is done. The data must be used to manage the process. When you find out a process is out of control, search for and eliminate the special cause (more information on how to do this in chapter 12).

Process Measurements Must Be Timely

The information learned from collecting and analyzing process performance data must be timely so appropriate actions can be taken. The sooner a problem can be detected and addressed, the fewer products or services will be affected by the problem.

Display Process Measurements

Process measurements do little good stashed away in someone's desk. Making process measurements visible in a work area serves many benefits. First, the data are visible to all members of the team (all those involved with the process being measured). This visibility allows everyone to participate in the analysis.

The process measurements also can serve as a source of pride for the team. Charts visible in a work area demonstrate the team's commitment to process improvement. Favorable changes in process performance levels can also be visible for others to see. This type of enthusiasm can be contagious.

Use Measurement Data to Make Process Decisions

Process performance data allow decisions to be made based on facts—management by fact. You no longer need to make decisions based on hunches and guesses. Use the data to tell you what you need to know about process performance. Data analysis can be the basis for your decisions to hire another worker, stop purchasing from a specific vendor, buy another computer, and so forth.

I have participated in several meetings where a team's recommendations have been accepted because of the sound rationale presented based upon its data analysis. Recommendations accompanied by data are hard to refute.

The information resulting from process analysis also should be used to verify that changes implemented are having the desired effect. Do not shift your attention away from a specific process improvement until you have continued to monitor the data and verify that your action did improve the process. It is possible for a solution to have an adverse effect on the process or cause other performance problems.

SUMMARY

All of the activities performed as part of the *plan for customer satisfaction* and *understand processes* steps of the continuous process improvement cycle are conducted in preparation for the *measure performance* step. Collecting and properly analyzing meaningful process performance data allow the process to be managed by fact.

The result of this analysis probably will be the identification of problems to solve or improvements to implement. The final step of the cycle, *take action to improve,* provides a structured means for implementing improvements.

REVIEW QUESTIONS

Use the questions in Figure 11.11 to review your progress and make sure you are ready to continue on to the next chapter.

NOTES

1. Robert T. Amsden, Howard E. Butler, and Davida M. Amsden, *SPC Simplified: Practical Steps to Quality* (White Plains, N.Y.: Quality Resources, 1989).

2. Howard Gitlow, Shelley Gitlow, Alan Oppenheim, and Rosa Oppenheim, *Tools and Methods for the Improvement of Quality* (Homewood, Ill.: Irwin, 1989).

☐ Is the process in control or out of control?

☐ What identified the process as out of control?

☐ What is the special cause?

☐ Is the process capable?

☐ Are the team's recommendations supported by data?

Figure 11.11. Review questions.

SOLVE PROBLEMS

The result of measuring process performance often is the identification of problems to solve or other improvements to implement. The *take action to improve* step of the continuous process improvement cycle builds upon the previous cycle steps and provides a structured approach to problem solving.

OVERVIEW OF THE PROBLEM-SOLVING APPROACH

Problem solving requires a structured approach. Without such an approach, efforts often are random and/or misguided. The five steps listed in Figure 12.1 can be applied to any type of problem, regardless of its complexity.

Complexity of the problem does, however, have an effect on how formally the steps should be followed. The more complex or difficult the problem, the more rigidly the steps should be followed. Simpler problems, while not requiring the formality of following each of the steps, should still utilize the concepts present in the approach.

The remainder of this chapter describes the steps in detail.

DEFINE THE PROBLEM

A specifically defined problem provides focus to your problem-solving efforts. So, the first step in solving a problem is to define exactly what the problem is. It is possible to set out to solve what the problem is thought to be, only to find out later that the wrong problem is being addressed.

The answers to the questions listed in Figure 12.2 define the problem.

1. Define the problem	2. Identify the root cause	3. Select the best solution	4. Develop an action plan	5. Verify plan results
• What is the problem?	• List possible causes	• Identify selection criteria	• Document planned activities	• Monitor implementation results
• Where is the problem occurring?	• Test possible causes	• Generate solution ideas	• Identify potential problems	
• When is the problem occurring?		• Compare solution ideas	• Revise the plan	
		• Analyze risks	• Follow the plan	
		• Select the best solution		

Figure 12.1. The five-step problem-solving approach.

Answers to each of these questions reveals different, additional information necessary to completely define the problem. The more specific the answers, the more tightly defined the problem is. The aim of this step is to bound the problem by defining it as succinctly as possible. This focus allows future activities to be directed toward solving the problem at hand.

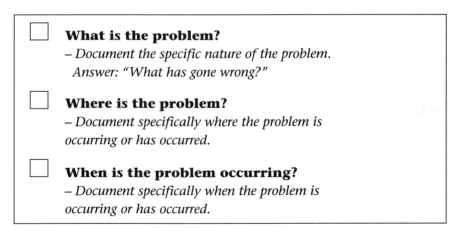

☐ **What is the problem?**
  – *Document the specific nature of the problem.*
  Answer: "What has gone wrong?"

☐ **Where is the problem?**
  – *Document specifically where the problem is occurring or has occurred.*

☐ **When is the problem occurring?**
  – *Document specifically when the problem is occurring or has occurred.*

Figure 12.2. Problem definition questions.

What Is the Problem?

The starting point in defining the problem is to specifically describe the problem. Examples include

- The roof is leaking.
- The copy machine is jammed.
- The checkbook does not balance with the bank statement.
- The trend in the data reveals that the process is out of control.
- The number of new accounts has declined by 20 percent over the last year.

Remember, the problem should be described as specifically as possible! For example, it is not clear enough to say there is a problem with the copy machine. As we have all experienced, copy machines can have many different problems. The machine could be jammed, it could be out of paper, it may need to be filled with toner, it may require some type of maintenance, and so on. If the problem is that the machine is jammed, say so.

Information from a Control Chart. An out-of-control condition on a control chart points to an unusual situation. The performance of the process is significantly different than what you expected—either better or worse. When the performance is better than expected, you should find out what caused this pleasant situation and try to duplicate it. If the performance is worse than expected, you have a problem.

When a problem exists, useful information about what the problem is can be gained by considering what signaled the out-of-control situation. Use the table on page 194 to help answer the "what" question. By answering the questions in the table, your "what" portion of the definition will be complete.

For example, knowing the duration of a cycle identified on a control chart helps define the problem. A cycle lasting several days is a very different situation from one repeated several times a day. Knowing and documenting the cycle duration as part of the *what* portion of the definition adds clarity to the problem definition.

Where Is the Problem Occurring?

Additional clarity can be achieved by documenting where the problem is occurring as part of the problem definition. There are two levels of "where" questions.

Geographic Location. First, describe where geographically the problem is occurring. This step may require some research to identify everywhere the problem is occurring. Take the time, as the information gained can be very helpful in defining (and ultimately solving) the problem. If a copy machine is jammed, where is the machine (on the ninth floor, in

Out-of-control indicator	Questions to ask
Nonrandom patterns	
Cycle	• What is the duration of each cycle? • What is the height of each cycle?
Mixture	• What is the difference between the levels? • How many points are observed at each level?
Shift	• What is the difference between the levels? • Is the shift toward or away from the preferred value?
Trend	• Is the trend upward or downward? • What is the slope of the trend?
Out-of-control rules	• Which of the rules has been violated? • Do the offending points lie above or below the centerline?

the sales office, outside the lunchroom, etc.)? Be as specific as possible, details can help pinpoint the problem. Other examples include

- Every office on the second floor
- On the north side of the building
- Every Ford dealership in Arkansas
- In the northwest branch office

Local Location. Secondly, describe where locally the problem is occurring. Where within the copy machine is the paper jammed (for example, in the paper tray or in the output sorter)? Other examples include

- The lock on the front, passenger side door
- The "7" key on the telephone
- On the first page of each statement

When Is the Problem Occurring?

Finally, by listing when the problem occurs, the definition of the problem is complete. The "when" question may be answered by a specific day, time, month, weather condition, season, or event (such as a shift change). This question will be answered differently depending on whether the problem has occurred only once, or if it is an ongoing problem.

Single Occurrence Problems. For a single occurrence, the answer to the "when" question should document the day and time the problem occurred. It also is helpful to document what was happening at the time of the problem. Be as thorough as possible. Some events may seem insignificant or unrelated to the problem, but record everything you can think of—you never know what will be meaningful in your problem solving efforts. Answers may include the following:

- Thursday, December 17 at 2:30 P.M.
- Right after Tom washed the floor
- As soon as the lights were turned off
- After supplies were received from a new vendor
- As soon as the typewriter was plugged in

Recurring Problems. For recurring problems, answers to the "when" question document the events that seem to be related to the problem. Answers may include

- At 3:00 P.M. every day
- Every Friday afternoon
- Every time it rains
- At every shift change
- Every time Bob makes the coffee
- Only when the outside temperature exceeds 100° F.
- On the first day of each month
- Only when Mary is absent
- Every time paper is loaded into the copy machine

Using Control Chart Notes. Control chart notes are a good source for determining when a problem is occurring. Because notes document special events taking place at the time of the measurement, they should provide clues about what was happening when the problem occurred. For example, a note may document when a new secretary started work, new software was installed, the regular employee was gone on vacation, and so on. These notes may provide the information you need to know to determine what unique events were occurring at the time of the problem (out-of-control condition).

The Problem Definition Worksheet

Use the problem definition worksheet on page 197 to record the answers to the what, where, and when questions.

Example. Study the completed problem definition worksheet for someone having trouble getting their car started (see page 198). Notice that as much information is recorded as possible. It is impossible to know at this point what information may be useful, so list everything you think may help define the problem.

IDENTIFY THE ROOT CAUSE

Permanently solving a problem requires you to get at the root of the problem. The second step in solving a problem is identifying the root cause. The root cause of a problem is the cause that itself has no cause. It is possible for a problem to have more than one root cause.

By identifying and correcting the root cause of the problem, the *root* or source of the problem is addressed and eliminated.

The Importance of Determining the Root Cause

Consider the example of an investigator assigned to a criminal case. The investigator's job is to understand the crime, then identify and follow the trail of clues back to the guilty party. Solving a problem is similar. The aim in problem solving is to understand (or define) the problem, then identify the trail of causes that leads to the real culprit—the root cause.

Periodically, newspapers report stories of someone being freed from jail after being wrongly convicted of a crime. In these cases, the investigator somehow misinterpreted a clue or did not completely follow the trail of clues all the way to point to the real criminal. The real criminal may continue to break the law while the wrong person was tried and jailed. The similarity between criminal investigations and problem solving continues. Addressing the wrong cause not only can be a waste of resources, but can allow the original problem to continue occurring.

ROOT CAUSE
The cause that itself has no cause; the source of the problem.

List Possible Causes

An analysis of the problem description provides a starting point for listing possible causes. Start by explaining why the problem

- Is *what* it is and nothing else
- Happens only *where* it does and not at any other location
- Happens only *when* it does and not at any other time

Answers to these questions may begin to provide hints about the cause of the problem.

For example, consider the information gained about the cause of a problem once you realize it (whatever the problem is) is happening only

Problem Definition Worksheet

DESCRIPTION

WHAT is the problem? (Describe what has gone wrong.)	_____ _____ _____ _____ _____ _____ _____
WHERE is the problem occurring? (Describe where the problem is occurring—list both the geographic and local location.)	_____ _____ _____ _____ _____ _____
WHEN is the problem occurring? (Describe when the problem was first noticed and the events that seem to have an impact on when the problem occurs.)	_____ _____ _____ _____ _____ _____

Problem Definition Worksheet

DESCRIPTION

WHAT is the problem? (Describe what has gone wrong.)	My car will not start. It sounds like it is starting to "turn over," but it does not start.
WHERE is the problem occurring? (Describe where the problem is occurring—list both the geographic and local location.)	In the office parking lot and in the parking lot at the mall.
WHEN is the problem occurring? (Describe when the problem was first noticed and the events that seem to have an impact on when the problem occurs.)	The problem started last week. Since then we have had very hot, dry weather. I notice the problem most in the afternoon.

in the offices on the north side of the building (where) every time it rains (when). No other office is experiencing the problem, and the offices with the problem only notice it when it rains. Analysis of this information often results in a list of possible causes.

Descriptions of other helpful methods follow.

Creative Thinking. The methods of creative thinking are especially helpful in problem solving. One of the uses of creative thinking is the identification of potential root causes. Without using the techniques of creative thinking, problem solvers are likely to revert to familiar causes. Identification of a problem's root cause often requires a different way of thinking. How many times have you been faced with solving a problem that was supposedly solved at least once before? This situation is more common than we would probably like to admit. The reason for this is really quite simple, thinking of new ideas for problem causes and solutions can be difficult. This is why training in the techniques of creative thinking is so important. Chapter 13 provides instructions for specific techniques that may be used in expanding the list of possible root causes.

Ask Why. Why does the problem exist? Asking "Why?" several times can sometimes help lead to the identification of the root cause of the problem. (This technique may be painfully familiar to parents of preschool children—kids seem to have a knack for asking "Why?". Maybe this is another chance for us to learn something from them.) Be persistent. Keep asking: "Why has this happened?" As a rule of thumb, answer why at least five times before you think about considering the cause to be a potential root cause. Figure 12.3 shows an example of how this simple technique can be used.

In this example, it is easy to assume Mary is the cause of the problem. Without following a structured approach to problem solving, one may conclude the solution is to reprimand Mary. In fact, the problem has little if anything to do with her, the real cause to address is the problem with the new software.

Cause/Effect Diagrams. Cause/effect diagrams are used to identify possible causes of a problem and their relationships with each other. Stated another way, cause/effect diagrams document the causes of an effect. Cause/effect diagrams also are called fishbone diagrams (because of their shape) or Ishikawa diagrams (after their inventor, Kaoru Ishikawa). (See Figure 12.4.)

The power of a cause/effect diagram is in its ability to force problem solvers to think of possible causes in a variety of categories. In this way, possible causes are identified that otherwise may not have been suggested.

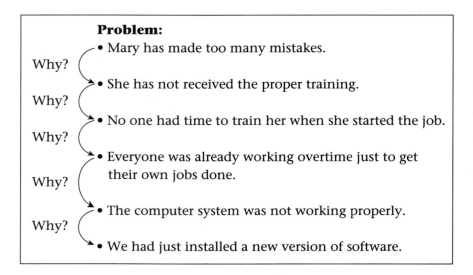

Figure 12.3. The "asking why" technique.

CAUSE/EFFECT DIAGRAM

A problem-solving tool used to identify possible causes of a problem and their relationships with each other. Forces problem solvers to think of possible causes in a variety of categories. Also called fishbone diagrams or Ishikawa diagrams.

There is no right choice for the categories used as the bones in the diagram (Methods, Machine, Human Resources, and Materials in the figure). Just remember that the purpose of the categories is to stretch the scope of possible causes to be considered.

The following steps are provided as guidelines in constructing cause/effect diagrams.

1. Write the problem (or effect) being solved on the right side of the paper. Use information from the problem definition to describe the problem. Draw a box around the statement (this box will be the head of the fish) and draw a horizontal arrow pointing into the box. This arrow is the spine of the fish.

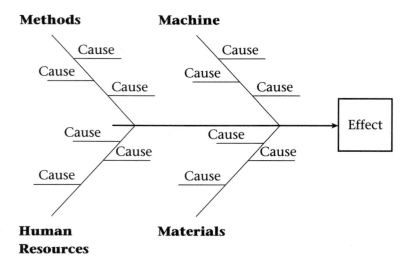

Figure 12.4. A cause/effect diagram.

2. Identify the major causes of the problem. This step is very important because these major causes form the structure of the diagram. These causes are listed at the end of diagonal lines (the fish bones) drawn from the spine. It is often difficult to identify the major causes of a problem until further analysis has been performed. A common method of identifying major causes is to use common, universal major causes. One such list is called the 6 Ms and includes Man, Machine, Material, Method, Measurement, and Mother Nature (the environment or weather conditions).

3. Identify all of the possible causes that can lead to the major cause listed at the end of the bones. List these causes on horizontal lines branching from the diagonal major cause bones. Use brainstorming or any other creative thinking technique to identify all of the possible causes.

4. Continue step 3 to identify the causes of the causes just listed. At this point, a cause/effect diagram can get very crowded. Two options should be considered to continue further. First, a new cause/effect diagram could be constructed with one of the causes listed in step 3 listed as the effect. This new diagram could then serve as a means to identify the causes of this effect. This step could be continued for each cause identified in step 3. Figure 12.5 shows an example of this approach.

The second option is to consider using a relationship diagram.

RELATIONSHIP DIAGRAM

A graphic representation of the chain of events that result in a problem. Aids in identifying the root cause(s) of the problem.

Relationship Diagrams. Relationship diagrams provide a way of graphically showing the chain of events that result in a problem. These diagrams are especially helpful since rarely does a single event or cause result in a problem. Most of the time there are a series of interrelated events that cause the problem. In these cases, it is helpful to understand the sequence of events that lead to the problem. By following this trail back from the problem, the real sources or root causes of the problem can be identified.

The following steps are provided as guidelines in constructing relationship diagrams.

1. Write the problem statement in the center of a large piece of paper. Use the information from the problem definition to describe the problem. Circle the statement with a bold line.

2. Use brainstorming or any creative-thinking technique to identify the causes of the problem stated. Write the causes on the paper surrounding the problem statement. Circle each of the causes written.

Note: Consider using the causes listed on the cause/effect diagram created for the same problem as this first level of causes. Remember, the cause/effect diagram is very helpful in identifying causes because of the thinking required to identify causes in each of the major cause categories.

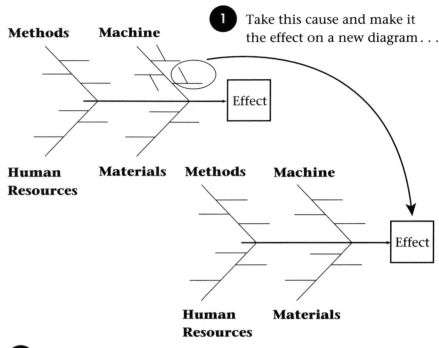

Figure 12.5. Using multiple cause/effect diagrams.

3. Draw arrows connecting the causes to their effect (arrows pointing from the cause to the effect). Frequently, a single cause can lead to many effects. In these cases, draw an arrow for each cause/effect relationship.

4. Identify the causes for each of the causes listed. Write and circle each cause on the paper near its effect.

Note: At this point, the diagram can become very messy. Don't worry too much about the appearance. Just make sure you (and everyone involved) can tell where the arrows point.

5. Repeat steps 3 and 4 until no additional causes can be identified.

6. Analyze all causes that have no arrows pointing into them. These are candidates for the root cause.

The result of this step should be the identification of possible root causes to consider or analyze further. An example of using a relationship diagram to determine the root cause of a classroom's lack of student participation is shown in Figure 12.6.

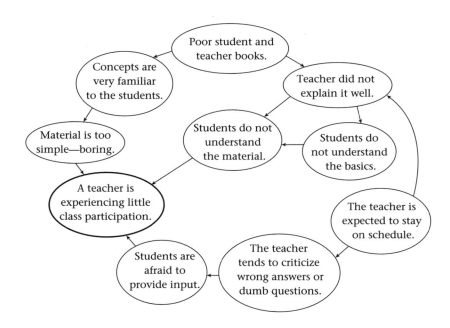

Figure 12.6. A relationship diagram.

In this example, the relationship diagram identifies two possible root causes (bubbles with no arrows pointing in): "Poor student and teacher books" and "The teacher is expected to stay on schedule." Further analysis of the class participation problem should focus on these possible causes.

These diagrams can get very large—that is a good sign! Large diagrams indicate the trail between problem and root cause(s) is being documented. Don't let the size of your paper (or any physical resource) limit your analysis. Get large flip pads, rolls of butcher paper, or tape pages together. Do whatever you need to identify the root cause.

Test Possible Causes

Testing the possible causes you have identified before proceeding can save you from trying to address the wrong cause. So, at this point it is a good idea to compare the possible causes identified to the problem definition developed earlier. The cause or causes being considered must be able to account for the problem as described in the problem definition (what, where, and when). Can the causes under consideration address all portions of the problem definition? Carefully consider the following questions for each cause.

- Can the cause explain why the problem is *what* is being experienced *and nothing else?*
- Can the cause explain why the problem is happening *where* it is *and nowhere else?*
- Can the cause explain why the problem is happening *when* it is *and at no other time?*

If the answer to any of these questions is no, then the cause under consideration is suspect. Time spent addressing a cause that cannot pass the test is wasted.

Pay particular attention to the last part of each of the questions. Refer to the *when* question, for example. Make sure the cause explains only when the problem is noticed, and no other time! If the cause can explain the time the problem occurs, but also would cause the problem to be noticed at other times when the problem is not occurring, eliminate the cause from consideration.

For example, "road under construction" may be considered as a cause for an ongoing employee tardiness problem (we all know road construction can significantly affect the amount of time required to get somewhere). Because this cause cannot explain when the problem is occurring (the employee was late even before the road was under construction), it should not be considered. If the employee and management agree to blame the road construction for the tardiness problem, will the problem be eliminated even after the road construction is completed? No, because a solution was implemented for the wrong root cause. Causes that cannot account for the problem as described by the problem definition must be eliminated.

Take this step seriously, it can save you a lot of time. Done correctly, this test will keep you from implementing solutions to the wrong cause.

Continue with the steps described in the remainder of this chapter for the causes that pass this test.

SELECT THE BEST SOLUTION

After the root cause of the problem has been identified, the next step is to select the best solution for the problem being experienced. This section introduces and discusses the steps required for selecting the best solution for the problem being addressed. Figure 12.7 shows the steps involved in selecting the best solution.

The reasons for following these steps and specific how-to information follow.

Identify Selection Criteria

What is important to you in selecting the best solution to implement? How will you make the selection? These are two key questions to answer. The criteria that will be used to select the best solution need to be identified and listed. Identify the factors that are important in segregating possible alternatives. All solution ideas generated in the next step will be compared against this criteria to identify the ones that best satisfy these factors.

List the Criteria. Identify and list all of the criteria that will be used to select the best solution alternative. These selection criteria represent the

1. **Identify the selection criteria**
   to document the factors to be used in the selection.

2. **Generate solution ideas**
   to consider all possible solution options.

3. **Compare solution ideas**
   to identify the "best" solution.

4. **Analyze the risks**
   to consider potential obstacles to implementation.

5. **Select the best overall solution**
   to implement the solution offering the best combination of performance and acceptable risk.

Figure 12.7. Select the best solution steps.

SELECTION CRITERIA

The criteria used to select the best solution. The factors that are important in segregating possible alternatives.

requirements for the solution that eventually will get selected. Selection criteria may include these characteristics.

- Cost
- Size
- Delivery schedule
- Appearance (color, format, and so on)
- Location

Let's consider an example. A local mortgage company has noticed that many of its customers are refinancing their loans with other mortgage companies. Even though they offer competitive rates, the number of active loans from their company has dropped from 150 to 115 in just the last six months. Analysis of the problem has revealed that one of the root causes is the poor service offered to customers. The customer service department of the company has received numerous complaints about the time required to talk to a service representative to obtain information on their mortgage. Their customers complain that when they try to call for information, they either get a busy signal or are placed on hold "forever." In trying to identify the best solution to this problem, they may identify the following selection criteria.

- Lowest purchase/implementation cost
- Provide fastest response to customers
- Provide accurate account status information
- Project a "we care about you" attitude
- Provide up-to-date payment information
- Provide latest interest rate information

The selection criteria development worksheet is provided as a means for documenting your criteria list. Specifically list all of your decision criteria (see page 207). Ignore the "Weight" and "Mandatory?" columns for now.

Note: The worksheets in this section are provided solely to help reinforce the concepts of the decision making model presented. Use of the worksheets is not mandatory. Many find the structure provided by the worksheets to be helpful, while others find them limiting. Use them if they are helpful, don't use them if they are not. The same caution applies to the use of the numbers used to represent the weights and scores. Assigning the numbers obviously is not an exact science (for example, how do you really know whether to assign a seven or an eight?). Use the results of the mathematics as a guide in your decision making. Remember, the concepts introduced are important, the method you select to carry out the process is not as important (as long as it is compatible with the concepts).

Assign Criteria Weights. Not all of the selection criteria are equally important. Because some of the criteria are more important than others, a method for assigning weights to the criteria must be used. A 10-point scale provides the level of detail needed to differentiate between different importance levels. Review the criteria and assign a 10 to the criterion that is the most important. (It is possible to have two or more equally important criteria that are all assigned a weight of 10.) Review all of the other criteria, and assign a weight relative to the one(s) assigned a 10. A criterion that is important, but not quite as important as the one(s) assigned a 10 would receive a 9. One that is about half as important would be assigned a weight of 5, and so on. Assign a weight to each of the criteria and record the weights on the selection criteria development worksheet.

Avoid the tendency to assign high weights (7–10) to all or most of the criteria. We all tend to think everything is important, especially when we are close to the situation. A clustered group of criteria weights can make it difficult to differentiate between solution alternatives later. Carefully analyze each criterion to select an appropriate weight. It is a good idea to review your weights after you have completed the assignments to make sure they are not top-heavy.

Identify Mandatory Requirements. You may have mandatory performance levels for some of the criteria. For example, one of your criterion may be lowest cost. But, you may have a not-to-exceed budget amount of $1000. This means, no matter how good the solution is, it will not be considered if it costs more than $1000. It is important to document any mandatory performance levels you have for the criteria. These manda-

Selection Criteria Development Worksheet

Criteria	Weight	Mandatory? (If the criteria are mandatory, describe the required level of performance.)
_____	_____	_____
_____	_____	_____
_____	_____	_____
_____	_____	_____
_____	_____	_____
_____	_____	_____
_____	_____	_____
_____	_____	_____
_____	_____	_____

tory requirements will be used as a filter to eliminate any solution ideas that do not pass the test. Record your mandatory requirements, if any, on the selection criteria development worksheet. Examples of mandatory requirements include

- Provides response within 15 seconds
- Compatible with existing computer equipment
- Available within three days

Be careful in establishing the mandatory requirements. They can serve as excellent guides to selecting the solution idea that best satisfies your requirements, but they also can eliminate ideas from consideration. If you state that the solution must cost less than $1000, you better be sure. What if an idea that satisfies all of the rest of your criteria costs $1100? Would you consider the idea? If you list $1000 as a mandatory requirement, the idea will be eliminated from consideration.

It may seem like any criterion with a corresponding mandatory requirement should automatically be assigned a weight of 10. This is not necessarily the case. Continuing the example above, assume you have a mandatory requirement that the solution cost less than $1000. You may have some requirements that are more important to you than cost (as long as the cost is less than $1000). The length of the warranty may be the most important criterion to you (therefore assigned a 10) and cost a lesser criterion (maybe a 7 or 8).

Example. The selection criteria development worksheet on page 209 has been completed for the mortgage company suffering from customer complaints about the time required to get information on their mortgage.

Generate Solution Ideas

A key step in selecting the best problem solution is the generation of as many solution ideas as possible. This is the time to let your creative juices flow. It can be too easy to jump to conclusions and select the first solution that comes to mind. Several possible solutions should be considered. Make sure ideas are requested from several experts on the subject, the creative thinkers within your company or department, and even some outsiders who may suggest ideas that others very close to the problem may not consider. The more ideas suggested the better!

Use brainstorming or any of the other creative-thinking techniques described in chapter 13 to generate solution ideas. Don't give up too easily in preparing the list. Often, the best ideas are not the first ones a team will think of. The first few ideas often are obvious alternatives that may have been tried in the past.

Selection Criteria Development Worksheet

Criteria	Weight	Mandatory? (If the criteria are mandatory, describe the required level of performance.)
Accurate account status information	10	*100% accurate*
Up-to-date payment information	8	
Latest interest rate information	7	
Fastest response to customers	6	
Project a caring attitude	6	
Lowest cost	5	*total cost < $35,000*
Easy implementation	3	

Compare Solution Ideas

The next step is to compare all of the solution ideas generated against the criteria already identified. The best solutions are those that most completely satisfy the selection criteria. This comparison takes place in two steps.

Check Against Mandatory Requirements. First, rule out any solution ideas that do not satisfy all of the mandatory requirements. Any idea that does not satisfy a mandatory requirement should not be considered further. By definition, a solution idea cannot be accepted if it does not satisfy all mandatory requirements. So, if one of your mandatory requirements is the implementation cost must be less than $35,000, research the implementation cost for each of the solution ideas you have identified. Any that cost more than $35,000 should be eliminated from further consideration.

Check Against Selection Criteria. Secondly, score the ability of each solution to satisfy each of the criteria. The solution comparison worksheet is provided as a means to record the information from the previous steps and to compare the solution ideas against each other to begin selecting the best solution to implement. The worksheet has room to compare two solution ideas. In most cases, you will have more than two ideas to compare, so use additional copies of the form for additional ideas (mark through ideas 1 and 2 and record them as 3 and 4). Use the following steps as guidelines in completing the worksheet (see page 212).

1. Record the criteria and their corresponding weights down the first two columns (from the selection criteria development worksheet).

2. Record the solution ideas being considered across the top.

3. Analyze the first criterion. Assign a score of 10 to the solution idea that best satisfies this criterion (it is possible to have two solution ideas that equally satisfy the criterion so they both get a 10).

4. Analyze each of the other solution ideas for this criterion. Determine how each of the other ideas compare to the idea(s) assigned a 10. Assign each of the solution ideas a score relative to the 10. An idea that satisfies the criterion about half as much as the one assigned a 10 should receive a score of 5. Get input from everyone involved. Do not worry too much about whether to assign a 7 or an 8, the difference is not really that significant. Do spend time discussing the cases where some suggest a score of 3 while others suggest an 8. Discuss the reasoning behind the suggested scores and come to a decision by consensus. Continue this step until each solution idea has a score recorded for the criterion.

5. Repeat steps 3 and 4 for all of the remaining criteria. At the completion of this step, every solution idea should have a score recorded for each criterion.

6. Calculate a weighted score for each solution idea and criterion. For each criterion, multiply the weight (column A) by the score (column B or C) and record the result in the "Wt. Score" column.

7. Total each of the "Wt. Score" columns at the bottom of the page.

Example. Let's continue with the mortgage company example to see how the solution comparison worksheet can be used to compare possible solution ideas (see page 213). The criteria and their corresponding weights documented on the selection criteria development worksheet have been recorded in the first two columns. The team analyzing the problem has identified many possible solution ideas. For the purpose of this example, two ideas have been recorded across the top of the worksheet.

For the first criterion ("Accurate account status information"), solution idea 2 was deemed to best satisfy the criterion. It received a score of 10. Solution idea 1 was almost as good at satisfying the criterion, so it received a score of 9. For the second criterion ("Up-to-date payment information"), both solution ideas can satisfy equally, so they both received a score of 10. This analysis continued for the remaining criteria.

From this analysis, solution 1 (hiring an additional service representative) seems like the best idea because its score at the bottom of the page is higher than solution 2. But, the risks associated with implementing these ideas should be analyzed before selecting the solution to implement.

Analyze Risks Associated with Implementation

Before settling in on the best solution, the obstacles or risks associated with implementing the solution must be considered. The solution ideas that scored the highest during the comparison just performed should each be analyzed for risk. Ask, "What could go wrong?" Also, look at the criteria for which the idea received low ratings. Then, identify preventive actions that could be taken to reduce or eliminate the possibility of the risk occurring and/or contingent actions that could be taken in the event the risk does occur.

Take some time with this step. From experience, I know it is tempting not to take this step seriously. Realize the time spent now can save a lot of time (pain, anguish, embarrassment, and so on) later if the risk occurs.

I was once part of a small group responsible for selecting a vendor for a critical piece of equipment to be used in a new, automated assembly line. After a considerable amount of time invested in identifying and analyzing potential vendors, we selected the best product. One problem was that we did not consider the risks associated with selecting the company. The company with the best product was a very small company

Solution Comparison Worksheet

		Solution ideas			
		1. _____		2. _____	
Criteria	A. Weight	B. Score	B × A Weight score	C. Score	C × A Weight score
_____	____	____	____	____	____
_____	____	____	____	____	____
_____	____	____	____	____	____
_____	____	____	____	____	____
_____	____	____	____	____	____
_____	____	____	____	____	____
_____	____	____	____	____	____
_____	____	____	____	____	____
_____	____	____	____	____	____

Solution Comparison Worksheet

COMPLETED

Criteria	A. Weight	Solution ideas 1. *Additional rep.* B. Score	B × A Weight score	2. *Computer-voice* C. Score	C × A Weight score
Accurate accounts status information	10	9	90	10	100
Up-to-date payment information	8	10	80	10	80
Latest interest rate information	7	10	70	10	70
Fastest response to customers	6	7	42	10	60
Project a caring attitude	6	10	60	3	18
Lowest cost	5	6	30	10	50
Easy implementation	3	10	30	3	9
			402		387

and this was their first product. (The red lights and sirens are probably sounding in your head—it all seems so obvious, now.) We had all kinds of problems with the company and the product. The entire project was significantly delayed because of these problems. After several months, we had to switch vendors. All of this could have been eliminated, or at least the impact minimized, if we had taken the time to analyze the risks.

The risk analysis worksheet provides a structured way to anticipate the risks associated with implementing a solution being considered. Follow the guidelines below in completing the risk analysis worksheet (see page 215).

1. Document the solution being considered for implementation at the top of the worksheet.

2. Identify the risks (or obstacles) associated with implementing the solution. Make a thorough list; try to think of everything that could go wrong. The time spent now trying to anticipate what could go wrong probably will smooth implementation greatly.

3. Document actions that could be taken to prevent the risk from occurring in the preventive action column. What steps could be built into the implementation plan to eliminate the problem from ever occurring?

4. Document actions that could be taken in the event the risk does occur to minimize its impact in the contingent action column. Some risks either cannot be avoided entirely (like lightning) or are so unlikely that you may not want to put steps in place to eliminate them. In these cases, it is worth the time to plan what will be done in case the event does happen.

Example.   The risk analysis worksheet on page 215 has been completed to show what risks may be associated with hiring a new service representative for the mortgage company. The risks associated with implementing any of the top-scoring ideas should be analyzed. Because this is just an example, the risks for only one solution idea are analyzed.

Select the Best Overall Solution

The solution that provides the best combination of performance and acceptable risk should be selected. Should you select the solution idea that scored the highest, even though you have identified several elements of risk? Or, should you select the idea that may not have scored as high, but is much safer? This is a judgment call that you will have to make. You must balance performance against risk. How much risk are

Risk Analysis Worksheet

Solution: _____

Risk	Preventive action	Contingent action
_____	_____	_____
	_____	_____
	_____	_____
_____	_____	_____
	_____	_____
	_____	_____
_____	_____	_____
	_____	_____
	_____	_____
_____	_____	_____
	_____	_____
	_____	_____
_____	_____	_____
	_____	_____
	_____	_____

Risk Analysis Worksheet

Solution: _Hire an additional service representative_

Risk	Preventive action	Contingent action
Rep. may not be polite	_—offer customer service training_ _—test for politeness in job interviews_	_—send apology card_
Trained worker may quit	_—show appreciation_ _—recognize outstanding performance_	_—be prepared to promote from within_
People get sick/miss work	_—offer complete benefits package_ _—recognize those with excellent attendance records_	_—have employees on call to fill in_

you willing to accept? How much risk are you comfortable with? How likely is the risk? What is the impact of the event should it actually occur? The aim of the previous steps is to provide all of the information necessary for you to select the best solution.

DEVELOP AN ACTION PLAN

An often forgotten part of problem solving is the development of an action plan—a document listing the actions that need to be performed for success. All of the work performed up to this point can be wasted if the implementation of the selected solution is not systematic. This section describes the purpose and methods for developing an action plan for systematically implementing a solution to a problem.

Document Planned Activities

List the activities that need to be performed to solve the problem. For each activity, list

- The specific task to be performed in a manner that is measurable (Is the task complete or not? What percent complete is the task?)
- The individual or team responsible for performing the task
- The time frame in which the task is to be performed (include both planned start and completion dates, if appropriate)

A convenient method for documenting and providing status of activities is a Gantt or milestone chart. The objectives should be further analyzed to identify potential problems during implementation.

Identify Obstacles

Take the time to anticipate problems with the implementation plan. After the original plan has been completed (a plan is never really complete since it should always be updated to include current activities), the planned tasks should be reviewed to identify high-risk areas or obstacles. The best time to find and address potential problems is before they happen. What could go wrong during implementation of the plan? This type of proactive approach allows the implementation plan to contain the actions necessary to eliminate or minimize the effect of these obstacles.

Identify obstacles by reviewing the activities documented in the plan to determine which could be sources of problems. Use the suggestions from Figure 12.8 to begin your analysis.

For the critical plan steps identified, answer the following questions.

- What events might cause this activity to fail?
- How likely is the event to occur?
- If the event does occur, how serious is the impact?

Look for objectives that

☐ Require a specific, specialized skill

☐ Have a tight schedule

☐ Are assigned to new or inexperienced employees

☐ Rely on new or untested methods

☐ Require coordination of several people or departments

☐ Involve a complex technology or method

☐ Require a skill, machine, or any resource from outside the organization

☐ Rely on the use of old or unreliable equipment

Figure 12.8. Potential obstacle identification suggestions.

Activities with an unacceptable level of risk should be further analyzed. Determine the likely causes of the events and build solutions to these causes into the plan.

There are two types of actions: preventive actions aimed to keep a problem from occurring, and contingent actions aimed to minimize the effect should a problem exist.

PREVENTIVE ACTIONS

Actions that can be taken *now* to prevent the problem from happening later.

Plan Preventive Actions. Planning preventive actions minimizes the chance the problem will occur. The aim is to decide what can be done now to prevent the problem from happening later. Examples of preventive actions include rescheduling the tasks to allow more time for a risky task, assigning an experienced employee to help an inexperienced employee, and allowing more time and resources to test a new method.

CONTINGENT ACTIONS

Actions to be taken in the event a problem does occur. Minimizes the impact of the problem.

Plan Contingent Actions. Some problems just cannot be prevented. For these problems, develop contingent actions to be taken if the problem does occur. Think how you will react if the problem occurs. The purpose of these actions is to minimize the impact of the problem in the event that it does happen.

Revise the Plan

Since the preventive and contingent actions identified in the previous step were not part of the original plan, the plan needs to be updated to include these actions. This type of analysis strengthens a plan by proactively addressing potential problems.

Follow the Plan

Do it! Follow the steps called for in the plan. During execution of the plan, changes that need to be made to the plan may be identified. Make the changes. An up-to-date plan not only charts planned future activities, but records actual steps taken.

VERIFY THE SOLUTION RESULTS

A very important step in the problem-solving process is the verification of solution results. Has execution of the plan resulted in the desired outcome? Did the attempted solution fix the problem?

Monitor the success of the solution implementation to ensure the results are as planned. Avoid the temptation to leave the problem behind since it has been solved. The problem is not really solved until you are absolutely convinced it will not surface again.

SUMMARY

Taking action to improve work processes requires a systematic approach to problem solving. This chapter has provided a systematic problem solving approach and identified several techniques to be applied to determine and eliminate the root cause of a problem. The steps to follow in making a decision also have been covered.

Key elements of any problem-solving effort are identifying the root cause and generating a list of possible solution ideas. Both of these steps can be greatly aided by the application of creative thinking techniques. Chapter 13 presents methods anyone can use to generate creative ideas.

REVIEW QUESTIONS

Use the questions in Figure 12.9 to review your progress and make sure you are ready to continue on to the next chapter.

☐	How was the root cause identified?
☐	Were multiple solution possibilities considered?
☐	How was the best solution determined?
☐	What selection criteria were used?
☐	What risks were identified?
☐	What actions have been planned to eliminate or minimize the impact of the risks?
☐	Does the selected solution completely address the root cause?
☐	Is the process still monitored to verify solution results?

Figure 12.9. Review questions

USE CREATIVE-THINKING TECHNIQUES

Few people consider themselves to be creative, but almost everyone agrees that creativity is very helpful (if not necessary) in problem solving.

The purpose of this chapter is to provide a way for noncreative people to experience the benefits of creative thinking as applied to problem solving. First, the role of creative thinking in problem solving is discussed, then specific techniques for creative thinking are introduced.

THE ROLE OF CREATIVE THINKING

Creative thinking may have an obvious link to problem solving, but exploring the reasons behind this link will provide helpful background information.

Escape from Patterns

Have you ever felt in a rut? Have you ever had difficulty thinking of new ideas and wondered why? The answer is in your mind and the way it works. Your mind is a pattern-making system; it creates and looks for patterns. Sometimes you need to do something different to break out of your mold. The creative-thinking techniques introduced later provide a means to escape from your existing patterns.

Provide a Means for Restructuring

The patterns our minds make are strongly influenced by the sequence in which events occur. As our minds absorb information, the pieces are placed and the pattern is created. A pattern may develop in one way, but had all of the information been available at the same time (rather than gradually over time), the pattern may have been quite different. Sometimes, the information needs to be restructured to create a better and more effective pattern.

A simple example will help demonstrate this point. I will provide you with some letters, one at a time. Your task is to make a single word from all of the letters provided so far. Take a little time now to complete the table below.

Letter	Word	
A	_____	(use only one letter)
T	_____	(use two letters)
C	_____	(use three letters)
S	_____	(use four letters)
K	_____	(use all five letters)

After the first four letters, most have formed the word CATS. The sequence in which the letters were introduced made it simple to create this pattern. The introduction of the fifth letter, though, required the existing pattern to be restructured to make the word STACK.

Everyone has probably heard the phrase: "We've always done it this way." This phrase is an obvious signal that a pattern exists. Just because a work process has always been performed a certain way does not mean that the method is the best way. In fact, with what we now know about patterns in our mind, we can say with great confidence that any method followed without revision for a long period of time is probably not the best method. As you gain more information about the process over time, you should analyze the process to identify a way to restructure the existing patterns. The techniques of creative thinking provide a means of restructuring existing patterns to create better patterns.

Challenge Assumptions

Assumptions are patterns that go unchallenged. As we have already seen, all patterns need to be challenged and analyzed for their usefulness. Everyone probably agrees with the need to challenge assumptions. The difficulty is in identifying the assumptions.

Creative-thinking techniques will generate many ideas, some of which will sound crazy or ridiculous. One reason the ideas seem crazy is that they conflict with the assumptions you have made. Probably the best way to challenge your assumptions is to think about why an idea seems crazy. Ask yourself

- What makes you think that the idea suggested is crazy?
- Why couldn't the idea work?

The answers to these questions may reveal your hidden assumptions. After you have identified your assumptions, challenge them! Challenge your assumptions by asking

- Are the assumptions accurate?
- Do the assumptions serve a constructive purpose, or do they just serve as limiters?

Be Careful in Challenging the Assumptions.   It is very easy to accept existing assumptions as accurate and necessary. In many cases, the assumptions are neither accurate nor necessary. Do you remember when personal computers were tools only for business people to use in their offices? Well, not any more! Now we use them at home to play games and balance our checkbooks, and take them on airplanes to do our work 20,000 feet above the ground.

Paradigms.   A new word recently has entered the business lexicon: *paradigm.* Joel Barker, the author and management consultant generally acknowledged as the paradigm expert, defines paradigm as

> A set of rules and regulations (written or unwritten) that does two things: (1) it establishes or defines boundaries; (2) it tells you how to behave inside the boundaries so as to be successful.[1]

This concept of paradigms fits well into a discussion of the need to challenge assumptions. Barker's message to American businesses is that they need to realize they are restricted by paradigms they may not even know exist. Management must identify and challenge the paradigms that govern the decisions they make.

An example of a simple paradigm may help. For years, I mowed my yard with a side-discharge lawnmower. With the bag attached, I was limited to how I approached a tree or fence and still mow as close as possible. After mowing the same yard with the same mower for several years, I developed certain patterns that I unconsciously followed in mowing the yard. When it was finally time to replace my mower, I purchased a "rear bagger" model. Even though I could now approach the trees and fences from either direction, what patterns do you think I followed? One day I finally found myself going out of the way to approach a tree from a certain direction when I realized I no longer needed to be limited to this approach (this realization, by the way, came a few months after I began using my new mower). I was initially bound by my *mowing paradigm.* Only after I challenged my assumptions about how I needed to mow my yard was I able to use a much more efficient approach.

Challenging Assumptions May Not Be Popular. Challenging assumptions is not always the popular thing to do. Do you remember from your high school science class how Copernicus was ridiculed for stating that the sun, not the Earth, was the center of our universe? (He was challenging the ideas that had been dogmatically accepted since Aristotle.) You may find some members of management are resistant to your challenges of existing assumptions. After all, they may think, the methods worked well enough for them to get promoted.

TECHNIQUES

Some say creativity cannot be taught. This saying may be true (I'm not going to argue the point one way or the other), but techniques that can be applied to generate creative ideas most certainly can be taught. Several techniques for creative thinking will be discussed.

Application

There are two primary uses for creative-thinking techniques within problem solving: identifying possible causes and identifying possible solutions. The focus is different for these two uses.

While trying to identify possible causes, your focus is on the problem as defined in your problem definition (what, where, and when). After the possible causes have been identified, your focus shifts to identifying possible solutions for the causes. The following techniques can be applied for either use.

Brainstorming

Brainstorming is a common and effective creative-thinking technique. Brainstorming is a way to get a large number of ideas from a group in a short period of time. Participants use their collective experiences and points of view to generate ideas. Follow these steps to conduct a brainstorming session.

BRAINSTORMING

An effective creative thinking technique. Used to get a large number of ideas from a group in a short period of time.

---

1. Announce the purpose of the meeting to everyone on the team. In problem solving, the purpose of the meeting will be either to generate a list of possible causes or solutions.

2. Describe the rules of brainstorming.

   a. Do not criticize the ideas suggested by others. Criticism may be conveyed verbally or by gesture. No criticism of any type can be allowed. No matter how bad or crazy the suggestion may seem, it may spark an idea for someone else. There will be time allocated later for questions and clarification.

   b. Encourage wild ideas. It is easier to tame wild ideas than it is to add excitement to old ideas. Do not hesitate to suggest an idea because you think it may be wild or silly. It might not only be a good idea, it may cause someone else to think of another idea. Remember, one of the aims of creative thinking is to escape from existing patterns. Wild ideas can help everyone break from these patterns. So, speak up.

    c. Each participant should suggest just one idea at a time. This will allow everyone to hear the idea and have a chance to participate. This rule can help keep one person from dominating the idea generation time.

3. Proceed around the room allowing everyone the chance to voice an idea.

4. Write all of the ideas suggested on a flip chart to allow everyone to see them as they are suggested. Post the chart paper around the room as each page is filled up.

5. Encourage everyone to participate. Anyone can pass their turn if they don't have an idea to suggest. Each pass is a one-time event, because they may have a suggestion the next time it is their turn. Continue these steps until everyone has suggested everything that comes to mind.

6. Once all of the ideas have been mentioned and recorded, take time to answer questions and clarify the suggestions as needed.

Brainstorming sessions can sometimes become dry. Many ideas may be suggested at first, but then it becomes increasingly difficult to think of new ideas to mention. This situation is common with brainstorming sessions. Brainstorming is an excellent way to get started with generating ideas, but often additional techniques are needed to get over this dry spell. The following techniques are provided as a way to continue to generate new ideas.

Reversals

REVERSAL
A creative thinking technique used to help problem solvers change the way they look at a problem. Elements of the problem description are reversed to help spark new ideas.

It is possible to become so familiar with a problem that identifying creative solutions can be difficult. Changing the way you look at a problem frequently provides new perspectives resulting in new ideas.

Consider the following situation. You are responsible for scheduling the games for a softball league tournament. There are 48 teams in the league. The tournament is single-elimination (a team is eliminated as soon as it loses one game). How many games must be played to determine the league champion? Take a few minutes to figure the answer. Most people try to figure out how many games are required to produce one winner. This approach works, but it can be time consuming to draw a diagram, pair the winning teams, and count the games. Another way to approach the problem is to reverse the situation. Instead of trying to figure out how many games must be played to produce a winner, figure out how many games must be played to produce 47 losers (since 47 teams must lose to determine the one winner). Since it takes 47 games to produce 47 losers, the answer can be achieved much faster.

Reversing part of the situation is one way to change the way you look at a problem. Follow these four steps to use the reversal technique.

1. Review the subject (either the problem definition or cause) to clarify in your mind the problem for which you are searching for ideas.

2. Write a reversal statement. There are two simple ways to create a reversal statement. One method is to substitute a key element with a word that has the opposite meaning (for example, change improve to degrade, never to always). The other method is to change the direction of the action described in the statement (change "our customers never call us" to "we never call our customers," "the students do not listen to the teacher" to "the teacher does not listen to the students," and so on). Try to generate some reversal statements. The more statements, the more different approaches to the problem are provided.

3. Identify causes of or solutions to the problem presented in the reversal statement. List several actions. If the reversal statement is: "We never call our customers," list the possible reasons (causes) why you would never call your customers (too busy, don't have their phone number, or always get put on hold).

4. Analyze each of the causes of or solutions to the reversed problem to identify actions you could take for the real problem. If you have identified "not having their phone number" as a reversal cause, consider that your customers may have difficulty finding your phone number as a possible cause to your problem.

Two worksheets are provided to help apply the concept of reversal to your problem solving efforts. The reversal to identify causes worksheet is provided to document the results of the reversal technique in identifying possible causes for a problem (see page 227). The starting point of this worksheet is the problem definition. The reversal to identify solutions worksheet on page 228 is meant to help you in your efforts to identify possible solutions to the causes you have identified (for this reason, the reversal to identify causes worksheet always is used first).

As with any worksheet, a completed form is not nearly as important as the information gained from conducting the activity. By all means, do not feel locked in to using the forms. Do not let the forms limit you. There is nothing magical about two reversals per page or three reversal causes per reversal. The worksheets are provided as an aid in applying the reversal technique. Use them however they are helpful to you.

Reversal to Identify Causes Worksheet

1. Problem definition:

   What: _____

   Where: _____

   When: _____

   _____

2. Reversal: _____

   _____

3. Reversal cause: 4. Problem cause:

   A. _____   A. _____

   _____   _____

   B. _____   B. _____

   _____   _____

   C. _____   C. _____

   _____   _____

2. Reversal: _____

   _____

3. Reversal cause: 4. Problem cause:

   A. _____   A. _____

   _____   _____

   B. _____   B. _____

   _____   _____

   C. _____   C. _____

   _____   _____

Reversal to Identify Solutions Worksheet

1. Cause: _____

_____

_____

2. Reversal: _____

_____

3. Reversal solution: 4. Cause solution

A. _____   A. _____

_____   _____

B. _____   B. _____

_____   _____

C. _____   C. _____

_____   _____

2. Reversal: _____

_____

3. Reversal solution: 4. Cause solution:

A. _____   A. _____

_____   _____

B. _____   B. _____

_____   _____

C. _____   C. _____

_____   _____

An example of how to use the reversal technique may be helpful. For this example, assume a computer manufacturer's help-line representatives are reporting that some of their customers are hanging up while on hold before they receive help from the representatives. The representatives may use the reversal technique to identify reasons why the customers are hanging up. Because the representatives are attempting to identify possible causes to their problem, they have used the reversal to identify causes worksheet. Their completed worksheet appears on page 230.

Notice that the two reversal statements are very different. The first reversal changes the concept of the customers hanging up to the customers calling several times a day. The other reversal changes the direction of action. Instead of the customer hanging up, the service representative is hanging up on the customers. Remember, even though these statements may seem ridiculous, their aim is to generate new ideas.

Given the reversal statements on this sample worksheet, you may have thought of different reversal causes or different problem causes. You may even wonder how anyone could think of the reversal and problem causes listed. This diversity is good! You should expect everyone to think of different ideas, that is the purpose of creative-thinking techniques. By changing the problem to one that is probably ridiculous, you are removing the barriers and paradigms that can limit your thinking. You want everyone to think of different ideas so you can generate more relevant ideas (either problem causes or solutions).

Also notice that in one case, two problem causes were listed for a single reversal cause. This is often the case. List anything that comes to mind, even if the idea is not obviously related to the current discussion topic.

Characteristic Changing

The characteristic changing technique starts with an identification of the parts that make up a key element of the problem statement. The parts are then further divided into the characteristics that describe the parts. The characteristics are the sales features and differentiators for the parts. For example, the characteristics of a computer monitor would include its size, color options, resolution, and range of ergonomic adjustments. Once the characteristics are identified, think of ways to change them to help with the problem. To identify problem causes, ask "What about the (characteristic) could cause a problem with the (part)?"

To identify possible solutions, ask "What could we do about the (characteristic) of the (part) to eliminate the problem cause?"

The characteristic changing technique is especially helpful for challenging assumptions. Challenge each of the characteristics identified. Why does the package need to be rectangular? Why does the cover have to be black? Why do the buttons need to be so small?

The division of the key element of the problem statement can be depicted by a tree diagram. The concept of a tree diagram has been used

CHARACTERISTIC CHANGING

A creative thinking technique used to challenge assumptions about existing characteristics.

Reversal to Identify Causes Worksheet   COMPLETED

1. Problem definition:

What: Some customers hang up before a service representative can get to them.

Where: In our midwest office.

When: All throughout the month.

2. Reversal: Some of our customers call several times a day!

3. Reversal cause:

A. Our representatives are so friendly that the customers call just to talk to them.

B. Our customers like the music we play while they are on hold.

C. Each caller's name is placed in a drawing.

4. Problem cause:

A. (1) Our representatives are rude.
(2) Customers don't like talking to machines.

B. Customers find our hold-music boring or offensive.

C. Customers get little benefit from calling.

2. Reversal: Our representatives hang up on our customers before the customers have completed their business.

3. Reversal cause:

A. The representatives are attempting to satisfy their quotas of calls/hour.

B. The representatives get impatient with "dumb" questions.

C. The representatives get tired of repeatedly answering the same questions.

4. Problem cause:

A. Customers have many things to do so they choose to not wait on hold.

B. Customers have received some incorrect answers in the past.

C. Customers feel like they receive "canned" answers, not relevant to them.

on the characteristic changing worksheet (see page 232). The worksheet is structured to allow the key element to be divided into five parts, and each part divided into five characteristics. This layout should provide sufficient space for many situations. Any time you can identify more than five parts or five characteristics, use another piece of paper to create your own tree diagram. Do not let the worksheet limit your thinking.

For example, you may be experiencing problems with your computer. The characteristic changing worksheet on page 233 has been completed by identifying the parts of a computer and the characteristics of each of the parts.

To identify possible causes of the problem with the computer, ask "What about the (characteristic) could cause a problem with the (part)?"

Table 13.1 contains some of the questions that could be asked for this computer example, and includes some possible causes.

Some of the questions and possible causes may seem ridiculous, but don't worry. The purpose of any creative thinking technique is to generate ideas. No matter how crazy an idea may seem, it may have merit on its own or it may spark another, more practical idea. In fact, some of the possible causes listed may have little or nothing to do with the question being asked. It doesn't matter how the possible causes are identified, just capture all of the ideas suggested.

Questions	Possible causes
What about the *resolution* could cause a problem with the *monitor?*	The software may require a higher resolution than the monitor is capable of producing. Poor resolution may make interpreting graphs difficult.
What about the *size* could cause a problem with the *monitor?*	The monitor may be too heavy to set on the main unit (causing an electrical short in the case). The monitor may be so small that you misread some of the text.
What about the *storage capacity* could cause a problem with the *disk drives?*	There is not enough room on a disk to save the work. There is so much room on the disk that it is difficult to find files.

Table 13.1. Questions and possible causes.

Characteristic Changing Worksheet

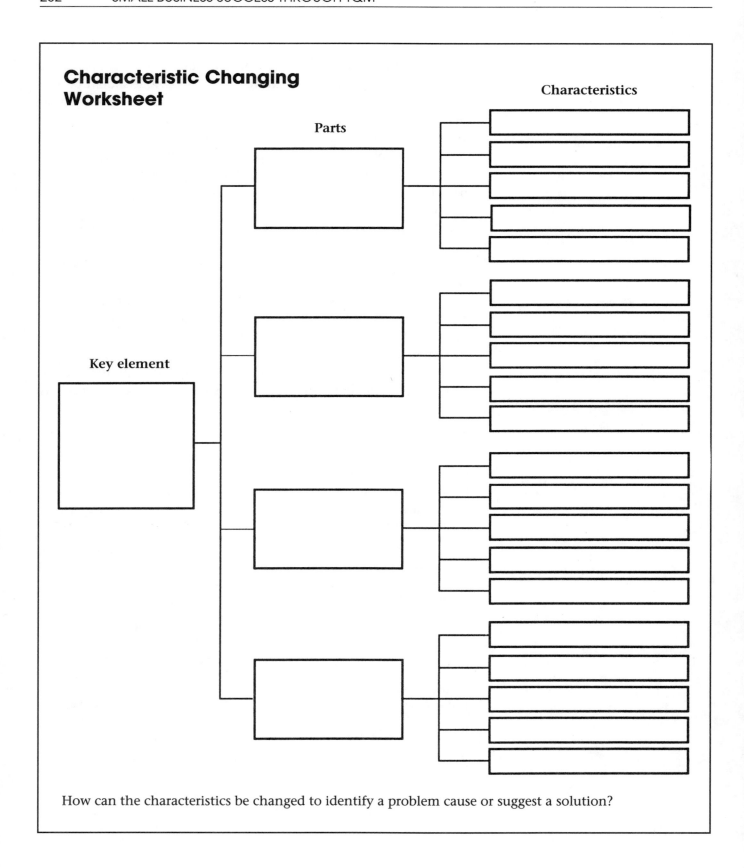

Parts

Characteristics

Key element

How can the characteristics be changed to identify a problem cause or suggest a solution?

Characteristic Changing Worksheet

COMPLETED

Parts

Characteristics

Key element

Personal computer

Monitor
- Resolution
- Size
- Color options
- Ergonomic positioning
-

Keyboard
- Key location
- Ergonomic positioning
-
-
-

Disk drives
- Number of drives
- Drive capacity
-
-
-

Central processing unit
- Type of processor
- Amount of memory
- Speed
- Math coprocessor
- Number/type of slots

How can the characteristics be changed to identify a problem cause or suggest a solution?

SUMMARY

The creative-thinking techniques presented in this chapter can be used by anyone to help generate new, creative ideas. The techniques can help you escape from the patterns we all get trapped in, provide a means for restructuring the situation you find yourself in, and challenge the assumptions that tend to limit your thinking.

Even though *take action to improve* is the final step of the continuous process improvement cycle, it is certainly not the last step in your journey for quality improvement. At this point, you should have a good idea about how to analyze and improve your work processes, and you should have applied the concepts and techniques to your work. Continue what you have started. You have many more work processes to analyze and improve. You need to continually talk to your customers and receive performance feedback from them. You need to always make sure you are focusing on what is important to your customers. In short, you have a lot of work to do! Remember, the cycle provides the structure to help you on your quality improvement journey. Next time you wonder what you should do, review the steps of the continuous process improvement cycle.

NOTE

1. Joel Arthur Barker, *Future Edge: Discovering the New Paradigms of Success* (New York: William Morrow and Company, 1992), 32.

MAKE QUALITY EVERYONE'S JOB

Quality is not part of your job. You do not do quality for a while, then get back to your "real" job. Quality is your job; it is everyone's job. Sometimes you can tell how far a company is on its quality journey by how its management talks about quality. Listen to their words. Some executives trumpet the number of teams they have formed or proudly claim that quality is an agenda item for every meeting. Conversely, mature companies actually sound like they deemphasize quality. You are not likely to hear braggadocios claims about quality from them. These companies have grown to the point where quality is everything to them, not something extra. Quality is ingrained in everything they do. Quality, to them, is everyone's job.

You have taken the first step toward making quality everyone's job by getting and reading this book. If you have not done so already, begin planning how everyone in your organization can receive the training prescribed here. Do what you can to encourage the application of the techniques documented in this book throughout your organization.

There are two additional subjects to which you should be introduced that can assist you in your efforts to make quality everyone's job: ISO 9000 and the Malcolm Baldrige National Quality Award. Even if you have no intention or requirement to receive ISO 9000 certification or desire to apply for the Malcolm Baldrige National Quality Award, important lessons can be learned from their study. This chapter is not meant to be a complete text on either of these subjects, but will provide you with enough information to be familiar with each subject and to determine if you want to do more reading on either subject.

ISO 9000

A key aim of TQM, as mentioned throughout this book, is customer satisfaction. The focus of customer satisfaction, in turn, is understanding and meeting or exceeding customer requirements. A system is required to ensure that the requirements are continually and consistently adhered to. The system contains documentation so exact that anyone assigned to perform a job can be trained in the same, precise manner as the previous person on the job. There can be no lapse in quality just because the person performing the process has changed. The existence or need for quality systems certainly is not new, companies around the world have been developing their own quality systems for years.

ISO 9000 is a series of international quality standards. Figure 14.1 lists the purpose of each of the documents. The advantage of the ISO 9000 series of standards is in their established, widely accepted clauses. Each of the documents, ISO 9001 through ISO 9003, include clauses describing elements of a quality system for different types of companies. The clauses documented in ISO 9001 are shown in Figure 14.2. After someone says they have received ISO 9001 certification, for example, you already know something about their quality system.

The importance of a documented quality system increases as a company matures to the point where quality is everyone's job. Everyone in the company is now involved in activities like process control, corrective action, quality records, and internal quality audits. The quality system ties these activities together across the entire organization.

Uses

ISO 9000 certification is being required by an increasing number of companies worldwide. In order to continue to do business with some

---

ISO 9001   *Quality systems—Model for quality assurance in design, development, production, installation, and servicing*

ISO 9002   *Quality systems—Model for quality qssurance in production, installation, and servicing*

ISO 9003   *Quality systems—Model for quality assurance in final inspection and test*

Figure 14.1. ISO 9000 documents.

4.1	Management responsibility
4.2	Quality system
4.3	Contract review
4.4	Design control
4.5	Document and data control
4.6	Purchasing
4.7	Control of customer-supplied product
4.8	Product identification and traceability
4.9	Process control
4.10	Inspection and testing
4.11	Inspection, measuring and test equipment
4.12	Inspection and test status
4.13	Control of nonconforming product
4.14	Corrective and preventive action
4.15	Handling, storage, packaging, preservation and delivery
4.16	Control of quality records
4.17	Internal quality audits
4.18	Training
4.19	Servicing
4.20	Statistical techniques

Figure 14.2. ISO 9001 clauses.

of your existing customers, you may be required to achieve certification. This fact alone is a good reason for many companies to pursue ISO 9000 certification. There is, however, another reason for small businesses to consider studying the ISO 9000 documentation: it provides an outline for a complete quality system.

Document Your Quality System.   If you do not have a documented quality system, use the clauses documented in the ISO 9000 document applicable to your business as a basis for your quality system. The documents can serve as excellent guides as you develop and document your system.

Assess Your Quality System.   If you do have a documented quality system, use the ISO 9000 documentation to assess the completeness of your system. This review may reveal some ways in which you can enhance your existing documentation.

TQM and ISO 9000

Because of ISO 9000's emphasis on quality system documentation, there are many steps for a company to work through before pursuing certification. The company should have all of its processes defined and documented and know everyone's responsibilities and have them documented. During the audit (required for certification), any employee is a candidate to be audited and must be able to describe what he/she does and provide documentation showing that what he/she is doing is in compliance with company procedures.

Following the steps prescribed in this book will prepare you to document your quality system and work toward certification. Team members will know what they are responsible for and work processes will be documented with process flow diagrams.

MALCOLM BALDRIGE NATIONAL QUALITY AWARD

The Malcolm Baldrige National Quality Award (MBNQA) is the United States' highest business award. The award is presented annually by the president of the United States to recognize U.S. companies that excel in quality management and quality achievement.

The award does much more than recognize a few excellent companies each year. For most companies, the strength of the MBNQA is not in applying or winning the award, it is in the information available from the award recipients and the criteria itself.

Learn from the Best

How do other businesses, in and out of your industry, excel in quality management and quality achievement? There are lessons for all of us from the companies recognized for achieving world class quality.

Recipients of the MBNQA are expected to share information about their successful quality strategies with other U.S. organizations. This information can be a great aid to you and your efforts to improve the quality of your products and services. Figure 14.3 lists the companies that have received the award so far. As the figure demonstrates, the award has three eligibility categories: manufacturing companies, service companies, and small businesses (defined as complete businesses with not more than 500 full-time employees).

I have written to many of the winners offering my congratulations and requesting information on their quality strategies. Each company that I have made such a request to has been very prompt in mailing me a packet of information. The packet contents vary considerably from company to company, but I have found all of them interesting and helpful. As you would expect, approaches to implementation vary, while some elements (like customer satisfaction) exist in every approach. I recommend that you write some of the winners, especially from the small business category, and request a packet of information. I have called information for the city listed to get a mailing address, and addressed my request to the attention of the Malcolm Baldrige National Quality Award Response Center. This center may or may not exist, but addressing my requests in this manner has worked for me.

Study the information you receive. Look for ideas you can implement directly, or with some modification, in your business. Be careful not to take ideas blindly from one company, and expect them to work with instant impact in your business. Companies have different cultures and industries have different regulations, just to mention two factors that affect implementation success. Instead, use the ideas as thought starters for your business. How could you take the idea and make it work in your business?

1993 Award Winners
Manufacturing
    Eastman Chemical Co.
    Kingsport, Tenn.
Small Business
    Ames Rubber Corp.
    Hamburg, N.J.

1992 Award Winners
Manufacturing
    AT&T Network Systems Group
    Transmission Systems Business Unit
    Morristown, N.J.
    Texas Instruments, Inc.
    Defense Systems & Electronics Group
    Dallas, Texas
Service
    AT&T Universal Card Services
    Jacksonville, Fla.
    The Ritz-Carlton Hotel Company
    Atlanta, Ga.
Small Business
    Granite Rock Company
    Watsonville, Calif.

1991 Award Winners
Manufacturing
    Solectron Corp.
    San Jose, Calif.
    Zytec Corp.
    Eden Prairie, Minn.
Small Business
    Marlow Industries
    Dallas, Texas

1990 Award Winners
Manufacturing
    Cadillac Motor Car Company
    Detroit, Mich.
    IBM Rochester
    Rochester, Minn.
Service
    Federal Express Corp.
    Memphis, Tenn.
Small Business
    Wallace Co., Inc.
    Houston, Texas

1989 Award Winners
Manufacturing
    Milliken & Company
    Spartanburg, S.C.
    Xerox Business Products
    and Systems
    Stamford, Conn.

1988 Award Winners
Manufacturing
    Motorola, Inc.
    Schaumburg, Ill.
    Westinghouse Commerical
    Nuclear Fuel Division
    Pittsburgh, Penn.
Small Business
    Globe Metallurgical, Inc.
    Cleveland, Ohio

Figure 14.3. MBNQA winners.

The materials should encourage you more than anything. You will find that you are not the only small business wanting to improve the quality of your products and services. In fact, other small businesses have been able to excel by emphasizing quality.

Assess Your Performance

The award criteria serve as an excellent guide for self-assessment. The criteria are divided into the following seven categories.

1.0 Leadership

2.0 Information and analysis

3.0 Strategic quality planning

4.0 Human resource development and management

5.0 Management of process quality

6.0 Quality and operational results

7.0 Customer focus and satisfaction

Many companies, of all sizes and from many industries, use the criteria to assess their performance. As you study the Baldrige documentation, you will see how everyone in your company must be involved to satisfy the criteria. Regularly scheduled assessments, conducted against a thorough set of evaluation criteria, can provide the objective data required to monitor your progress.

Individual copies of the award criteria can be obtained free of charge from

> Malcolm Baldrige National Quality Award
> National Institute of Standards and Technology
> Route 270 and Quince Orchard Road
> Administration Building, Room A537
> Gaithersburg, MD 20899-0001
> Telephone: 301-975-2036
> Fax: 301-948-3716

The MBNQA criteria can be used to assess any organization. This type of introspection can offer helpful information as long as everyone involved is completely honest and unbiased in their research and reporting. The assessment can result in the identification of areas of strength to build upon and weaknesses requiring improvement.

Some organizations choose to use an independent consultant to conduct their assessments. A qualified consultant not only offers experience in TQM implementation and assessment techniques, but also provides an independent, unbiased point-of-view free from internal politics. If you consider using a consultant, make sure you understand the criteria the assessment will be based upon (MBNQA or other), the method by which the assessment data will be gathered (personal observation, personal interviews, meetings, questionnaires, and so on), and how the final results will be tabulated.

Regardless of who performs the assessment, remember that any assessment is a report of your status at only one point in time. Assessments should be performed regularly (perhaps annually or every 18 months) to allow you to monitor your progress and make the necessary adjustments.

NOW IT'S UP TO YOU

Although it is true that quality is everyone's job, someone must lead the way. If you are the owner, president, or CEO of your company, you should be leading the way. Be active. Be visible. Be vocal. Lead by example. Everyone in the organization will be watching. After everyone sees your commitment to and involvement in quality, they will be more likely to participate. Quality cannot be everyone's job until they first see that it is your job.

This type of demonstration is important for you regardless of your title. When this type of leadership is demonstrated by the president or CEO, you are well on your way to success. However, you can provide this type of leadership in your organization even if you are not the CEO. Don't let the lack of commitment to quality from a CEO get in the way of progress. You have a sphere of influence (even if you think it is small). Apply the concepts and techniques documented in this book to your job. Your results will be noticed.

EPILOGUE

You are ready. The prescription documented in this book will work for your business. Use the continuous process improvement cycle as a guide on your quality journey.

Plan for customer satisfaction. Everything you do should focus on your customers and their satisfaction. Who are your customers? What do you provide to them? What do they think of the work you provide to them? Stay in touch with your customers. Make it easy for them to provide you feedback, both positive and negative, on your performance. Remember, the exciters you provide to them today become their basic expectations tomorrow. How are you going to excite them then? You better plan these exciters now, because there is a good chance your competition already is.

Understand processes. After you know what your customers want and expect, you need to understand the processes you perform to produce your products and services. What are your processes? Are all of your processes documented? Are the processes documented accurately? What could you do today to improve your processes? A well-defined and documented process is a start toward improvement.

Measure performance. Measurement data provide a means to objectively evaluate process performance. How are your processes performing? Are they able to satisfy your customers' requirements? Are they getting better? Process performance data allow you to manage your processes based on objective feedback.

Take action to improve. The result of measuring the performance of your processes often is the identification of problems to solve or actions to take. Remember the structured approaches to problem solving and decision making presented. Use the creative-thinking techniques introduced to help you break from your old molds and generate new ideas.

If you are anything like me, you have been tempted to skip some of the activities and ignore my advice to apply the concepts and techniques described here as you have read the book. If this is the case for you, now is the time for action! Reading this book, without taking action to improve your work processes, has done little for you other than increase your understanding of the concepts and techniques of TQM. If you haven't done so already, get started. Take action in the part of the company for which you are responsible. Share your ideas and enthusiasm with others. Pass this book on to co-workers (or better yet, buy them their own copy since you'll want to keep this copy for a reference). Whatever you do, get started.

Total quality management can be implemented with outstanding results in small businesses. Reading this book has prepared you to successfully implement TQM in your business. You know what to do, now it is up to you. Just do it.

BIBLIOGRAPHY

Amsden, Robert T., Howard E. Butler, and Davida M. Amsden. *SPC Simplified: Practical Steps to Quality.* White Plains, N.Y.: Quality Resources, 1989.

Barker, Joel Arthur. *Future Edge: Discovering the New Paradigms of Success.* New York: William Morrow and Company, Inc., 1992.

Brown, Mark Graham. *Baldrige Award Winning Quality: How to Interpret the Malcolm Baldrige Award Criteria,* 3d ed. White Plains, N.Y.: Quality Resources, 1993.

de Bono, Edward. *Lateral Thinking: Creativity Step by Step.* New York: Harper & Row, 1970.

Gitlow, Howard, Shelley Gitlow, Alan Oppenheim, and Rosa Oppenheim. *Tools and Methods for the Improvement of Quality.* Homewood, Ill.: Irwin, 1989.

Guaspari, John. *I Know It When I See It: A Modern Fable About Quality.* New York: AMACOM, 1985.

ISO-9000 Handbook of Quality Standards and Compliance. Bureau of Business Practice. Waterford, Conn.: Prentice Hall, 1992.

Katzenbach, Jon R. and Douglas K. Smith. *The Wisdom of Teams: Creating the High-Performance Organization.* Boston, Mass.: Harvard Business School Press, 1993.

Sewell, Carl, and Paul B. Brown. *Customers for Life: How to Turn That One-Time Buyer into a Lifetime Customer.* New York: Pocket Books, 1990.

VanGundy, Arthur B. *Idea Power: Techniques & Resources to Unleash the Creativity in Your Organization.* New York: American Management Association, 1992.

INDEX

Accuracy, requirement for, 84
Action plan, 219
    contingent actions, 218
    documenting planned activities, 217
    identifying obstacles, 217–18
    preventive actions, 218
Activity sheets
    average and range charts, 162–67
    c chart, 155–58
    check sheet, 131
    control chart selection, 173–74
    histogram, 138
    individuals control charts, 168–71
    for out-of-control conditions, 180–85
    output requirement listing, 40
    p chart, 150–53
Administrative tasks
    assessment checklist, 102
    minimizing, 101–2
Appropriate personal initiative, 8
    assignable cause, 117
Assumptions, challenging, 222–24
Attributes control charts, 147, 154
    c charts, 154–58
    p charts, 147–53
Average and range ($\overline{X}$–R) chart, 162, 164, 165
    activity, 162
    control limit calculations for, 163
    example using, 161
    steps in preparing, 159–61

Baldrige, Malcolm, National Quality Award (MBNQA), 235–41
    address for, 240
    award criteria, 240–41
    winners of, 239
Barker, Joel, 223
Basic customer expectations, 27–28
    versus customer exciters, 30
Brainstorming, rules of, 224–25
Business, activities valuable to, 99–100

Capable. *See* Process Capability
Cascading plan elements, 64
Cause/effect diagram, 199–201
    guidelines in constructing, 200–201
    using multiple, 202
c chart, 154
    activity, 158
    control limit, calculations for, 157
    example using, 154–55
    steps in preparing, 154
Centerline, 176
    calculations for, 152, 157, 163, 170
Changes
    evaluating impact of, 111
    process flow diagrams for analyzing, 95
Characteristic changing, 229, 231–33
    worksheet for, 232, 233
Check sheet
    activity, 131
    definition of, 128

location, 129
steps, 128
Checklist
    for administrative task assessment, 102
    for continuous improvement, 6
    for customer satisfaction, 4
    for process simplification, 103
    and standardization, 107–8
    for total quality management, 9
    for value-added assessment, 99
Checks and inspections, minimizing, 100–101
Comment cards, 48
Common causes of variation, 117
Competition, as reason for quality improvement, 10–11
Consensus decision making, 7
Contingent actions, 218
Continuous improvement, 5–6
    checklist for, 6
Continuous process improvement cycle, 17, 19
    focus of first time through cycle, 20–21
    focus of subsequent cycles, 21–22
    measuring performance, 19
    need for, 15–17
    planning for customer satisfaction, 18
    taking action to improve, 20
    understanding process, 18–19
Continuous quality improvement (CQI), 2
Control chart, 145
    attributes, 147–58
    control limits in, 147
    definition of, 146
    for identifying out-of-control conditions, 172–86
    for problem definition, 193, 195
    selecting most appropriate, 172, 173, 174
    uses for, 145–46
    using process measurements in, 188–89
    variables, 159–71
    zones in, 176
Control limit
    calculation of, for average and range charts, 163

calculation of, for c chart, 157
calculation of, for individuals control charts, 170
calculation of, for p chart, 152
definition of, 147
and process capability, 186–87
Correlation, 140
Cost/benefit analysis, 6
Costs, as reason for quality improvement, 11–12
Creative thinking, 221
    application of, 224
    brainstorming in, 224–25
    to challenge assumptions, 222–24
    characteristic changing in, 229, 231–33
    to escape from patterns, 221
    and problem solving, 199
    for restructuring, 222
    reversals in, 225–29
    techniques, 224
Critical process performance characteristics identification methods, 120
Current level of satisfaction, with input requirements, 85
Customer
    activities valuable to, 99
    definition of, 36
    developing lifetime, 24–25
    external, 25
    fickleness of, 24
    identifying, 36, 38
    internal, 25–27
    listing of, 36–38
    in mission statement, 55
    quality as defined by, 23–24
    as reason for quality improvement, 9–10
    team as, 26
Customer delight
    achieving, 30, 31
    versus satisfaction, 27, 28
Customer desires, 28–29
Customer exciters, 29–30
    versus basic customer expectations, 30
Customer expectations, 27–28
Customer feedback, methods for receiving, 46–49

Customer list, 36
    worksheet for, 37
Customer meeting
    conducting, 43
    customer reception of, 41
    determining requirement
        importance, 44–45
determining the current level of
        requirement satisfaction,
        45–46
    false expectations in, 43
    methods for receiving customer
        feedback, 46–49
    verifying output requirements,
        43–44
Customer requirements, under-
        standing, 18, 32
    identifying output requirements,
        38–41, 42
    listing customers, 36–38
    listing team outputs, 32–35
    meeting with customers, 41,
        43–50
Customer satisfaction
    checklist for, 4
    versus delight, 27, 28
    ensuring, 2–3
    external, 26
    planning for, 18, 21
    and quality improvement, 12
Customer satisfaction/delight
        model, 28
    sequence in, 30–32
Customers' point of view, and
        process performance
        measurement, 120–21
Cycles, 143, 175, 194
Cycle time and quality improve-
        ment, 12
Cycle time reduction, 105
    analyzing queues, 105
    conduct activities in parallel,
        106
    modify the sequence of activities,
        106
    time deadlines, 106–7

Decision making, consensus, 7
Decision points, analyzing, 104–5
Defect versus defective piece,
        147–48

Defective, 148
Defective piece versus defect,
        147–48
Deming, W. Edwards, 17
Deming cycle, 17
Desires. See Customer desires
Diversity, valuing, 7
Documentation
    of action plan, 217
    of measurement decisions,
        121–22
    of objectives, 62
    of obstacles for goals, 60
    of processes, 18–19, 89–96
    of quality system, 237
    of responsibilities, 63, 65
    of strategies for obstacles, 62
    of time frames, 63

Effectiveness, measurement of,
        118–19
Efficiency, measurement of, 119
Empowerment, 7–8
Exciters. See Customer exciters

False starts, avoiding, 16
Fishbone diagrams. See Cause/effect
        diagram
Focus group
    for customer feedback, 49
    definition of, 49
    pros and cons regarding, 46
Forms, and standardization,
        107–8
Foundation, building stable,
        16–17
Functional process flow diagram,
        91–92

Goal
    definition of, 59
    documenting obstacles for, 60
    examples of, 59
    in team plans, 58–60
    time frame for, 59

Histogram
    activity, 138
    caution, 137
    definition, 133
    steps, 133

stratified, 135
uses, 134
"How are plans used" survey, 54
How do you treat your internal
    customers test, 27

Improvement, evaluating need for,
    111
In control, 146
Individuals control charts (*X–R*),
    166, 169, 171
    activity, 168
    control limit calculations for, 170
    example using, 167
    steps in preparing, 166–67
Information, as output, 33
Input features, 84
Input requirements
    identifying, 83
    and level of importance, 85
    and level of satisfaction, 85
    negotiating, 85
    and supplier feedback, 83–85
Inputs, identifying, 73
Inspection, role in quality, 3
Inspection challenge questions, 100
Internal customer, 25–26
    self-test on treatment of, 27
Internal customer/supplier relation-
    ships, 25, 26
Internally required activities, opti-
    mizing, 103
Interrelationships and dependencies,
    process flow diagrams for
    understanding, 94
Interviews
    for customer feedback, 47
    definition of, 46
    pros and cons regarding, 46
Ishikawa, Kaoru, 199
Ishikawa diagrams. *See* Cause/effect
    diagram
ISO 9000, 235, 236
    documents, 236
    total quality management,
    238
    uses of, 236–37
ISO 9001, 236
    clauses in, 237
ISO 9002, 236
ISO 9003, 236

Layout process flow diagrams, 92
Loss
    realistic view of, 116
    traditional view of, 114–16
Lower control limit (LCL), 147, 176
    calculations for, 152, 157, 163,
    170

Mandatory requirements
    checking solution ideas against,
    210
    for selection criteria, 206, 208
Markets, in mission statement, 55
Measurement decision documenta-
    tion worksheet, 122, 123
Measurements. *See* Process
    management
Methodology, need for, 15–17
Mission
    definition of, 55
    flowdown of, 56–57
Mission statement
    elements of, 54–55
    level of detail in, 56
    overlaps or gaps in, 57
Mixtures, 143, 175–76, 194

Nonassignable causes, 117
Nonrandom patterns, 175
    cycles, 175
    mixtures, 175–76
    and problem definition, 194
    shifts, 176
    trends, 176
Nonvalue-added activity, 99–100
    measurement activity as, 120

Objective
    definition of, 62
    documenting for each strategy,
    62
    in team plans, 62–63
Obstacle
    definition of, 60
    documenting for each goal, 60
    documenting strategies for each,
    62
    in team plans, 60
    types of, 60
Obstacle identification in action
    plan, 217–18

Operations process flow diagram, 90–91
Organization, understanding the team's role in, 57
Organizational process map, 75–76
Out-of-control condition, 179–85
  identifying, 172, 175–79
Out-of-control processes, working with, 186
Out-of-control rules, 176–78
  and problem definition, 194
Output
  calculating priority of each, 49–50
  definition of, 32
  grouping similar, 69–70
  listing team, 69
  types of, 33–34
Output list, 32
  detail in, 34
  development of, 34
  keeping current, 34
  types of outputs, 33–34
Output requirement
  customer additions to, 44
  and customer point of view, 39
  determining current level of satisfaction with, 45–46
  determining importance of, 44–45
  identifying, 38–39
  listing activity, 40
  verifying, 43–44
  worksheet, 39, 41, 42, 50, 51

Paradigms, and challenging assumptions, 223
Pareto chart
  definition, 130
  steps, 130
  stratified, 132
Patterns
  escaping from, 221
  restructuring, 222
p chart, 147–48, 151, 153
  activity, 150
  control limit calculations for, 152
  example using, 149–50
  steps in preparing, 148–49
Performance feedback, 110–11
Performance measurement, 19, 21

Performance targets, setting meaningful, 111
Periodic process reviews, 96
Personal accountability, process flow diagrams for increasing, 94
Personal initiative, encouraging, 7–8
Plan-do-check-act (PDCA) cycle, 17
Plan-do-study-act (PDSA) cycle, 17
Planned activities, documenting, 217
Preventive actions, 218
Problem definition, 191–92
  what, 193
  when, 195
  where, 193–94
  worksheet for, 196, 197, 198
Problem solving, 191
  defining problem, 191–96
  developing action plan, 217–19
  diagrams used for, 199–203
  five-step approach, 192
  identifying root cause, 196–204
  selecting best solution, 204–17
  verifying solution results, 219
Process(es)
  analyzing additional, 22
  broadening emphasis on, 22
  definition of, 4
  documentation of, 18–19, 89–96
  highlighting variance between actual and planned, 94
  managing, 3–4
  naming of, 70–71
  understanding, 18, 21
Process activities
  combing similar, 104
  listing, 71, 73
  modifying sequence of, 106
  serial versus parallel, 106
Process boundary, 71
Process capability
  definition of, 186
  determining, 186–88
Process definition, 67–68
  defining process boundaries, 71
  grouping similar outputs, 69–70
  identifying inputs, 73
  listing process activities, 71, 73
  listing team outputs, 69

naming process, 70–71
  worksheet for, 71, 72, 73, 74, 75
Process documentation
  flow diagrams for, 89–96
  selection, 89
Process flow diagrams, 89
  definition compatibility in, 90
  definition of, 90
  functional, 91–92
  layout, 92
  level of detail in, 89
  operations, 90–91
  and performance measurement,
    121
  symbols in, 90, 91
  types of, 90–92
  updating, 95–96
  uses of, 92–95
Process improvement
  cycle-time reduction in, 105–7
  prioritizing processes for, 76–79
  process simplification in, 103–5
  standardization in, 107–8
  taking action for, 20, 21
  waste reduction in, 97–103
Process map, 75–76
  areas of duplication in, 76
  definition of, 75
  gaps and overlaps in, 76
  verifying output/input matches
    in, 76
Process performance
  collecting and analyzing data, 19
  monitoring of, 21
Process performance measurement,
    109, 121, 188
  developing, 19, 118
  displaying, 188
  documenting decisions, 121–22
  for effectiveness, 118
  for efficiency, 119
  identifying critical characteris-
    tics, 119–21
  to make process decisions,
    188–89
  and process variation, 112–18
  purposes of, 110–11
  timeliness in, 188
  types of, 118
  for work versus people, 109–10

Process priority, 76–77
  calculating scores, 77
  inputs to calculating totals, 77
  list worksheet, 80
  scoring worksheet, 78
Process simplification, 103
  analyzing decision points, 104–5
  combining similar activities, 104
  steps checklist, 103
Process variation, 118
  common causes of, 117
  definition of, 112
  examples of, 112–13
  losses due to, 114–16
  measurement of, 146
  special causes of, 117–18
  treatment of causes, 118
  is undesirable, 114
Product in mission statement, 55
Profit, quality chain reaction, 12
Proposed changes, process flow dia-
    grams for analyzing, 95

Quality
  customers defining, 23–24
  reasons for improving, 9–12
Quality improvement, 9–12
  competition in, 10–11
  costs in, 11–12
  customers in, 9–10
Quality/profit chain reaction, 12
Quality system
  assessing, 237
  documenting, 237
Questionnaires for customer feed-
    back, 48
Queue times, analyzing, 105
Range, 159
Recurring problems, 195
Relationship diagram
  definition of, 201
  in determining root cause,
    202–3
  guidelines in constructing,
    201–2
Requirements, 39
Responsibilities, documenting, 63, 65
Reversal, 225–29
  to identify causes worksheet,
    226, 227, 230

to identify solutions worksheet, 226, 228
Risk analysis
    for solution selection, 211, 214
    worksheet for, 214, 215, 216
Root cause
    definition of, 196
    importance of, 196
    listing possible causes, 196–203
    testing possible causes, 203–4
Run chart
    definition, 141
    patterns, 143
    steps, 141

Scatter diagram
    correlations, 140
    definition of, 139
    steps, 139
    uses, 139
Schedules, setting meaningful, 111
Selection criteria
    assigning weights to, 206
    checking solution ideas against, 210–11
    definition of, 205
    development worksheet, 206, 207, 209
    example for, 208
    identifying, 204–8
Service companies, effect of technology on, 11
Services
    in mission statement, 55
    as outputs, 33–34
Sewell, Carl, 24, 34
Shifts, 143, 176, 194
Sigma, 146
Single occurrence problems, 195
Solution comparison, 211
    worksheet for, 210–11, 212, 213
Solution ideas
    comparing, 210–11
    generating, 208
Solution results, verification of, 219
Solution selection
    best overall solution, 214
    comparing ideas, 210–11, 212–13
    generating ideas, 208

identifying selection criteria, 204–8, 209
    risk analysis, 211, 214, 215, 216
    steps, 205
Solutions worksheet, reversal to identify, 228
Special causes of variation, 117
Special features in mission statement, 55
Standardization, 107
    developing standard report formats, 107
    reviewing/creating work procedures, 107
    use of forms, worksheets, and checklists, 107–8
Standard report formats, 107
Statistical data analysis, 19, 145
Storage activities, minimizing, 102–3
Strategies
    definition of, 61
    documenting for each obstacle, 62
    examples of, 61–62
    in team plans, 60–62
Stratification, definition of, 132
Stratify
    histogram, 135
    Pareto, 132
Supplier
    dependence on, 82
    relationship to internal customers, 25, 26
    team as, 26
Supplier feedback, 18
    conducting meeting for, 86
    input requirements, 83–85
    providing regular, 86, 88
    steps leading to providing, 81
    worksheet for, 86, 87
Survey. *See* written survey
Symbols in process flow diagram, 90, 91
Systematic process review, 5

Team, 6–7
    boundaries for, in mission statement, 55
    as both customer and supplier, 26

definition of, 6
developing mission for, 54–57
goals associated with mission, 59
listing of outputs, 32–35
process flow diagrams for understanding jobs on, 94
understanding role in organization, 57
Team notebook
creating, xxvi
customer list worksheet in, 37
output list worksheet in, 34
updating, 50
Team plans, 18, 58
cascading elements, 64
to communicate purpose and direction, 65
to document responsibilities, 65
elements of, 58
goals in, 58–60
objectives in, 62–63
obstacles in, 60
purpose of, 53–54
receiving and understanding team mission, 54–58
relationship between elements, 63
strategies in, 60–62
updating, 65
Technology, effects of, on competitive boundaries, 10–11
Time deadlines, and cycle time reduction, 106–7
Timeliness
in process measurements, 188
requirement for, 84
Total quality leadership (TQL), 2
Total quality management (TQM)
applicability of, to small business, 8–9
checklist for, 8, 9
continuous improvement, 5–6
encouraging personal initiative, 7–8
ensuring customer satisfaction, 2–3
ISO 9000, 238
key elements, 2
managing processes, 3–4
teamwork in, 6–7

Training, process flow diagrams for, 94–95
Transportation activities, minimizing, 103
Trends, 143, 176, 194

Upper control limit (UCL), 147, 176
calculations for, 152, 157, 163, 170

Value-added assessment, 97
to business, 98–99
checklist for, 99
to customer, 98
nonvalue-added activities, 99–100
Variables control charts, 159
average and range charts ($\bar{X}$–R), 159–65
individuals charts (X–R), 166–71
Variances, process flow diagrams for highlighting, 94
Variation. *See* Process variation

Waste reduction, 97
minimizing administrative tasks, 101–2
minimizing checks and inspections, 100–101
minimizing storage and transportation activities, 102–3
optimizing internally required activities, 103
and quality improvement, 11
value-added assessment, 97
What question in problem solving, 193
When question in problem solving, 193–94, 195
Where question in problem solving, 193
Why question in problem solving, 199, 200
Work procedures, 107
Worksheets
changing characteristics, 232, 233
customer list, 37
measurement decision documentation, 123

output list, 35
output requirement, 42, 51
problem definition, 197, 198
process definition, 72, 74
process priority list, 80
process priority scoring, 78
reversal to identify causes, 227, 230
reversal to identify solutions, 228
risk analysis, 215, 216

selection criteria, 207, 209
solution comparison, 212, 213
and standardization, 107–8
supplier feedback, 87
Written survey, 47
aim of, 47
analyzing the numerical responses, 48
customer instructions for, 47–48
definition of, 47
pros and cons regarding, 46